MW01516737

Closing the Doors

CLOSING THE DOORS

The Failure of Refugee Protection

David Matas
with Ilana Simon

Summerhill Press, Toronto

© 1989 David Matas and Ilana Simon

Published by Summerhill Press Ltd.
52 Shaftesbury Avenue
Toronto, Ontario M4T 1A2

Distributed by University of Toronto Press
5201 Dufferin Street
Downsview, Ontario M3H 5T8

Cover design by Images Art Direction and Design Inc.
Printed and bound in Canada

Canadian Cataloguing in Publication Data
Matas, David
Closing the doors: the failure of refugee protection
Includes index.
ISBN 0-920197-81-7
1. Refugees - Government policy - Canada. 2. Refugees - Legal Status,
laws, etc. - Canada. 3. Refugees - Government policy. I. Simon, Ilana,
1963-. II Title.

HV640.M3 1989   362.8'7   C89-094270-6

Contents

5

Part Three:
THE UNITED STATES' REFUGEE POLICY

Part Four:
INTERNATIONAL RESPONSE TO
REFUGEE PROTECTION

Preface

I am a lawyer, in private practice in Winnipeg since 1973. When I began practicing, my cases ranged over a wide variety of legal fields. Immigration and refugee law was just one of the many types of work that came into the office.

But from the very first refugee case I took, the problems facing refugees both dismayed and bewildered me. I was dismayed that refugees in apparent danger back home were denied the most elementary procedural protections granted automatically in every other area of law. Refugee claimants were virtually alone among those seeking legal redress in Canada in being denied the right to a hearing, the right to know the case they had to meet, access to counsel at initial stages, a meaningful appeal, and an explanation of the reasons for a judgement against them.

I was puzzled. Why were people who faced possible death or torture back home if their claim was rejected in Canada given fewer procedural protections than someone questioning, say, a parking ticket? Through my practice, my writing, and my volunteer work I attempted to discover the reasons why this perverse cruelty was inflicted by the state in which refugees sought protection.

This book sets out my own answer to this puzzle. It describes some of the cases I litigated on behalf of refugee claimants. It presents a history and explanation of recent legislative changes in Canada. It discusses the legal systems in Europe and the U.S., and the international system of protection for refugees. It puts all of this into the context of an explanation

9

I have developed about what is happening to refugees and why it is happening.

As bad as matters were for refugees when I first began doing refugee work, matters have since, in some respects, become much worse. I have ceased to wonder why, but my dismay, my concern, have increased. The book contains many arguments against what is happening to refugees and many suggestions for improvements to make the lot of refugees a safer one.

There are a number of people I have to thank for this book. There is first of all Ilana Simon. This book is drawn from speeches, submissions, articles, and legal representations I have written throughout the years. Putting it all together in one readable, coherent whole was a mammoth task. Without her contribution, this book would never have been written.

There is the refugee legal community in Canada. Barbara Jackman, Melvin Weigel, Joyce Yedid, Pierre Duquette, Lorne Waldman, Ken Zaifman, Renate Krause, Mendel Green, Maureen Silcoff, Michael Schelew, Michael Bossin, Bill Sloan, Jim Hathaway, Juanita Westmoreland Traore, and Lisa Gilad have all helped me a good deal. My conversations with them on legal refugee issues taught me much that is reflected in this book.

There was the Task Force on Immigration Practices and Procedures, of which I was a member. Lloyd Axworthy, then Minister for Immigration; Joe Stern, the Minister's Assistant for refugees; Susan Davis, United Nations High Commission for Refugees legal representative at the time; Gerry Robinson, Chair of the Task Force; and Ed Ratushny, Carter Hoppe and Manon Vennat, the other members of the Task Force, helped me with the report I wrote for the Task Force in 1981, and in developing my own thinking on refugees.

There is the refugee support community in Canada. Tom Clark, Margaret Third Tsushima, Anne Paludan, Rivka Augenfeld, Bert Foliot, Winn Leslie, Pat Doern, George Cram, Kathleen Ptolemy, Stephen Foster, Peter Bisson, Nancy Pocook, Nancy Nicholls, John Jones, Cornelia Johnson and countless others inspired me with their own dedication and commitment.

Their practical everyday insights gave me an appreciation of refugee problems I would not have otherwise achieved.

There is B'nai Brith. Many of my submissions on refugee issues described in this book were made on behalf of B'nai Brith. Many of the speeches I presented on refugee issues I presented as a spokesman for B'nai Brith. Ellen Kachuck, the professional responsible for international affairs; Frank Dimant, the executive director; Moishe Smith, the president; and the office, the executive and the general membership supported me in the volunteer and advocacy refugee work that led to this book.

Finally, I want to mention Susan Charendoff, Gordon Montador and Clifford Maynes. Susan, who coauthored *Justice Delayed: Nazi War Criminals in Canada* with me, provided many helpful suggestions for this work. Gordon Montador of Summerhill Press went above and beyond a publisher's duty in his efforts for the book. Clifford Maynes, the copy editor, gave invaluable advice on improving the text. Also, a thank you must be extended to William Marantz for use of his quality printer.

Throughout *Closing the Doors* the masculine *he* is used in place of the more appropriate he or she purely for reasons of brevity. In fact, all general uses of *he* refer to both male and female persons.

Although this book is intended for a general readership, the endnotes are in legal style, and will be of interest mainly to lawyers.

CLOSING THE DOORS: THE FAILURE OF REFUGEE PROTECTION

The world is awash with refugees. In the early 1960s, when 1.2 million refugees sought protection worldwide, countries were still optimistic the problem would be resolved. Now, the world refugee population has swelled to a staggering 12 million and the world refugee system is in crisis.

Refugees come from places as diverse as Iran, El Salvador, Vietnam and Pakistan, fleeing war, civil strife, revolution or strong-fisted rule. Their circumstances vary, but these desperate refugees share a deep-seated fear for their own safety. Fleeing persecution in their home country may be their last hope for staying alive.

No corner of the globe has been left untouched. Every country is either the source of exodus, a temporary refuge, a place of resettlement, or a financial contributor to the system.

Refugees should be protected. They should not be returned to countries where their lives or freedoms are imperilled. If the world learned anything from Nazi oppression and the Holocaust, it was the life-and-death necessity of asylum.

THE ROLE OF EASTERN EUROPE

The Refugee Convention was originally designed by the West to provide refuge to anti-communists fleeing Eastern Europe after the Second World War. Ironically, today's refugee crisis can itself be traced to Eastern Europe, which has turned the tables and applied the Convention against the West.

In recent years, East Germany began to allow the entry of large numbers of Third World refugees. Visa requirements were waived and travel made cheap. East Germany intended not simply to earn foreign currency, but also to force West Germany into closing off Berlin. West Germany views Berlin as a unified city and allows free travel in and out of the Non-Communist zone. East Germany views Berlin as a divided city and has built a wall around the Communist zone. Refugees were brought to East Berlin, but directed to West Berlin and the West German refugee protection system. East Germany's flood of Third World refugees was used to try to coerce the West Germans to back off their commitment to Berlin as an open city, and to close off access from East Berlin to West Berlin.

West Germany maintained its commitment to Berlin as a united city, despite this refugee influx. Instead it has tried to cut off the flow of refugees in another way by setting up disincentive schemes. Claimants have been denied work, education, freedom of religion and their native diet. They have been exposed to extreme crowding and restricted in mobility. The refugee definition has been restrictively applied in the courts. Claimants have been forced to lead lives of idleness and despair, waiting for positive determinations which never come.

The disincentive schemes worked, not to send the refugees back to their homes, where they feared civil war or persecution, but to drive them elsewhere in Europe and North America. The Tamils that came to Canada by ship in the summer of 1986 and the Sikhs that came by ship in the summer of 1987 were part of this group.

14

As refugees fanned out from West Germany throughout Europe and North America, or simply skipped West Germany to go to other countries with less harsh systems, these other countries in turn reacted to the overflow by setting up disincentive schemes and removing procedural protections.

By using economic leverage, West Germany eventually talked East Germany into imposing visa restrictions on the Third World. The refugee flow through Berlin has decreased, but the damage has been done. Once the West got caught up in this game of competitive destruction of safeguards, the contest could not be stopped.

Of course, the refugee problem is not just a Berlin problem. Even without Berlin as a political pawn, the world refugee problem would have tested the West's generosity. But Berlin led to the fall of the first domino, West Germany, and all other dominoes fell in sequence.

THE HOLOCAUST AND THE COLD WAR

Two historical events are of major significance to the present international refugee structure. One is the Holocaust, the other the Cold War. The Holocaust showed the failure of voluntary, humanitarian resettlement refugee policies before and during the Second World War, and exemplified the need for refugee obligations.

The failure of the voluntary system was manifested by Evian. Following an intergovernmental conference at Evian, France in 1938, governments of 32 nations formed an intergovernmental committee to assist refugees leaving Nazi Germany and Austria.[1] The Evian system was unsuccessful: everyone favoured resettlement, but no one was prepared to offer it.

Without legal recourse available to refugee claimants, anti-Semitic or anti-alien immigration officials could prevent Evian's good intentions from having concrete results. The Canadian Immigration Department, headed by Fred Blair, was motivated by anti-Semitism to prevent every single Jewish refugee from entering Canada.[2] The U.S. State Department under Breckenridge Long, Assistant Secretary for Special Problems, was compelled by an anti-alien attitude to block entry of Jewish refugees to the U.S., and even suppressed news of the Holocaust to further this goal.[3]

In order to appease Arab leaders, Britain was determined to keep quotas for Jews entering British mandated Palestine at a minuscule level. British mandate officials turned away ship after ship of Jews from Palestine.

If the Holocaust disclosed the need for an obligatory rather than voluntary system, the Cold War led to a desire for condemnation. Prior to the Nazi phenomenon, refugees had been described simply as people who no longer enjoyed the protection of their governments.[4] Nazism led toward a definition of refugees in terms that judged the governments of the countries fled. The 1938 Geneva conference excluded as refugees people who left for "purely personal convenience." In other words, refugees were people forced to leave by their governments. The 1943 Bermuda conference defined refugees as people who had to leave because of "danger to their lives or liberties."

With the collapse of Nazism, these judgemental definitions temporarily disappeared. The United Nations Relief and Rehabilitation Administration (UNRRA) was established in 1943 to assist displaced persons, victims of war. Its object was to secure their repatriation or return. But emphasis on repatriation quickly collided with the problem of Ukrainians and Balts who did not wish to return to Soviet rule. Humanitarianism led to a mitigation of this forced repatriation.[5]

The International Refugee Organization (IRO), which replaced UNRRA in 1947, allowed a person to refuse repatriation if he had been persecuted or feared persecution. The stress on resettlement not only accommodated humanitarian demands. It also condemned communist regimes as persecutors of their citizens.

Eighteen states ratified the IRO Constitution between May, 1947 and March, 1949. Eastern European countries did not join the IRO because they did not wish to share in their own condemnation. Several Western countries did not join because they were not ready to join in open condemnation of the Eastern bloc.

The United Nations Convention on Refugees, signed in 1951, received greater acceptance from states. The definition was more restrictive: to be defined as a refugee, a person had to have a well-founded fear of persecution. A simple fear of persecution was not sufficient. Eastern European countries, believing they were again being condemned, did not sign. The West, by and large, did.

One exception was the United States, which had played a key role in drafting the refugee definition and pushing it through the UN General Assembly.[6] The U.S. did not sign because it opposed distinguishing between refugees and those fleeing Eastern Europe for economic reasons, who were excluded from the UN definition.

This system of resettlement and condemnation was meant to discredit the East by showing that its people were prepared to flee.[7] Eastern European refugees became tools for psychological warfare, and in theory could be used to conduct sabotage, engage in guerilla warfare, or establish governments in exile. Defections removed people valuable to Communist regimes.

With the continuation of the Cold War and the 1956 Soviet invasion of Hungary, it became clear that the problem of refugees from Eastern Europe was not just a Second World War phenomenon. The 1951 Convention had been restricted to refugees forced to flee because of events before 1951. In response to the enduring refugee problem, a 1967 Protocol was signed that deleted the 1951 cut-off date. As of March 28, 1989, 106 countries had signed the Convention or Protocol, including the United States. Of the Eastern European countries, only Yugoslavia and Hungary have signed.

THIRD WORLD REFUGEES

The explosion of Third World refugees presented the Western World with an unanticipated dilemma. Following the Second World War, decolonization in the Third World was marked by turbulence and civil war. The West had little desire to condemn these newly independent governments for their political behaviour. Third World governments are often military allies, trading partners and ideological colleagues of Western countries.

By expanding the refugee definition, the problem of condemnation could be solved. The 1969 Convention of the Organization of African Unity defines as a refugee anyone compelled to leave by reason of external aggression, occupation, foreign domination, or events seriously disturbing public order. The notion of persecution is side-stepped altogether.[8]

However, the West has not wanted to broaden the refugee definition and increase refugee admissions. On the contrary, the larger-than-expected number of people who meet the current restrictive refugee definition has more than exhausted Western willingness to absorb refugees.

We are left with a contradiction: refugee determination systems founded in obligation coupled with a political reluctance to recognize and grant the right to remain, particularly to Third World refugees. Inevitably, distortions occur such as a lack of fairness in refugee determination procedures. Western democracies say they accept the principle of protection, but they deny it in practice.

The overall argument of *Closing the Doors* is that refugee protection is accepted in principle, but denied in fact. Few principles meet with such widespread general agreement among the countries of the world as the policy of refugee protection. Governments have signed treaties, Parliaments have passed laws and even enacted constitutional provisions to commit themselves to this policy. Intergovernmental organizations have been established to ensure refugee protection. Non-governmental organizations, both religious and secular, work to promote it.

Yet few principles are so widely violated. Governments pass laws to curtail the number of refugee claims. Refugees are forcibly returned to countries where their life or freedom is threatened because of race, religion, nationality, membership in a particular social group or political opinion. Refugees are also discouraged by more subtle government-orchestrated obstacles, deterrents, or administrative hurdles which make successful refugee claims nearly impossible.

Governments say one thing about refugees and do another. This is not mere confusion, but calculated hypocrisy. The purpose of *Closing the Doors* is to expose this hypocrisy. The book looks at how the gates have been shut to refugee protection in Canada, the United States and Europe, which are leaders of the world in advocating the principles of refugee protection. The book proposes that these gates must be re-opened so that genuine refugees receive the protection they deserve.

TECHNIQUES OF DENIAL

The first part of the book "Techniques of Denial" shows what techniques are used to deny protection to refugees in fact, while maintaining lip service to the principle of protection.

Chapter 1, "Racism in Canadian Immigration", focuses on requirements and procedures for admission to Canada neutral in appearance, but discriminatory in fact. This discrimination has the effect of denying admission in a racist way. The chapter traces the history of overt racism in Canadian immigration policy to its present superficial neutrality. This chapter is general in nature and looks at attitudes to all newcomers — immigrants and refugees. Racist attitudes about immigrants in general have obvious implications for refugees even though refugees are not immigrants and the two groups are processed separately.

The government sets targets, not quotas, for the overall immigration system. For 1989, the immigration target was 150,000 to 160,000, up from 125,000 to 135,000 in 1988. Refugees are included as subcompartments of immigration totals. In 1989, Canada will accept 13,000 government-sponsored refugees selected from refugee camps abroad, 10,000 privately-sponsored refugees, and another 7,000 refugees who make claims from within Canada.

Chapter 2, "The Refugee Definition", shows how the narrowness of the refugee definition is used to justify excluding whole categories of refugees from protection. As it is applied, the definition denies protection to large numbers of people fleeing man-made danger. The chapter discusses how the definition could be changed to encompass persons fleeing generalized violence.

Another technique of denial is the lack of fairness in refugee determination procedures. Chapter 3, "What Fairness Requires", details how an unfair procedure leads to inaccurate results and real refugees being rejected in error and forcibly returned to danger. The chapter proposes twelve standards of fairness refugee determination systems must meet.

Deterrence schemes are another technique of denial, described in Chapter 4, "Refugee Deterrence". Refugee claimants are presented with so many difficulties while making their claims that they are discouraged from remaining in the resettlement country until a decision is reached. This chapter examines the difficulties in family reunification and the problems claimants face getting work permits, permission to go to school, access to medicare, legal aid, welfare, family allowance, and driver licensing. Visa requirements are another deterrent which prevent claimants from ever arriving in Canada.

The final technique of denial, described in Chapter 5, "Diplomatic Asylum", is the denial by Canadian diplomats of a grant of asylum to refugees in Canadian embassies abroad. In theory, diplomatic asylum is an avenue of protection open to refugees. In practice, it is not available.

CANADA AND THE WORLD'S REFUGEES

Part One draws its examples of techniques of denial from the Canadian scene. Part Two, "Canada and the World's Refugees", delves more thoroughly into how these techniques of denial have developed in Canada. This part focuses on the new Canadian refugee laws, how the demand for them arose, how they were changed in the legislative process, and what is wrong with them.

Chapter 6, "Canada's Old and New Refugee Determination Systems," describes the old system in place from April, 1978 until January 1, 1989, and briefly the new. The old system was complex and full of unnecessary delays that created an incentive for abuse. Phony refugee claimants travelled to Canada in order to take advantage of the delays. However, the new system is almost equally complex.

Fairness can be denied when a claimant is not given an oral hearing. Chapter 7, "Oral Hearings for Refugee Claimants", describes the battle in the courts to win claimants the right to present their claims orally. Although a number of government reports over the years recommended oral hearings be instituted, the old system did not allow for them. Eventually, the Supreme Court of Canada ruled that oral hearings were constitutionally required.

Chapter 8, "Refugee Mistakes", is a critical look at the new Canadian refugee determination process. Because the Refugee Reform Act removes common sense procedural protections, mistakes will be easy to make, impossible to correct, and catastrophic. Oral hearings are now part of the law, but a number of other procedural safeguards have disappeared.

In 1988, the Canadian Parliament passed another law to make matters worse for refugees. Chapter 9, "A War Measures Act for Refugees", looks at the Refugee Deterrents and Detention Act. The law deters refugees from coming to Canada, penalizes those in Canada who would try to help these refugees, and provides for prolonged detention of claimants.

The last chapter in this part, Chapter 10, "The Senate Response to the Refugee Bills", describes what the Senate amended — and what it ignored — when reviewing the government bills. At first the Senate was principled in its objections to the Refugee Deterrents and Detention Bill, Bill C-84. Its response to the Refugee Reform Bill, Bill C-55, was abjectly political.

THE UNITED STATES REFUGEE POLICY

Part Three "The United States Refugee Policy" presents the problems refugees face obtaining protection in the U.S. Chapter 11 "United States Refugee Determination System", sets out in particular the obstacles Guatemalan and Salvadoran refugees endure in seeking refuge in the U.S.

The U.S. sanctuary movement was formed in 1982 to protect refugees from El Salvador and Guatemala who were systematically being denied protection by the U.S. government. Chapter 12 "The U.S. Sanctuary Movement and Sanctuary Trial", reports on how the American government attempted to shut down the movement.

The existence of the sanctuary movement in the U.S. and the sanctuary trial raises questions for Canada. What would the legal status be of a Canadian sanctuary movement offering protection to refugees in defiance of Canadian law? Chapter 13 "A Canadian Sanctuary Movement?", attempts to answer that question.

INTERNATIONAL RESPONSE TO REFUGEE PROTECTION

Failure of refugee protection is a world-wide phenomenon, not singularly or even primarily a North American problem. Part Four, "International Response to Refugee Protection", looks at the international weakening of procedural safeguards for refugees.

Chapter 14, "Europe's Denial of Protection to Refugees", examines refugee determination procedures in seven Western European countries. As in North America, the absence of procedural safeguards in Europe leads to the rejection of genuine refugees.

When governments are disinclined to protect refugees, intergovernmental organizations offer little resistance. Canada has attempted to get international endorsement of its own weakening protection for refugees at the United Nation's High Commission for Refugees Executive Committee and the International Civil Aviation Organization. Chapter 15 "Canada and the UNHCR", tells this international story.

To combat the co-ordinated efforts of governments internationally to weaken and restrict protection for refugees, non-governmental organizations must also join forces in the same international fora. Chapter 16 "Non-Governmental Organizations and the UNHCR", sets out what NGOs can do to counter these intergovernmental efforts at weakened refugee protection.

CONCEPTS AND PRINCIPLES FOR REFUGEE PROTECTION

How can the general acceptance of human rights *principles* be used to generate acceptance in *practice* for the principles of refugee protection? Should the countries of Western Europe and North America offer first asylum to spontaneous arrivals, or only secondary resettlement to selected refugees chosen from camps abroad in countries of proximate refuge? Should refugees be protected? Part Five "Concepts and Principles for Refugee Protection", attempts to answer these general questions.

The existence of mass exoduses of refugees has been used to strengthen human rights standards and institutions. But human rights standards have not had a beneficial effect on refugee protection. Chapter 17, "Human Rights and Mass Exoduses", discusses the linkages between human rights standards and mechanisms and refugee outflows.

For governments in North America and Western Europe the issue is not so much the protection of refugees in the abstract as it is the protection of spontaneous arrivals. The West is less and less inclined to open its doors to refugees seeking asylum. Western governments favour choosing refugees to come to their countries from refugee camps abroad. Chapter 18 "Resettlement or Asylum? The Safe Third Country Concept", argues the West should serve as a place of first asylum, not only a place for resettlement. As well, refugees should not be sent back to countries of provisional asylum they have left.

The public at large often raises the general question of why refugees should be protected. This final chapter, Chapter 19 "Why Protect Refugees?" argues for the protection of refugees on both legal and moral grounds.

PART ONE

TECHNIQUES OF DENIAL

Chapter 1

RACISM IN CANADIAN IMMIGRATION

A brief historical review of Canada's attitude toward newcomers helps us to understand the current treatment of refugees. In a word, this attitude has been racist. Indeed, to talk of racism *in* Canadian immigration policy before 1978 is being over-generous. Rather, we should talk of racism *as* Canadian immigration policy. Canada's immigration policy was guided by a bias against Asians, Jews and other minorities and in favour of Western Europeans.

REFUGEES DIFFERENT FROM IMMIGRANTS
Refugees are different from immigrants. While immigrants are pulled, refugees are pushed. Immigrants want to come and stay once they have arrived. Refugees do not want to leave their home country and flee only to avoid persecution. Refugees, at least initially, want to return once the danger subsides.

27

According to the 1951 United Nations Convention on Refugees, refugees are defined as those with a well-founded fear of persecution by reason of race, religion, nationality, membership in a social group or political opinions who are outside their country of nationality or habitual residence and are unable or unwilling to return. Immigrants who come to Canada are those who seek permanent residence in Canada.

Although refugees and immigrants are conceptually different, practically Canada assimilates the two categories. Refugees admitted for resettlement to Canada come as landed immigrants. Refugee claimants who come to Canada to seek protection are required to seek landing once recognized as refugees or face deportation.

This government policy of forced transformation of refugees into immigrants leads Canadian authorities as well as the Canadian public to view refugees as immigrants. Artificially assimilating refugees and immigrants has a number of consequences — most significantly the spillover of racist attitudes towards immigrants onto refugees.

In any case, racism is a general attitude. Both immigrants and refugees will be the objects of racism even from those who understand the differences between the two groups, but who have racist sentiments.

While the distinction between refugees and immigrants is now legally and conceptually clear cut, that was not always the case. Before the Second World War there was no separate legal regime for refugees. Not only in the public's mind were immigrants and refugees one and the same category, but in national legal systems as well.

IMMIGRANTS PROHIBITED ACCORDING TO RACE

Racial intolerance first surfaced in the Canadian Immigration Act of 1910, which boldly gave Cabinet power to prohibit immigrants on racial grounds.[1] The wording of the legislation may have changed from time to time, but that sweeping power was to remain intact for almost seventy years. It wasn't until 1978 that a new immigration policy came into effect, formally removing the power to rebuff immigrants to Canada on the basis of race.

In 1919, the law permitted Cabinet to bar from Canada immigrants of any race on the grounds that they were considered undesirable, "owing to their peculiar customs, habits, modes of life and methods of holding property and because of their probable inability to become readily assimilated."[2]

In a March 14, 1919 Order in Council, this authority was used to prohibit German, Austrian, Hungarian and Bulgarian or Turkish immigrants, except with the permission of the Minister of Immigration. A separate prohibition denied entry to those who had been "enemy aliens" during the First World War.[3] That same year, the power was again invoked to prohibit Dukhobors, Hutterites, and Mennonites from landing in Canada.[4]

Asians were denied entry into Canada from 1923 until 1956. Exceptions were made for farm labourers, domestics, and a Canadian male's Asian wife and their children under age 18. In 1930, the exceptions for farmers, farm labourers and domestics were revoked, making immigration possible only for members of families.[5] In 1956, this general prohibition was replaced by government-to-government agreements limiting annual entry to 150 from India, 100 from Pakistan, and 50 from Ceylon, in addition to immediate relatives of Canadian citizens.[6] In 1958, the figure was increased to 300 from India. These limitations remained in effect until 1962.

Cabinet did not need to pass Orders in Council explicitly prohibiting citizens of particular countries from entering Canada. Nationals of all but a few countries were implicitly prohibited. The 1954 immigration regulations limited admission to citizens of the U.K., Australia, New Zealand, South Africa, Ireland, the U.S., and France.[7] Citizens of these countries had only to have sufficient means to maintain themselves until they secured employment to become Canadian immigrants.

In 1956, citizens of other Western European countries were added to the welcome list, provided they were coming to Canada for a government placement or the government had approved their employment. People from Europe, the Middle East or the Americas could come if they had extended family here. Others, notably those from Africa and Asia, could come only if they had immediate family here.[8]

Prohibition by implication lasted until 1962, when any person who could show he was able to successfully establish himself in Canada could come.[9] Even with this change, however, preference was given to people from Europe, the Middle East, or the Americas, who were eligible for admission to Canada if they had *extended* family here, including a son, daughter, brother, sister, or unmarried nephew or niece under the age of 21. All other applicants were required to have *immediate* family members in Canada, including a husband, wife, unmarried son or daughter under 21, fiance(e), or grandparent.

FINANCIAL BARRIERS
In addition to prohibiting immigrants explicitly and implicitly, the Immigration Act also allowed Cabinet to restrict entry to Canada by applying racist criteria. The Immigration Act of 1906 stated that Cabinet could require immigrants, as a condition for entry, to possess a prescribed minimum amount of money, which varied according to the race of the immigrant.[10]

That power was first used as a racial barrier in 1908. A January Order in Council had already required every immigrant to Canada to possess $25. In June the minimum requirement was raised to $200 for all Asiatic immigrants, with the exception of those from China and Japan, who were regulated by a separate set of discriminatory rules. The 1908 Order in Council speaks for itself in its comments on Asian immigrants: "Their language and mode of life render them unsuited for settlement in Canada, where there are no colonies of their own people to ensure their maintenance in case of their inability to secure employment."[11]

The Canadian Immigration Act of 1910 reiterated Cabinet's powers to restrict access to immigrants possessing a prescribed minimum amount of money, and to vary the amount according to race.[12] That power was to remain intact until 1956.

In 1914, Cabinet passed an Order in Council requiring an immigrant of any Asiatic race to possess $200 in his own right. This regulation became the subject of a bizarre course of

30

litigation that went all the way to the British Columbia Court of Appeal. The case, *Singh v. Immigration Authorities of Canada*[13] gives a crystal clear picture of the intent of Canadian law — the attitude that immigrants and refugees have confronted.

Munshi Singh appeared at the Canadian Port of Vancouver in May, 1914, a few months after the Order in Council had been passed, with only $20 in his pocket. He was subsequently detained and ordered deported on the basis that he was of an Asian race and had less than $200 with him. Mr. Singh appealed this order to the Supreme Court and to the Court of Appeal of B.C. He lost at both courts.

In a long judgement in the Court of Appeal, Justice of Appeal McPhillips said:

> The better classes of the Asiatic races are not given to leave their own countries...and those who become immigrants are...undesirables in Canada. Their ways and ideas may well be a menace to the well being of the Canadian people.
>
> The Parliament of Canada...may well be said to be safeguarding the people of Canada from an influx which it is no chimera to conjure up might annihilate the nation...introduce Oriental ways as against European ways...and all the results that would naturally flow therefrom.
>
> In their own interests their proper place of residence is within the confines of their respective countries in the continent of Asia, not in Canada, where their customs are not in vogue and their adherence to them here only gives rise to disturbances destructive to the well being of society...
>
> Better that people of non-assimilative...race should not come to Canada, but rather that they shall remain of residence in their country of origin, and do their share, as they have in the past, in the preservation and development of the empire.

THE HEAD TAX

A series of immigration laws were specifically directed against persons of Chinese origin. Chinese immigrants needed not only to have money in their pocket, but to pay it over to immigration officials in the form of a head tax. Under the Chinese Immigration Act of 1885,[14] the head tax was first set at $50, increased to $100 in 1900,[15] and increased again to $500 in 1903.[16] Entry to Canada or landing of persons of Chinese origin or descent was banned altogether in 1923,[17] irrespective of allegiance or citizenship or cash up front. The only exceptions were diplomats, Chinese born in Canada, merchants and students. That statute remained on the books until 1947.

THE CONTINUOUS PASSAGE RULE

Cabinet also exercised another power, which was neutral on the face of it, but discriminatory in intent. This was Cabinet's authority to impose a "continuous passage" rule,[18] a power that survived until 1978.

Cabinet used this power to pass a 1914 Order in Council prohibiting any immigrant from landing in Canada unless he had come by continuous journey from his native country or a country where he was a naturalized citizen. The only way to comply with the law was to produce a through-ticket purchased in that country or prepaid in Canada. It is no coincidence that in those days it was impossible to purchase a ticket in India for a continuous journey from India to Canada, or to prepay for one in Canada.

Munshi Singh — the same person who was ordered deported because he had only $20 rather than $200 in his pocket — was also ordered deported because he had not made a continuous journey from India. He stopped at Hong Kong first. The Court of Appeal also ruled that Mr. Singh was validly ordered deported under the continuous passage provision.

JAPANESE CANADIANS

In form if not in effect, the most racist immigration measures were directed against the Japanese during and after the Second World War. Under the authority of the War Measures Act instituted by Order in Council in 1942, Japanese citizens were restricted entry from abroad. Further, Canadian-born citizens of Japanese descent were subject to deportation. If a natural-born

British subject of Japanese race, 16 years of age or over and resident of Canada, requested repatriation,[19] his wife and children could be ordered deported along with him, regardless of whether they wanted to leave.

This regulation was challenged before the Supreme Court of Canada and the Privy Council in England on appeal on the ground that Canada could not deport citizens born in Canada. However, both courts ruled that the Canadian government had the power to deport its own citizens.[20]

DISCRIMINATION AGAINST JEWS

Canada's discrimination against the Jews was evidenced before, during and after the Second World War. In *None is Too Many*,[21] Harold Troper and Irving Abella recount in chilling detail the determination of Canadian immigration authorities to keep out every single Jew, fleeing first Nazi persecution, then the Holocaust, and finally the aftermath of the Holocaust.

Legally, Jews were not singled out for discrimination. There was no Jewish Immigration Act to prohibit Jews from entering Canada, no financial requirements, head tax, or continuous passage rule. And yet, discrimination against Jews was incontestable. Jews who met all the normal immigration requirements were not admitted.

This discrimination was achieved not through the exercise of express powers, but through abuse of powers. Canada's Immigration department was headed by Fred Blair, an avowed anti-Semite. Blair transferred responsibility for processing Jewish applicants from other government offices to his own, where he personally scrutinized each application, deciding its eligibility and virtually always turning them down.

RACISM TODAY

The Jewish experience is illuminating. It shows that we do not need racist laws to have racial discrimination in immigration — all we need is unlimited discretion. With an unsympathetic public, unmotivated public leadership, or racists in office, racism can make its way into the immigration process even with laws that appear neutral and fair.

This lesson is particularly relevant today because all racist overtones have disappeared from our immigration laws. One of the obligations under the present Immigration Act, enacted in 1978, is "to ensure that any person who seeks admission to land is subject to standards of admission that do not discriminate on the grounds of race, national or ethnic origin, colour, religion or sex." The power to prohibit entry by race is gone. The power to impose a financial requirement by race is gone. The continuous passage rule is gone. Yet the danger of racism remains.

Tannis Cohen has written about the present immigration system that discrimination does not only occur in individual cases. In certain respects it is built into the immigration system itself. Discrimination can still exist because the universal system applies only to a narrow segment of the immigration process, and because rules which treat people the same do not necessarily treat them equally.[22]

Although the present Immigration Act is not intentionally discriminatory, it may allow and even generate systemic discrimination. Three areas of immigration policy deserve examination: visitor's visas, delays, and the points system.

VISITOR'S VISAS

Those who become permanent residents in Canada do not always come as immigrants. Sometimes they come as visitors and become landed immigrants after they have arrived. Refugee claimants may also come as visitors and claim refugee status either during their stay as visitors, or after their visitor status has expired. Racism towards visitors has an impact on both immigrants and refugees.

As a general rule, everyone must obtain a visa issued at a Canadian immigration post abroad before coming to Canada.[23] However, Cabinet has granted exceptions to this rule for visitors to Canada from sixty-five countries. Citizens of these countries can simply appear at the border and get a visitor's permit. U.S. citizens and permanent U.S. residents do not need visas at all.

It is easier to obtain a visitor's permit at the border than a visitor's visa abroad. Once a person has made a long trip to

Canada, it is much more difficult for an immigration officer to deny entry than if the person were still in his home country. Denial of entry may mean deportation, with extra cost to the government. As well, delays are shorter. A person granted a visitor's permit at the border usually has to wait only a few minutes in a queue while a person may have to wait months to be granted a visitor's visa at a Canadian post abroad.

Historically, for a select group of immigrants, visiting was particularly difficult. Before 1987, citizens of fourteen countries were required to obtain a visa even if they were in Canada in transit only — even if they never left the airport or the plane. People from these countries were prohibited from passing through Canada *en route* to another destination unless they had obtained a Canadian visa abroad. In 1987, the government extended this requirement to every country for which a visa requirement was imposed.

The Immigration Act imposes on airlines the costs of detention and removal of persons brought to Canada without visas, including transit visas, who should have them.[24] Some individuals with visitor's permits overstay their visits, requiring government enforcement action to remove them from Canada. A visa requirement is intended to cut down on this abuse because airlines, which want to avoid paying detention and removal costs, will not transport to Canada a person who does not fulfill his country's visa requirement.

It is unfair for anyone to be told he must get a visa before he enters Canada because Immigration believes on the basis of his nationality that he may overstay a visitor's permit. Assuming a person will abuse the system because of his country of origin flies in the face of equality provisions under the Charter, which guarantees "everyone" (not just citizens and permanent residents) the legal benefit of the law without discrimination based on national or ethnic origin.[25] To require nationals of one country to hold visas while exempting nationals of another is to discriminate on the basis of national origin.

A different problem exists for visitors from countries for which visas are not required: they are subject to selective examination as to whether they are genuine visitors. Many feel the selection process is discriminatory. *Equality Now,* a report produced by the Parliamentary Committee on Visible Minorities, noted that, rightly or wrongly, visible minorities widely perceive that treatment of minorities at the border discriminates on the basis of race or ethnic origin. One witness said, "Turbans attract attention." The Committee recommended Employment and Immigration Canada take appropriate steps to ensure members of visible minorities are not unduly singled out for unusual immigration procedures.[26] Any such procedures, the Committee added, should be adequately explained to arriving persons and their awaiting relatives and friends.

The government responded that it was well aware visible minorities perceived themselves as unduly singled out for a more intensive interview on their arrival here. The government committed itself to developing a cross-cultural training programme for its officers and improved liaison with ethnic communities.

DELAYS

The second contemporary concern is the delay in processing visas — not just the length of the delay but its distribution. For Canadian visa offices in some parts of the world, delays are relatively short, while in other regions, delays are excruciatingly long.

These delays have a direct impact on refugees. Refugees in Canada trying to sponsor their families from abroad suffer the delays that all family sponsors do. Refugees applying to come to Canada from abroad through a resettlement programme are also caught up in Canadian visa office delays.

Government tables indicating mean processing times of family class* immigration applications by overseas offices give some idea of this discrepancy.[27] Mean processing times were determined by charting the length of time it took to process immigration applications for family members sponsored by Canadian landed immigrants during the three-month period of October, 1987 to December, 1987.

---

* The family class consists of parents, spouses, fiance(e)s and unmarried children.

36

Mean processing time[†] is different from averaging processing time. Average processing time for refugee and immigration applications is typically a good deal higher than the mean. The mean figure artificially deflates the waiting time. For example, if there are twenty-one cases, eleven of which take six months to process and ten that take two years, the mean processing time is six months. For the same case numbers and processing times, the average would be fifteen months.

Also, sixty days were added to the processing time for sponsored applications to cover the contact time between Canada Immigration in Ottawa and overseas visa offices. When a refugee or immigrant is sponsored, the following steps occur: the immigrant's immediate family member or the refugee sponsorship group in Canada contacts Canada Immigration in Ottawa; the Canadian office contacts the foreign visa office; the visa office contacts the refugee or immigrant; and the refugee or immigrant replies to the visa office. The tables assume the four steps would take sixty days. However, in many countries initial contact between the visa office and the refugee or immigrant takes much longer.

A table published in 1982 by the Recruitment and Selection Branch of the Canada Employment and Immigration Commission for family class applications indicated the dimension of the problem at the time. The table reflects the mean processing time from application received to final disposition. An application took four and one half times as long to process in the Philippines as it did in the United Kingdom.

Five years later, the discrepancy between processing delays has improved, but not disappeared. The table covers government figures for family class applications, in the three months from October, 1987 to December, 1987. The table reflects the mean processing time from applications received to final disposition.

[†] The mean time is the middle figure in the list of waiting times ordered in numerical rank. The average waiting time is the total of all waiting times divided by the number of cases in the list.

Canadian visa office	1982 Mean Processing Time (days)	1987 Mean Processing Time (days)
London	94	101
Birmingham	93	94
Sydney	120	183
New York	176	190
Manila	380	191
New Delhi	324	204
Port of Spain	303	127
Hong Kong	289	284

One cause of this pattern of delays is visa office distribution.[28] In 1986, when Canada received 6,940 landed immigrants from India, the government had only one visa office, in New Delhi. It still has. Yet distances within India are great, and transportation is inefficient, time-consuming and expensive. Sponsored applicants generally must be interviewed at the Canadian visa office in New Delhi. In the Philippines, another large territory from which Canada received 4,102 immigrants, there was only one immigration office, in Manila. There still is.

In Great Britain, from which Canada received 5,088 immigrants, the government had three visa offices, in Glasgow, Birmingham and London. In France, from which Canada received 1,124 immigrants, the government had three visa offices, in Marseilles, Bordeaux and Paris. In the U.S., from which Canada received 7,275 immigrants, there were 11 visa offices. In 1986, the intake from India and the U.S. was about equal, yet the Canadian government had 11 times as many offices in the United States.

When questioned on this discrepancy by the Parliamentary Committee on Visible Minorities, the government of Canada attributed the lengthy delays to factors such as the lack of reliable record-keeping systems in the country of origin. The Committee recommended the government conduct a general review of its policy concerning the location of offices and procedures for processing applications.[29] The government said it would open seven new points of service in existing Canadian missions in developing countries, and that it would closely monitor processing times of posts.

THE POINTS SYSTEM

A third factor contributing to discrimination in immigration is the points system. Independent immigrants[§] are admitted to Canada depending on how many points they receive, calculated according to skill, education, experience and training. Under current rules, independent immigrants must have a job for which no Canadian is available, have a highly skilled occupation, buy a business that employs at least one Canadian, start or buy a business for which there is a significant demand, or make a financial investment of a certain amount.[30]

A Canadian employer who used a hiring system like this would need an affirmative action programme to overcome its discriminatory effects. Needless to say, for immigration there is no such thing as an affirmative action programme.

Of course, the systemic discrimination of the point system can only be tested or proven if the appropriate statistical data is collected. If we compare all those who came in as individual independent immigrants, is it more difficult for a black to meet the points requirements than a white? For an Indian than an American? In the absence of data, which the government does not make available, we cannot make any conclusions with certainty. However, it would be surprising if the points system did not work in favour of some racial groups and against others. This discrimination tax has an impact on refugees since refugees being resettled from abroad must show they can successfully establish in Canada.

As a nation, we should not have an immigration system that discriminates by intent or effect. Internationally, Canada is vigilant that groups of people are not discriminated against. At home, Canada should be as watchful concerning immigration and protection of refugees. We cannot hermetically seal our-

---

[§] Independent immigrants are immigrants who come to Canada on the basis of their potential contribution to the Canadian economy.

selves off from the value system we preach to others. We must apply the same values within our borders. Do we as a community want to combat racism? If the answer is yes, we must be aware that if discrimination in immigration and refugee protection is condoned, eventually discrimination will permeate throughout Canada's entire value structure, legal system, and judicial process.

Chapter 2

THE REFUGEE DEFINITION

D elays in granting visas, maldistribution of visa offices and other practices with racist effects prevent refugees from obtaining protection from the dangers they fled. Another way in which real refugees are denied protection is an overly narrow application of the refugee definition. Those who are refugees, by any common sense application of the term, are denied refugee status because they do not fit the technical legal definition.

The refugee system in place world-wide is intended to protect persecuted people — a noble and worthy goal. Yet the system has led to difficulties: people in real danger are denied protection. The UN Convention refugee definition, with its emphasis on persecution, leads to a denial of protection for three reasons. Firstly, the refugee definition is applied only to those suffering from individualized persecution, not generalized persecution. Secondly, political considerations come into play for condemnation of the persecuting countries. Thirdly, the emphasis on persecution results in resettlement countries viewing the permanent exile of refugees as the most likely scenario. In turn, these countries fear unmanageable numbers of refugee inflows and set up disincentive schemes to halt the flows.

REFUGEE DEFINITION NARROWLY APPLIED

The 1951 UN Convention on the Protection of Refugees, defines a refugee as someone who has a well founded fear of persecution because of race, religion, nationality, membership in a social group, or political opinion. A person who is persecuted for an unlisted reason is legally not a refugee.

The concept of social group was meant to be flexible and cover all types of persecution by a tyrant. In practice, that has not happened. For instance, young, urban males persecuted because they refuse to join the military have been found by Western courts not to fall within the concept of social group, or the definition of refugee.

It's not enough to be the victim or potential victim of *generalized* violence. The violence must be directed towards the claimant. A villager who is shot at because of his political opinion can be a refugee; villagers who are bombed from the air because, for example, they live in guerilla-controlled territory are not thereby considered refugees.

Thus, millions of people fleeing life-threatening conditions at home do not fall within the United Nations definition of refugee as it has been applied. In any practical use of the term they are refugees, but according to the refugee determination systems of states they are not. These people may be denied refugee protection, forcibly returned to the conditions they have fled, or held in intolerable conditions outside their home country waiting for solutions that never come. Ironically, the more generalized the violence in a particular country, the less likely a person from that country is to be considered a refugee.

The notion of persecution implies that refugees must be victimized by *governments*. A person victimized by the *opposition* is not legally considered to be within the refugee definition. However, people flee all perils, not just government or state-tolerated dangers. People under attack by the opposition are as likely to flee their home countries as people who are persecuted by a government. Basing the refugee definition on the source of danger is arbitrary and unfair.

Some scholars have argued that the refugee definition even in its present form is broad enough to cover all man-made dangers. For instance, Arthur Helton of the United States has suggested that the concept of social group was meant to be flexible to cover all types of persecution which a tyrant might inflict.[1]

People under attack by the opposition are sometimes found to come within the refugee definition on the ground that the government has failed to protect them. Government is not just a few people in power, but a system of law and order. When that system collapses the government has failed in its duty of protection.[2]

Finally, it arguable that the definition does indeed include people fleeing generalized violence. If it can be shown that a group is under attack as a group, then the fact there are many victims rather than few should not, in principle, remove their eligibility for refugee status.

However, these arguments are, in many cases and in many countries, more theoretical than real. Whether the narrow application of the definition is right or wrong, the fact of the matter is that the definition is applied restrictively and genuine refugees fail to receive protection from asylum countries.

POLITICALLY-MOTIVATED REFUGEE DETERMINATIONS

Persecution involves a violation of human rights. If a person is deemed to be a refugee, his government is therefore deemed to be a human rights violator. However, asylum countries are reluctant to condemn a source country that is also a friend or ally. Thus, a refugee is more likely to receive protection in an enemy country than an allied country. Individual lives are sacrificed to preserve economic, strategic, and political ties.

The United Nations High Commission for Refugees was established and the Refugee Convention was drafted after the

Second World War essentially as an anti-Communist gesture. This linkage between the Convention and anti-communism is shown explicitly in two different ways. The Convention gave signatory states the option of limiting its refugee obligations to events in Europe.[3] The Convention also was limited at the option of signatory states to events occurring before January 1, 1951.[4] At that time, the significant refugee outflow was from Eastern Europe. The Western World wanted to condemn the Communist states as persecutors, and constructed the formal refugee system to do so. This anti-Communist bias in the system persists. Few Communist states have signed the Refugee Convention, and only Hungary and Yugoslavia from Eastern Europe. Hungary did not sign until 1989.

Western Bloc countries find it easier to grant refugee status to those fleeing Communist regimes than to those fleeing non-Communist regimes. Those fleeing right-wing anti-Communist regimes have a much harder time. The United States, which is vigorously anti-Communist, has treated refugees fleeing right-wing regimes with particular harshness, but Canada and other Western states are not immune from this bias. We end up with a world of unbalanced injustice.

The refugee system as applied not only excludes people it should include, but admits people it should reject. Genuine refugees in Canada are denied refugee status, and yet people who are not in any danger of any kind, either from individualized persecution or generalized violence, are recognized as refugees and receive unwarranted protection. They fill up scarce spaces and consume meager budgets theoretically designated for refugees.

People in this category, from Communist countries mainly, are leaving a political and economic system they reject out of personal belief. They have made an individualized decision that they cannot tolerate continuing to live under their country's system, which has become repugnant to them. They would rather make a personal sacrifice — loss of economic position, separation from family, breaking from their culture — than continue to live under a system they reject.

When people leave government positions to flee their country, they are called defectors. When they are common

44

citizens, they are called refugees. Unlike Convention refugees, and even those fleeing generalized violence, these refugees decide from the start to leave permanently. Only a change in the system of their home country would persuade them to return. Convention refugees or those fleeing generalized violence may end up having to leave permanently, but typically, at least initially, their decision to leave is a temporary one.

In many countries favourable treatment of those rejecting Communism is not explicit.* A country does not announce its desire to accept white Eastern Europeans. Immigration policies do not state today that educated refugees from Communist countries are preferred over Sri Lankan refugees with lesser skills. Rather the favourable treatment is implicit. Asylum-seekers from Communist countries have higher acceptance rates in the West than would be expected in light of conditions fled. Conversely, asylum-seekers from non-Communist countries have lower acceptance rates in the West than would be expected in light of conditions fled.

In the West, people who leave Communist states such as the Soviet Union simply because they reject Communism are often treated as refugees even if they are in no danger. People who leave pro-Western military dictatorships such as Paraguay under former dictator Alfredo Stroessner simply because they reject living under a dictatorship are not considered refugees. They are forcibly returned to the countries they fled.

In Canada, an ideologically explicit system exists for welcoming those fleeing Communist countries: the Self-Exiled and Indochinese Designated Classes. The Self-Exiled Class of refugees is comprised of people who have left Eastern Europe and do not want to return.[5] Provided they are unwilling or unable to return to their country of citizenship, and will be able to become successfully established in Canada, they can enter Canada. They can demonstrate their potential to establish

---

* In Canada, a Special Review Committee used to consider requests for the humanitarian landing of people who met specific criteria, including persons who had achieved success in their own country but who were willing to sacrifice to live in a democratic system. The Special Review Committee was abolished February 28, 1989.

45

themselves successfully by arranging either private or government sponsorship. In this way, Eastern Europeans seeking entrance into Canada do not have to show that they meet the refugee definition. Under the Indochinese Designated Class, citizens of the Communist countries of Indochina[6] — Laos, Vietnam and Kampuchea — have basically these same advantageous rules as citizens of Communist countries of Eastern Europe.

Offering refugee protection to those who are not refugees is not, in itself, objectionable. It is a form of generosity. However, it becomes objectionable when placed side by side with the rejection of people who are fleeing real danger. The unfairness of this system becomes all the more glaring and blatant when those accepted are less deserving than those rejected.

A BIAS AGAINST TEMPORARY PROTECTION

A persecuted person needs protection as long as he is still in danger in his home country. He does not necessarily want to take up permanent residence in the asylum country. In fact, the overwhelming majority of refugees would gladly return to their countries of origin provided the danger for them has subsided. However, the refugee system is biased against temporary protection.[7]

Canada, for instance, requires that refugees apply for landed immigrant status, implying their problems are permanent, not temporary. Once a claimant is recognized as a refugee, he must apply for landing within sixty days or else be required to leave.[8] There is no middle ground between landing and being deported. Yet, immigration is a permanent solution that may have been appropriate for post-war refugees fleeing Eastern Europe, but not for refugees of today.

Because those accepted as refugees become permanent residents, immigration officials are inclined to recognize as refugees people they would welcome as immigrants. Refugees who do not meet normal immigration criteria tend to be rejected. In Canada, this tendency is reinforced because an Immigration Department adjudicator is one of the decision-makers on refugee claims. Adjudicators may apply immigration criteria to determinations of refugee status. Immigration officials tend to view refugees as persons who have slipped through the immigration system, because they would not be landed as immigrants if not for their persecution.

Yet the confusion between refugees and immigrants is inappropriate: refugees do not choose to leave their countries of origin, as immigrants do. The confusion between refugees and immigrants works against Third World refugees. Third World refugees are less likely to have the skills, training, education, or wealth of Second or First World refugees, including those from Eastern Europe, and are thefore less likely to meet normal immigration criteria. Because of the anti-Communist bias, Third World refugees from non-Communist countries have an even harder time getting refugee protection. Yet today's refugee-producing countries are predominantly Third World nations.

The Convention, with its bias toward permanent resettlement, reflects the post Second World War conditions under which the Convention was developed. Post-war refugees, fleeing hostile Communist regimes, were viewed as a source of skilled immigrants, and an opposition in exile to help discredit the source country. But today, many refugee-producing countries such as Sri Lanka are not the hostile enemies characteristic of the Cold War period. The West may have wanted to discredit the governments of Eastern Europe. It has no desire to discredit the government of Sri Lanka and other Third World refugee-producing countries.

The bias in favour of keeping refugees in exile has ended up hurting the persecuted. It has led to an excessive demand for resettlement, beyond the capacity of resettlement countries. And this has helped to provoke a tightening up of the refugee system in these countries. Canada followed other traditional resettlement countries with the exclusionary policies included in Bill C-55. Like European countries and the U.S., Canada has become part of the trend toward dismantling procedural safeguards for refugees. Once one country makes it more difficult for refugees seeking protection, others fearing large influxes of refugees follow suit. The obligation of international burden-sharing of refugees is forgotten.

This emphasis on resettlement has been unworkable in practice. We have not yet abandoned the concept of providing protection to the persecuted, but the means to make the persecution concept work have been forsaken. Procedural rules are set up to deny protection to refugees in practice through unfair refugee determination processes.

CUSTOMARY INTERNATIONAL LAW

The legal definition of refugees in the Refugee Convention has not worked. It has excluded all sorts of people fleeing manmade danger who, according to common sense, are refugees.

A broader definition of refugees is needed to include those refugees excluded by the present definition. It is argued that this has already happened because of customary international law. Customary international law is not treaty law, but a practice the community of nations follows and regards as binding. A widespread acceptance is sufficient. Unanimity is not necessary.

This widespread practice is shown in a number of different ways. Canada has historically had a number of temporary humanitarian programmes to provide protection within Canada of persons from countries experiencing adverse domestic events. Past programmes have protected persons from Chile, El Salvador, Ethiopia, Guatemala, Iran, Iraq, Lebanon and Sri Lanka.

The United Nations High Commission for Refugees (UNHCR) has been given a mandate by the UN General Assembly to assist refugees, including those who do not meet the refugee definition. The only criterion is that the refugees have crossed an international border as a result of conflicts or radical political, social or economic changes in their countries of origin. No individual determination is required to determine whether the person falls within the United Nations Convention refugee definition.

This General Assembly authorization has come from a sequence of resolutions dating back to 1957. The U.N. Economic and Social Council and the Executive Committee of the UNHCR have passed similar resolutions. The UNHCR assists this broader category of refugees — sometimes called "mandate" refugees — and has intervened to ask asylum countries not to return these refugees back to the country of danger.

48

Latin America's Cartagena Declaration of 1984[9] and the Organization of African Unity Convention of 1967[10] accept an expanded definition of refugee to cover those fleeing generalized violence. A broader definition may not be part of international treaty law outside of Africa and Latin America, but, it is argued, a broadened definition of refugees is already part of customary international law.

True, refugees fleeing generalized violence are provided some form of protection, if not resettlement. But do states view the practice as binding? Many states seem to view protection as an obligation of other countries, and not necessarily as their own. The United States, for instance, will call upon Thailand to give protection to refugees fleeing generalized violence from Kampuchea and Vietnam. Yet the U.S. balks at giving the same protection to refugees fleeing generalized violence from Guatemala and El Salvador.

Can a customary international law arise when states view a practice as binding on others, but not themselves? Is there a customary international law of protection of "mandate" refugees? To my knowledge, no court in any country has confirmed the existence of such a law. Arguing the existence of a customary international law offering protection to "mandate" refugees is a fruitful but arduous area of litigation. International precedents worldwide would have to be marshalled.

INTERPRETATION

The distinction between refugees fleeing individualized violence and refugees fleeing generalized violence does not originate in the Convention itself, but in interpretations widely accepted throughout the Western world.

The West restricts the Convention refugee definition, not as the result of a close textual analysis, but for political reasons. Resettlement countries want to restrict their obligations to provide protection, and a narrow definition helps to achieve this goal.

But equally practical reasons exist now for moving to a broader version of the refugee definition. Persons fleeing generalized violence already may become *de facto* refugees —

refugees in fact — and therefore not forcibly returned to danger. However, they are not given the status and benefits of *de jure* refugees — refugees in law. These *de facto* refugees may be denied the right to work, attend school or travel within the country. They may be kept in refugee camps, denied freedom of movement, or denied family reunification. *De facto* refugees will almost certainly not be given documents that will allow travel outside the country. Changing the law to categorize *de facto* refugees as *de jure* refugees would improve their condition. It would not change the fact of protection. Protection that existed in fact could, with a change in law, exist legally.

Changing the Convention to incorporate the reality of *de facto* refugees as *de jure* refugees would be difficult. Changing the interpretation of the refugee definition within the existing legal structure would be much easier. Signatories would not have to approve a new Refugee Convention definition, only to accept a new interpretation.

Courts in the Netherlands broke new ground in this area. Until recently, asylum requests in the Netherlands would result in either "A" status or "B" status. "A" status was refugee status. "B" status was granted if the alien was not a refugee but there were valid objections to returning him to his country of danger, including compelling reasons of a humanitarian nature relating to the political situation in the country of origin. In February, 1988, the highest court in the Netherlands held it was not possible to make a distinction between "A" status and "B" status. Those granted "B" status are now considered to have been granted "A" or Convention status.[11]

THE FOURTH GENEVA CONVENTION

One technique to broaden the interpretation of the refugee definition is to use the Fourth Geneva Convention for Protection of Civilians in Time of War. In the case of internal rather than international armed conflict occurring in one of the signatory states, the Convention requires each party to the conflict to abide by certain minimum provisions. Torture, hostage-taking and extra-judicial executions are among the prohibited activities.[12] Each of the parties to the Convention undertakes to ensure respect for the Convention.[13]

A "protected person" is defined as someone who finds himself, in the case of a conflict, in the hands of a party to the conflict.[14] This Geneva Convention provides that "protected persons" may be transferred by the detaining power only to a country which is a party to the Convention. The country detaining the refugee must also have satisfied itself of the willingness and ability of the transferee country to apply the Convention.[15]

Counsel in the United States used the Geneva Convention for the Protection of Civilians in Time of War in litigation to argue for the duty of protection of "mandate" refugees from El Salvador. Counsel said Salvadoran Jesus Del Carmen Medina was a "protected person" because while in the U.S., he was in a country party to the conflict in El Salvador. Although U.S. Immigration Judge Michael Horn did not hold the United States to be a party to the conflict in El Salvador, he found Medina was a protected person under the Convention's minimum provisions.

The upshot of the case was that the requirement to prove persecution by a government was side-stepped. It wasn't necessary to show that torture, hostage-taking or extra-judicial execution were the responsibility of a government, only that they were happening.

In the end, Judge Horn refused a request to grant asylum in the U.S. and to withhold deportation to El Salvador.[16] He decided Medina's counsel had not clearly established that grave breaches of the Convention — willful killing, unlawful and wanton destruction, torture or inhuman treatment[17] — were occurring in El Salvador.[†]

[†] Horn decided the case based on evidence before him, not on the situation in El Salvador. Defence testimony simply addressed the armed conflict in El Salvador, the judge stated, and not whether grave breaches of the Convention had occurred. As well, he said, defence evidence was all secondary or derived. Evidence presented was conclusions rather than fact. Given the consistent pattern of human rights violations in both El Salvador and Guatemala, establishing grave breaches of the Fourth Geneva Convention should not be difficult. In fact, it can be used for virtually every trouble spot on the globe because, unlike the Refugee Convention, the Geneva Convention has received almost universal recognition by states. However, the U.S.

51

INTERNATIONAL COVENANT ON CIVIL AND POLITICAL RIGHTS

Another device for expanding the scope of refugee protection is the International Covenant on Civil and Political Rights (the Covenant). Like the Geneva Convention, the Covenant is not intended as a refugee instrument. Yet its provisions may be used to aid refugees. In particular, the Covenant states that every human being has the inherent right to life, and that this right must be protected by law. No one may be arbitrarily deprived of his life.[19]

When a refugee is denied protection, his right to life is not being protected by law. If he is forcibly returned to the country of danger and killed, he was arbitrarily deprived of his life. For countries like Canada that have acceded to the Covenant, an expanded refugee definition can be based on this provision in the Covenant.

EXPANDED REFUGEE DEFINITION

Let us assume no customary international law exists requiring protection to refugees fleeing generalized violence, and that the Geneva Convention and Covenant are not available alternatives.

One obvious suggestion is to change and expand the refugee definition in the Refugee Convention to cover everyone who has fled man-made danger, whether generalized violence or individualized persecution.

The definition of refugees in the Organization of African Unity Convention and Latin America's Cartagena declaration shows a willingness, at least within Africa and Latin America, to expand the refugee definition to include those fleeing generalized violence. Many governments, international bodies and experts in favour of a comprehensive definition of refugees have passed resolutions and recommendations on the subject.

Board of Immigration Appeals rejected Horn's interpretation of the Convention as did the U.S. District Court of Northern California. Both courts held that the U.S. had to be a party to the conflict before it was obligated by the Convention to protect refugees, and that it was not a party to the conflict in El Salvador.[18]

Ideally, the Refugee Convention definition would be changed to cast a wider net for refugees. Do we want to start a debate about changing the definition? There are dangers to that approach. The immigration bias that works against a fair application of the present restricted refugee definition would create a powerful force against expansion, and would work against a proper application of any expanded definition that was accepted. Once discussions of a definition start, there is a danger resettlement countries will attempt to narrow the definition even more.

The First World already thinks it gets too many Third World arrivals. An expanded refugee definition leading to an even greater number of Third World arrivals will be opposed by the First World in both theory and practice.

The Third World's consensus on an expanded refugee definition has been suggested as a starting point to develop a new international refugee legal order. However the Third World cannot change international law by itself. The West opposed the Third World proposal for a New World Economic order, and the proposal failed. A change in refugee definition cannot succeed without the support of the Western resettlement countries.

TEMPORARY REFUGE OPTION

One way to make an expanded definition acceptable is to link *temporary* rather than *permanent* refuge protection with the refugee group covered by the broader definition.

In fact, some countries currently denying refugee protection to those refugees fleeing generalized violence offer them a "B" or *de facto* refugee status, a form of temporary refuge. Linking an expanded refugee definition with temporary refuge for those covered by it would legalize the system currently in force. What is arguably customary international law already would become treaty international law.

However, problems lie with that suggestion too. Imposing temporary protection is far different from granting it on request. The refugees' plight is worsened when they are held at bay and told they will have to leave soon or be forced to leave at a certain time. In countries of refuge, they need to be welcomed and given a chance for integration.

Linking flight from persecution and permanent protection on the one hand, and flight from generalized violence and temporary protection on the other hand is inappropriate. Some public disorders last for years. A refugee forced to return years after he established himself in a resettlement country is not just being returned, but is undergoing one forced relocation after another.

Temporary refuge should be an option. Further, temporary refuge should be an option for all refugees, not just "mandate" refugees. Asylum states should not force return, nor should they create barriers to return. It should be a matter of choice. The notion of temporary refuge has a value to assist refugees, not to make a broader definition more acceptable to states.

Countries committed to refugee protection should move to eliminate the restrictive narrow refugee definition now in place. It is utopic to believe resettlement countries already feeling overburdened by the number of refugees seeking protection would favour an explicit expansion of the definition in the Convention to include refugees fleeing every man-made danger. However, broadening the interpretation of the present refugee definition may be possible. Changing the interpretation of the Refugee Convention definition is the most plausible step toward ensuring that those fleeing every man-made danger receive the refugee protection they deserve.

Chapter 3

WHAT FAIRNESS REQUIRES

n order for a person to be a refugee, he must have a well-founded fear of persecution. A fear of persecution alone is not enough. If the fear is without foundation the person is not a refugee. The state in which a refugee claimant seeks protection has to determine whether or not the claimant's fear is just. If the fear is unfounded, the state has no duty of protection.[1] If the fear is well-founded a duty of protection is owed.

Refugee determination systems have been established in protection states to make these determinations. Yet these systems are in one way or another procedurally unfair. Unfair determinations lead to inaccurate results. Real refugees are rejected in error. The commitment to protection is violated.

For protection states, a narrower definition of refugees has not been enough of a deterrent. Unfair procedures are yet another technique of denial of protection.

For a refugee wrongly rejected and returned to the persecuting country, death may await. A death squad could capture him upon his arrival in the home country. A person who fled and was unsuccessful in his refugee claim will be viewed by the persecuting government as a traitor. If the refugee's life was in danger before he left, it will be in even greater danger when he returns.

As a refugee lawyer in private practice in Canada, I meet genuine refugees who have come to Canada after having been refused refugee status elsewhere, only to be turned down here. I have talked to refugee lawyers in other countries who see what I see, that genuine refugees are denied refugee status, not occasionally or accidentally, but systematically and on a large scale.

Signatory countries shirk their responsibility to share the refugee burden. Instead, each tries to foist the rising tide of refugees on others. The number of refugees unable to find durable solutions continues to swell, while governments proclaim "new and improved" refugee determination processes aimed at keeping refugees out.

It is ironic that refugees fleeing persecution should face this universal denial of fairness in refugee determination systems. Refugees flee their home countries because they are victims of human rights violations such as kidnapping, harassment or torture by the military. They seek protection in countries of refuge because they believe they will find deference to human rights. Yet, when a refugee faces an unfair determination process, he faces a variation of the very human rights violation he has fled. At home, for example, he may have been denied a fair trial. In the country of refuge, he is likely to face exactly the same thing.

CAUSES OF UNFAIRNESS

The unfairness of the world's refugee systems stems not from mere sloppiness, but from five basic causes: political, economic, administrative, practical and numerical.

I. Political

Acceptance of a refugee claim is an acknowledgement that the claimant has a well-founded fear of persecution perpetrated by a foreign government. Political unfairness is bound to emerge when the foreign affairs department of the asylum country becomes involved in refugee determination. Any country's foreign affairs department works toward improved relations with its allies, and would be reluctant to imply their friends are human rights violators. For example, the U.S. State Department has been reluctant to imply that Guatemala and El Salvador are human rights violators because these countries are military allies. A condemnation of an ally, implicit in finding a person to be a refugee, would be contrary to the other responsibilities of the foreign affairs department.

2. Economic

The economic cause of unfairness is the suspicion that refugee claimants — many from Third World countries with inferior standards of living — are really economic immigrants attempting to circumvent immigration criteria. Most refugee claimants would not qualify to enter or remain in the asylum country as immigrants. Immigration enforcement officials, who constantly discover people attempting to enter their borders to take advantage of the better standard of living, inevitably bring immigration considerations to bear when these officials are part of the refugee determination process.

3. Administrative

Determination systems are often set up with a view to efficiency rather than fairness. An administrator's desire to cut costs and be expeditious can often result in an unfair administrative procedure. To conduct a proper assessment of some refugee claims may require procedures that are slower, more time-consuming or more costly than the bureaucracy wants. Up to a point, efficiency can be an element of fairness: genuine refugees reap no benefits from a slow, expensive determination process. Beyond that point, however, efficiency must be balanced against other needs. When efficiency is the sole concern, unfairness results.

4. Practical

There is also a practical reason for unfairness of the determination process. Once the claimant's case is rejected he is no longer present to complain of the system's unfairness. He leaves the country of asylum and may be forcibly returned to the country from which he fled. He can not practically contest the unfairness endured once he has been removed from the country of refuge.

5. Numbers

Lastly, unfairness in the refugee determination process is caused by the sheer number of refugees in the world today. Absorbing twelve million Convention refugees is obviously beyond the capacity of any one asylum country. Unfairly rejecting refugee claimants is a way of controlling numbers. The resettlement countries of North America, Australia and Europe are widely concerned that, with a refugee system easy of access and generous in spirit, each country would soon be flooded not with abusive refugee claimants, but with genuine refugees.

PRINCIPLES OF FAIRNESS

Standards of fairness or natural justice are legal requirements in many countries and represent common sense notions. I suggest the following twelve standards of fairness.

1. Structural Impartiality

The refugee system of a country must recognize refugees from all countries on equal terms. Making it easier for claimants from some countries to get refugee status by allowing them access to the deciding authority is unfair when claimants from other countries are not even allowed to make a claim. It is unfair when refugee procedures may be rigorous and the standards invoked by the deciding authority difficult to meet, and yet nationals of some countries may be presumed to be refugees without having to pass over the procedural hurdles or meet the standards.

2. Safeguards

The United Nations High Commission for Refugees (UNHCR) Executive Committee has said a claim must be rejected as manifestly unfounded only if it is "clearly fraudulent" or unrelated to the Refugee Convention criteria.[2] Claims could, however, be unfairly rejected as manifestly unfounded where there are no procedural safeguards in place to ensure the claim is, indeed, not bona fide.

The safeguards that are proposed in this chapter for a full hearing cannot be swept away for a "manifestly unfounded" claim. Unless the procedural safeguards are in place, it is impossible to be confident that the determination "manifestly unfounded" is accurate.

3. Access to Counsel

Refugee claimants who fear persecution in their own countries are often reluctant to speak freely to authorities in a would-be asylum country. Details of victimization may be repressed because they are painful to recall. Claimants will also be wary of saying anything to compromise or endanger family and friends they have left behind. Further, refugee procedures and laws of asylum countries are often complex and the official examining the claimant may not be well versed in refugee law or sensitive to difficulties refugees face. For all these reasons, counsel can be of invaluable assistance in representing refugee claims.

4. Opportunity to Respond

A claimant must have the right to know the objections to his claim and the opportunity to respond to these objections. Possible objections to a claim are that the claimant has been inconsistent, contradicted himself, concealed material facts, or made a misrepresentation. It would be unfair for a claim to be rejected on the basis of these objections before giving the claimant a chance to respond to them.

The *Handbook on Procedures and Criteria for Determining Refugee Status* published by the UNHCR in 1979, recognizes this need. "While an initial interview should normally suffice to bring an applicant's claim to light, it may be necessary for the examiner to clarify any apparent inconsistencies, to resolve any contradiction in a further interview and to find an explanation for any misrepresentation or concealment of material fact."[3]

In a 1985 judgement, the Supreme Court of Canada stated that fundamental justice requires that a claimant must know the case he has to meet.[4] The claimant must have an opportunity to explain apparent inconsistencies or contradictions in his own testimony, or challenge Department of External Affairs reports about human rights conditions in the country fled which may (wrongly) contradict his testimony.

5. Oral Hearing

A refugee determination requires a judgement of the applicant's credibility. In fact, many refugee claims are rejected on the grounds that they are incredible. However, it is unfair to make such a judgement without ever seeing the person, assessing his demeanour or listening to the manner in which he speaks. It is particularly unfair when the person is a refugee claimant in an alien environment, using an interpreter. The UNHCR executive committee recommends applicants be given a complete personal interview, wherever possible, by an official with the authority to determine refugee status.[5]

In systems without oral hearings, refugee claimants are sometimes examined by officers without authority to decide. A transcript or summary of the examination is sent to the officials who make the decision. In theory, this system is fair because the applicant has the chance to answer objections to his claim during a re-examination. In fact, this system is time-consuming, cumbersome and open to mistakes. The examining officer serves as an intermediary between the deciding officer and the refugee claimant. The deciding officer never meets face-to-face with the claimant. Instead, the examining officer passes questions and answers back and forth.

6. Benefit of the Doubt

The *UNHCR Handbook* says: "If the applicant's account appears credible, he should, unless there are good reasons to the contrary, be given the benefit of the doubt."[6] A refugee claimant is unlikely to arrive with extensive documentation supporting his claim. Witnesses who could corroborate his story may still be in the home country, subject to persecution if they say anything. To reject a claim where the claimant appears credible but can supply no independent proof is unfair.

7. Individual Consideration

Each claim must be assessed individually. This doesn't mean the claimant must establish he was singled out for persecution.

It does mean that the claim cannot be rejected out of hand based on the claimant's country of origin or membership in a group. The details of the individual claim must be considered.

8. An Independent Deciding Authority
An independent authority must be in place to decide refugee claims on their own merits. Yet virtually every country involves its immigration department or its external affairs department — or both — in the refugee determination process. The external affairs department may be reluctant to find in favour of a refugee claim if this implies that an ally is a human rights violator. The department of immigration may carry an inbred suspicion that refugee claimants are really economic immigrants in disguise.

9. A Qualified Examiner and Decision-Maker
In most countries, refugee interviewers are poorly trained, and their knowledge of international human rights is limited. Interviewers mix refugee work with other work. Examiners and decision-makers should know refugee law, understand conditions in the country from which the claimant has fled, and be sensitive to the difficulties refugees face.

10. An Appeal or Review Process
Despite the seriousness of the refugee decision, some countries deny court or government tribunal appeals to claimants. A deciding authority may have made a decision for the most obviously wrong reasons, but the error goes uncorrected without a right of appeal or review.

The UNHCR executive committee recommends, "If the applicant is not recognized, he should be given a reasonable time to appeal." The Committee urges the applicant be permitted to remain in the country pending the decision and the appeal from a negative decision unless the appeal is "clearly abusive."[7]

Even where the claim is manifestly unfounded and may be dealt with in a expeditious manner, the UNHCR recommends an unsuccessful applicant be allowed to appeal a negative decision before being removed.[8]

11. Reasons For a Negative Determination

Even if a claimant has a right to appeal or review, that right is of limited value if the original decision to reject is given with a scanty explanation or none at all. Reasons should include more than just stock phrases or conclusions. They should relate refugee law to the claim, deal with the substantial points raised, and relate the facts to the conclusions.

12. Systemic Impartiality

There are two main categories of discrimination: *structural*, for example, a system which openly denies access to Vietnamese refugees, and *systemic,* for example, a system which says it will consider all refugees, but in practice never admits Vietnamese refugees.

Even without direct evidence of discrimination, statistics may show it is easier for one race or nationality to get refugee status than another, leaving the system open to question. Faulty procedures, such as lack of independence or failure to consider cases individually, may introduce bias into the system. Fairness requires systemic impartiality.

Other criteria for fairness could be added: adequate translation or proper notice requirements, for example. But these twelve basic standards of fairness stand out because all of the many refugee determination systems I have examined fail to meet one or other of these criteria. This list is therefore a list of common failings.

International law does not require compliance with these twelve criteria of fairness. However, signatories to the Refugee Convention and Protocol are required to comply with the obligation not to return a refugee to a country where his life or freedom would be threatened. If these standards of fairness are met, the obligation not to return forcibly will likely be met. Where the standards are not met, the obligation will almost certainly not be met.

Rights without remedies are valueless. It is not enough to legislate the refugee definition. Unless fair procedures are established to determine refugee claims, genuine refugees will continue to be refused and forcibly returned to countries where their lives are in danger.

Chapter 4

REFUGEE DETERRENCE

Refugee claimants are among the most wretched people in Canada. They have fled countries where they have been imprisoned for their beliefs, where they may have been tortured or threatened with death. They have few or no friends in Canada and normally cannot speak either French or English. A refugee claim can take years to process before a final determination is reached, yet until a person is recognized as a refugee, he is not recognized as a resident. Despite this lengthy stay in Canada, he is treated as if he will be leaving in a week or two. There are few areas of life not regulated by government and few areas of government regulation where residency does not make a difference. Whenever residency does make a difference, a refugee claimant suffers. Refugees are made to lead such miserable lives in the country of asylum that they are deterred even from seeking protection.

Governments in Canada make no effort to help refugee claimants feel comfortable here. Quite the opposite. By and large, refugee claimants come from Third World countries lacking the standard of living and infrastructure of Canada. The government fears easy access to a Canadian standard of living would attract frivolous refugee claimants trying to benefit from a temporary stay in Canada. As a result, refugee claimants are made to suffer, not just by circumstance, but by design.

As a signatory to the Refugee Convention, Canada has an obligation not to return a refugee to a country where his life or freedom is threatened. But if a claimant is made to lead a miserable life in Canada, he may be discouraged from making a claim or be tempted to withdraw it, regardless of the possible consequences.

REFUGEE CLAIMANT PROBLEMS
Refugee claimants can encounter problems in the work permit system, their work search, the school permit system, medicare, legal aid, welfare, family allowance, in driver licensing and family reunification.

I. Work Permits
General rules dictate that a foreign worker must apply from outside Canada to get a work permit. The claimant must have a job offer and certification from the government of Canada that no Canadian is available for the position.

Refugee claimants are exempt from both of these rules. A refugee claimant may apply for and obtain a work permit from within Canada,[1] and doesn't need government certification that no Canadian is available for the job.[2]

Although refugee claimants are superficially advantaged by these exemptions, they are actually the root of much of their trouble. Refugee claimants are suspected of coming to Canada, not to seek protection, but to benefit from these exemptions. This suspicion may make their refugee claims harder to establish.

Refugee claimants may have been unemployed in their home countries or employed at wages significantly lower than the salaries they could earn in Canada. Even the minimum wage in Canada is a multiple of what could be earned back home. The very wealth of Canada, the availability of employment, and its high level of income compared to the Third World ends up undercutting the protection of refugees by generating suspicion about the claims.

The government has tried to counteract this temptation to claim refugee status simply in order to get a work permit by making work permits as hard as possible to obtain. Under the present system, work permits are not available immediately upon the making of a claim, but only after the claimant passes the first stage of the refugee determination process, the credible-basis step. Only after a claimant demonstrates that his claim has a credible-basis, a minimum foundation, is he eligible for a work permit.

A work permit is given to a claimant only if he would be destitute without it. He must establish to the satisfaction of immigration officials that any friends or relatives he might have in Canada are not willing or able to support him. If one member of the family is working, then other members of the family cannot work unless the family would be eligible for welfare, even with one family member working. In that case, a second family member will be allowed to work. However, if a claimant has a work permit for one job, he will be denied a second work permit for a second job. Again an exception is made only where the claimant would be eligible for welfare without the second job. These restrictions impoverish claimants. They are allowed to earn enough to keep off welfare, but no more.

Delay of eligibility for a work permit can mean destitution for refugee claimants who reside in provinces where claimants are not entitled to apply for welfare. Welfare is a matter of provincial jurisdiction, although the provinces and Ottawa cost-share welfare programmes fifty-fifty under the Canada Assistance Plan. A claimant eligible for neither welfare nor a work permit may not have any means of support. While abusive claims may be discouraged, so will genuine claims.

Prior to 1989, claimants' problems were complicated by the two avenues available for making a refugee claim: *in-status* and *out-of-status.* The problems a claimant faced depended on the kind of claim he made.

An in-status claim is made while the claimant is still a visitor in Canada. The claimant retains his status as a visitor until his refugee claim is determined through the refugee determination process. An in-status claimant is not subjected to Immigration enforcement procedures, and therefore cannot be ordered deported or excluded if the refugee claim fails. The claimant may leave voluntarily.

An out-of-status claimant is a person who has lost his visitor's status, or never had visitor status in the first place. He has no status in Canada, and is here solely pending determination of his claim. Thus, an out-of-status claimant is subject to deportation or exclusion if the refugee claim fails.

Beginning in 1985, an out-of-status refugee claimant became eligible to apply for a work permit once he made a claim at an inquiry.[3] In 1986, the government pushed back the eligibility date for work permits until refugee examinations were heard.[4] Claimants could no longer work between the date of inquiry and the date of examination.

The government said refugee claimants who started work after the inquiry were not showing up for their refugee examinations because they wanted to go to work instead. But I believe the government did not want to make Canada too attractive to claimants, and pushed back the date of eligibility as a disincentive. Postponing the date when work could begin made initiating a claim more of a hardship and less of a temptation. However, such disincentives affect real refugees and abusive claimants alike. They will not convince a genuine refugee to return to persecution, but they may make the protection he receives in Canada more grudging, more shoddy, more threadbare.

Whatever the logic behind the government position, the plan stopped working once the government stopped scheduling refugee claims. As the new system approached January 1, 1989, the old system stopped. Everyone in the old system, according to transition provisions in the new law, was funnelled into the new system. Unless their hearings had actually begun before the

Immigration Appeal Board, they were left in limbo to wait until the new system came into effect, and then start their refugee claim all over again.

Large influxes of refugees came to Canada in the months leading up to the new system's effective date in hopes that an amnesty would be announced for all those backlogged under the old determination system. The combination of the shut down of the system and the increase in claimant arrival caused an intolerable burden. Claimants who wanted to work, and had already found work, could not get work permits. Welfare expenditures for claimants increased by leaps and bounds.

The Department had no reason to worry that claimants would not show up for examinations if they were working, since no examinations were being scheduled until the new law took effect. Yet, work permits remained possible only after examinations.

Jose Marvin Campos came to Canada from El Salvador through the U.S. in March, 1988. When he arrived at the Canadian border, he was turned back and told to return to the U.S. until an adjudicator was available for an inquiry. His initial inquiry was held in April, 1988. He was not eligible for a work permit until his refugee examination.

The refugee examination was scheduled for November of the same year. But the Department realized everyone would be training for the new law at that time, and subsequently postponed Campos' refugee examination indefinitely. The eligibility of Campos to work was also postponed indefinitely.

On behalf of Campos, I asked the Federal Court to order the government to schedule the refugee examination of Campos. On November 16 at the court hearing before Federal Court Judge Max Teitelbaum, the government consented to schedule Campos a refugee exam.[5]

Campos got his examination and his work permit eligibility November 21, 1988, as originally scheduled. Anyone who wanted to go to court during this period could get a consent order. But a consent order is not a legal precedent, and only binds the government in the one case. Those who did not go to court continued waiting, without examinations and without work permits, many of them on welfare.

This insistence on postponing eligibility for work permits until an examination takes place — even after examinations were no longer being scheduled — showed the reason for the postponement had little or nothing to do with ensuring claimants were available for examination. The reason had everything to do with providing a deterrent to refugee claimants to discourage them from making or maintaining claims.

The refusal to schedule any refugee examinations even after the Campos decision — unless a court specifically required an examination to be scheduled — demonstrated the deterrence motivation even more clearly. The government simply did not want claimants to work.

For in-status claimants before January 1, 1989, the situation was even worse. Government guidelines for immigration officers said in-status claimants did not enjoy any of the employment privileges provided under the Immigration Act to an out-of-status claimant.[6] The Department could not even consider a work permit application by an in-status refugee claimant.

2. Work Search

Through the Canada Employment and Immigration Commission (CEIC), the government of Canada offers an employment service, matching job offers with job applicants. It is a heavily used service, particularly for unskilled labour. In the 1987-88 fiscal year, CEIC advertised 963,100 vacancies for jobs of more than one week, placed 666,800 people in jobs lasting for more than one week, and referred 2,952,800 people to regular employment.[7]

However, refugee claimants cannot take advantage of this service because they are not allowed to register with the CEIC. The government restricts the service to residents of Canada, forcing refugee claimants to find work on their own.

3. School

Under the new legislation, claimants may be prosecuted for attending school without authorization.[8] Everyone now requires permission to attend school, and adults are regularly denied permission.

Further, while refugee claimants are eligible to go to school, they are ineligible for any government training programmes.

CEIC finances training programmes at community colleges and on-the-job training to give Canadians the skills they need to find work. Refugee claimants are not permanent residents, and therefore need not apply.

Claimants may go to school only if they have permission from the Department of Immigration. The Department gives this permission only to minor dependents of refugee claimants, not to adult claimants. The Department says, "Studies are not considered necessary for subsistence while a claim is being determined." Before a minor dependent is given permission to go to school, the school must warrant that any non-resident fees have been paid. Schools do not have to charge refugee claimants non-resident fees, but if they do, the charges can be onerous.

If an in-status claimant who entered Canada as a tourist or a worker attends school without permission, he violates the terms and conditions of his entry and is subject to deportation. If he enters as a student and changes institutions, or even courses, without permission, he again violates the terms and conditions of his entry and is subject to deportation.

Until December 31, 1988, out-of-status claimants could go to school without authorization, simply because the law did not prohibit attending school without permission. Therefore, immigration officials had no say in whether out-of-status refugee claimants went to school.

It wasn't until April, 1984, that the Department of Immigration formally articulated its position on this question of school attendance. The Department added a section to the immigration manual titled *Refugee Claimants and their Dependents Attending School*[9] The manual states: "The fact that our legislation is silent on this matter (of school attendance of refugee claimants in the enforcement stream and their dependents) does not specifically prevent school attendance by such persons. Our present legislation does not require non-visitors to obtain a student authorization and such persons can, in fact, study without obtaining one."

The manual provided for a form letter to be signed by an immigration officer that the person concerned may attend school at the discretion of school officials. So after April, 1984 until January, 1989, refugee claimants and their dependents in the enforcement stream could attend school without permission, and not face prosecution, or even the threat of prosecution. The "no-objection" letter an immigration officer could issue clarified the situation to school authorities.

4. Medicare

Medicare eligibility is determined provincially, not federally, and can vary from province to province. In Manitoba, for example, the Manitoba Health Services Commission says a refugee claimant is eligible for medicare once he has one or more work permits totalling twelve months or more. A claimant becomes eligible as soon as he receives a work permit that will take him to twelve months. He does not need to have actually worked during this entire time. Since claimants do not find work as soon as they arrive in Canada, and may not get work at all, this leaves many people unprotected.

Private health insurance may not be available. Manitoba Blue Cross has a visitor health care plan, but the application must be received by the private insurer within seven days of arrival in Manitoba, and the term of the policy, plus all extensions, cannot exceed thirty-two days. Persons applying for immigrant status are not eligible for coverage.

Doctors and hospitals will provide medical help to refugee claimants for a charge. The cost may discourage refugee claimants from seeking necessary medical care.

5. Legal Aid

Eligibility for legal aid, like medicare, is decided by the provinces, resulting in varying rules across the country. In British Columbia, refugee claimants are not eligible for legal aid.

In the complex Canadian refugee determination process, a claimant without a lawyer can be at a serious disadvantage. Some lawyers volunteer their services when legal aid is absent, but lack of legal aid can discourage a claimant from even approaching a lawyer to act on his behalf.

6. Welfare

Theoretically, welfare is subject to national standards. Under the Canada Assistance Plan, which provides for federal cost-sharing of provincial welfare, need is the only criterion for eligibility. Legal residence in Canada is not required.

Nevertheless, individual provinces have imposed residency requirements. In B.C., a welfare recipient must be either a Canadian citizen or a permanent resident. The B.C. government appealed one case to the Supreme Court of B.C., which held that a refugee claimant is not a resident[10] and is therefore ineligible for welfare in the province.

The federal Minister of Employment and Immigration has sided with refugee claimants and against the government of B.C. on this issue. Yet, no action has been taken to limit federal funds paid to the province, and refugee claimants in B.C. are still ineligible for welfare.

7. Family Allowance

The Family Allowances Act states that to be eligible for family allowance, a person must be a citizen, a permanent resident, a visitor, or the holder of a Minister's Permit.[11] Before a person can be eligible as a visitor or the holder of a Permit, he must be authorized to remain at least two months and his income must be subject to income tax.[12]

Refugee claimants are placed in a no-win situation. Out-of-status claimants are neither visitors nor permit holders. In principle, they are not eligible for family allowance. In-status refugee claimants are visitors, and are therefore eligible for family allowances, provided they are authorized to remain at least twelve months and are subject to income tax.

However, until January 1, 1989 in-status claimants were denied work permits, simply because they were in-status. An in-status claimant was normally unable to earn the income and pay the income tax that would allow him to receive family allowance.

8. Drivers' Licence

Provincial highway traffic acts typically provide that a non-resident may drive without a provincially-issued licence for three months. A non-resident can use any licence he may have been issued by his former jurisdiction.

The acts do not say a person must be a resident to obtain a driver's licence, but in practice this is how they are interpreted.

Sometimes a licence may be granted on appeal to supervisory staff. However, the initial refusal may discourage claimants from going any further.

9. Family Reunion

Refugee claimants are often alone. If they came from a country with a visitor's visa requirement, a visa will not be issued to allow their spouse or children to join them.

Only permanent residents and citizens can sponsor their immediate family to come to Canada. Refugee claimants cannot. Since a refugee claim may take years to resolve, claimants are kept apart from their families for a prolonged period of time. Lengthy separations can lead to marriage breakdown and disintegration of the family unit. Spouses abroad are unaware of the complexities and delays of the refugee system, and may believe that claimant spouses are simply failing to send for them.

Canada's *Immigration Manual* favours speedy family reunification: "Once it has been determined that a refugee in Canada is a Convention refugee, the appropriate post abroad will consider the facilitation of early admission by way of Minister's permit, provided medical and background requirements have been satisfied...."[13]

However, Rabbi Gunther Plaut points out, "While this provision appears on its face to provide sufficiently broad and flexible mechanism, its application has been more restrictive. The Canada Employment and Immigration Commission sees the issuance of a Minister's permit as an exceptional measure to be exercised when the circumstances are such that the family of the refugee faces some danger and cannot await the normal processing of the necessary applications. It is therefore only in these cases that facilitation is recommended in practice."[14]

REDUCING REFUGEE MISERY

A 1984 Conference on Refugees and Settlement, held in Winnipeg, generated a number of important recommendations for lessening the misery of refugee claimants.[15] The conference recommended that:

- work permits not be denied because of permits held by spouses,

- work permits for additional jobs not be denied,
- work permits not be denied because a friend or relative is willing or able to assist,
- schools not charge non-resident fees to refugee claimants and their dependents,
- claimants and their dependents be given permission to attend school,
- refugee claimants be covered by medicare from the date of their claim,
- legal aid be available for refugee claimants,
- refugee claimants not be denied welfare by virtue of their status or lack of status in Canada,
- refugee claimants be entitled to family allowance on making their claim.

VISA REQUIREMENTS

Visa requirements have already been discussed in Chapter 1 as a racist technique of denial. Visa requirements are not only used indirectly as a form of racism, objective in appearance, discriminatory in impact. They are also used directly and overtly to prevent refugee claimants from coming to Canada.

A pattern has evolved in Canada's refugee system. When a repressive regime has generated a significant inflow of refugees into Canada, those claiming refugee status are refused in large proportions. The government of Canada assumes its refugee determination procedure is accurate, and therefore concludes the immigration system is being abused. The government prevents refugees from seeking protection here by requiring that a person from the country in question obtain a visitor's visa issued at a Canadian post abroad before he appears at a Canadian port of entry. In recent years, Canada has imposed visa requirements on Chile, Haiti, India, Sri Lanka, Guatemala, Peru and Guyana to stop nationals of those countries from coming here to claim refugee status.

As mentioned in Chapter 1, airlines will not transport to Canada a person without a visa who comes from a country with a visa requirement. The Immigration Act requires airlines to pay the cost of detaining and removing persons brought to Canada who should have visas but don't.[16]

Government officials claim that imposing a visa requirement does not stop refugee access to Canada altogether. In fact, by international standards, Canada accepts more than its share of the burden of refugee resettlement. A visa requirement merely regulates the flow: instead of refugees coming to Canada as their country of first asylum, they come when they are chosen by the government of Canada.

But that is not good enough. Like all signatories to the Refugee Convention, Canada has a duty of non-refoulement. A visa requirement violates this obligation. To the refugee, there is no difference between being forced to return from Canada to his country and not being allowed to come from his country to Canada in the first place.

A visa requirement is one technique for curbing abuse, but is not always appropriate. Genuine refugees are also prevented from seeking refuge in Canada. Amnesty International* believes the Canadian government has unnecessarily and unfairly imposed visa requirements on countries not generating significant refugee claimant abuse. This includes countries which are gross and flagrant violators of human rights, like Guatemala.[17]

A number of non-governmental organizations (NGOs) met in Toronto in 1984, sponsored by the Canadian Section of Amnesty International, to discuss the question of Canada as a country of first asylum. All the NGOs represented — the Canadian Council of Churches, the Canadian Labour Congress, the Canadian Jewish Congress, the Canadian Bar Association and Amnesty International — argued that Canada should be a country of first asylum for refugees who choose to come to this country. They also agreed that Canada should not impose a visa requirement on a refugee-producing country as a means of regulating refugee inflow to Canada.

The government of Canada alleges that a visa exemption allows oppressive regimes to expel their opponents. A foreign dictator may take advantage of a Canadian visa exemption to

---

*Amnesty International is a non-governmental organization opposed to torture, the death penalty and imprisonment of prisoners of conscience.

get rid of opposition forces by expelling them to Canada. A visa exemption, they say, can aid a foreign oppressor rather than refugees.

On the other hand, a visa requirement sends a message to an oppressive regime that the Canadian government is washing its hands of the problem. The government is saying it is not concerned with violations causing the refugee problem. Furthermore, a Canadian visa requirement can lead to retaliation in kind. This may hinder Canadians from travelling to other countries to assist the persecuted. Canadian doctors or aid workers will need visas, and may be denied them.

The NGOs which met in Toronto were most concerned with the visa requirement for Guatemala imposed by Canada in March, 1984. At that time, refugee inflow into Canada was small — 244 claims were made in 1983 — and abuse was minimal. There was an acceptance rate for claims of 70.5 percent. Nevertheless, Canada imposed a visa requirement. Guatemala countered by imposing a visa requirement on Canada.

The symposium concluded: where numbers of claimants are manageable, abuses are small, countries of origin are violating human rights in a gross and flagrant manner, and Canada is a logical and accessible country of refuge, a visa requirement should not be imposed. Guatemala met all of these criteria.

Canada has also imposed visa requirements on other refugee-producing countries in order to shut off refugee flows. In the late 1970s, Haitians coming to Canada and claiming refugee status through normal procedures were regularly refused status. Subsequently many Haitians came as visitors and stayed illegally, not bothering to make a refugee claim. At the time, the Lawyers Committee for International Rights reported Haiti consistently violated human rights in a gross and flagrant manner.

Canada responded to the buildup of illegal Haitian refugees here in a number of ways. First, the government closed the doors to future arrivals from Haiti by imposing a visitor's visa requirement. Second, Canada granted an amnesty to those Haitians in Canada illegally, provided they arrived prior to June

24, 1980 and came forward to regularize their status. In Quebec alone, an estimated 2,000 to 4,000 Haitians were able to regularize their stay without having to prove they were refugees, thanks to the amnesty. In the end Canada admitted a substantial number of Haitian refugees, but only by way of exception.

In 1980, the Progressive Conservative government imposed a visa requirement on Chile. They did this after the Conservatives had already been defeated in the House of Commons and the election had been called. When the Liberals formed the next government, they decided to retain the visa requirement for Chile.

Enforced misery or visa impositions are not appropriate abuse control mechanisms. Because these tactics make no distinction between the abuser and the genuine refugee, the legitimate refugee claimant suffers as much as someone who has come to Canada merely looking for a better way of life. A visa requirement can deny access to genuine refugees, and thus deny protection. The proper way to control abuse is speedy determination of refugee claims with proper safeguards. This would deny abusers any benefits from a long stay in Canada. Would-be abusers would not incur the expense of a trip to Canada if their stay were invariably short. Real refugees in Canada must be treated in a humane fashion.

Chapter 5

DIPLOMATIC ASYLUM

Diplomatic asylum could be an avenue of protection for refugees if it were open. Canada has made every effort to ensure it is not. Denying diplomatic asylum has become yet another technique of denying protection for refugees.

Diplomatic asylum for refugees could be granted by Canadian diplomats abroad to protect refugees in their home countries by sheltering them in Canadian embassies. Refugee status, on the other hand, is granted by Canada for protection in this country. While immediate asylum in a country of danger may be vital to a person's survival, Canadian policy, in effect, rejects the concept of diplomatic asylum. Foreign missions are discouraged from harbouring desperate refugees in Canadian embassies, even though diplomatic asylum may be a reasonable and expedient response to a cry for protection. Canada has not signed any agreement or convention obliging it to offer diplomatic asylum.

Canada's general asylum law and policy show bewildering inconsistency. In principle, a person claiming a grant of asylum should be treated the same no matter where he is when he makes his claim. Only the danger he faces and the reasons for the danger should be relevant. But in practice and in law, Canada treats a person far differently depending on where he is when he makes his claim.

KINDS OF ASYLUM

Canada can grant three kinds of asylum: *territorial asylum, secondary asylum* and *diplomatic asylum.*

1. Territorial Asylum

Territorial asylum entitles a refugee in Canada or at its borders to remain, provided he is not a subversive and has not been convicted of a serious criminal offence. Canada is a signatory to the Convention Relating to the Status of Refugees of 1951 and its Protocol of 1967, by which it agreed not to expel refugees within its borders.

2. Secondary Asylum

Canada also has an obligation under international law to co-operate in resettlement of refugees by absorbing its fair share of refugees from first asylum countries. This is called secondary asylum.

However, a refugee in provisional asylum in a foreign third country is not entitled to enter Canada as of right to seek secondary asylum. A refugee who is not in danger in the country of provisional asylum will be forcibly returned to that country if he enters Canada or appears at a port of entry. Canada has deported to Turkey a Cypriot refugee who had refugee status in Turkey.[1] A Hungarian refugee who had refugee status in Switzerland has been deported there by Canada.[2] A Czechoslovakian refugee has been deported by Canada back to the United States because he had refugee status there.[3]

3. Diplomatic Asylum

Canada has adopted a restrictive position on diplomatic asylum — the granting of asylum by Canadian diplomats and embassies abroad to persons in danger. Canada will grant only temporary diplomatic asylum, and only to persons who face a serious and imminent risk of violence against which the local authorities are unable to offer protection or which they themselves incite or tolerate.[4]

DIPLOMATIC ASYLUM VS. TERRITORIAL ASYLUM

In some respects, Canadian policy for diplomatic asylum is less restrictive than for territorial asylum. Canada will grant diplomatic asylum to a threatened person regardless of the cause. A common criminal fleeing a lynch mob would be eligible for Canadian diplomatic asylum. But territorial asylum will be granted only if a person has a well-founded fear of persecution because of race, religion, nationality, membership in a particular social group or political opinion.[5]

However, in every other respect, the Canadian policy of diplomatic asylum is more limited than that of territorial asylum. Most significantly, a person seeking diplomatic asylum must be in imminent danger. A person seeking territorial asylum need not be in imminent danger, but must have a well-founded fear of persecution.

If a Canadian embassy grants diplomatic asylum, the refugee will receive only temporary protection in the embassy until the immediate danger has passed. Further, Canadian diplomats will not provide safe escort for a refugee from the host country to Canada. They do not have the right.[6] A person granted territorial asylum, on the other hand, is entitled to remain in Canada once he is landed, even if the danger which prompted the granting of refugee status disappears.

A person will not be granted diplomatic asylum if he is in flight from the authorities, only if he is in flight from an unruly mob. This distinction is blurred but not obliterated by the policy that asylum will be granted to a person in flight from an unruly mob which is backed or tolerated by the authorities. Further, if the authorities later request his return, the Canadian embassy will hand him over.

But a person seeking territorial asylum will not be denied refugee status simply because he is in flight from authorities. On the contrary, for a refugee claim to succeed, the claimant must show the persecution he fears would be carried out by the government of the country fled, or by persons acting with knowledge or consent of the authorities.[7]

As well, a person will not be granted diplomatic asylum if the danger he flees is non-violent persecution. Danger must constitute risk to life, limb or liberty. But a person will be granted territorial asylum due to non-violent persecution such as arrest, interrogation, removal to a remote place, threats, systematic denial of employment, relegation to substandard dwelling out of political motives, exile, constant surveillance and longer than normal military service.[8] None of these sorts of persecution would justify a claim to diplomatic asylum.

Because a person has no right to claim diplomatic asylum, it is not incumbent upon Canada to accept the claim. Canada owes neither a duty to other states according to international law nor a responsibility to the person claiming diplomatic asylum. A person who is refused diplomatic asylum has no recourse, regardless of Canadian policy or the justice of his cause.[9] On the other hand, a person in Canada or at a port of entry has a right to claim territorial asylum and may appeal a rejection by leave to the courts.

CANADA'S APPROACH TO DIPLOMATIC ASYLUM

Canada's instructions to its consuls abroad about diplomatic asylum seem designed to restrict diplomatic asylum as much as possible. The Canadian government informs its missions that they may give temporary shelter on humanitarian grounds to persons whose lives, liberty or physical integrity are in imminent danger. Within these broad guidelines, the mission heads are on their own.

Canada believes its instructions conform to the international law of diplomatic asylum. But even if Canada's opinion is correct, Canada is not prevented from going beyond international law to grant asylum in other circumstances where it is deemed necessary. The Canadian government could and should state outright that its missions are allowed to grant asylum in situations where no right to grant asylum exists according to international law. It may be necessary, simply for the purpose of safe conduct of the asylum-seeker from the embassy out of the country, to have the local state's approval. But if that approval is forthcoming Canada should not object in principle to diplomatic asylum.

The Canadian government stresses the gravity of danger the person must face to be granted diplomatic asylum. On occasion, the government has referred to danger of life alone, rather than danger to life, liberty or personal integrity, as the criterion for granting diplomatic refuge.[10]

Furthermore, the Canadian government has gone so far as to say, "It is not clear that officials of the host state would be debarred from removing from the premises of such a diplomatic mission [a mission-granting asylum] a person who had been granted asylum but who was wanted by the host state."[11] This statement is questionable as a proposition of international law, but no doubt effective as an attempt to discourage Canadian missions abroad from granting diplomatic asylum.

NEED FOR REFORM

If Canada is right in its interpretation of the international law of diplomatic asylum, then this law needs reform. The territorial state should have a duty to assure the safe conduct of a refugee granted diplomatic asylum. Diplomatic asylum should be granted not only to someone fleeing an unruly mob, but also to someone in danger and fleeing authorities of the territorial state on account of his race, religion, nationality, political opinion or membership in a particular social group. The state granting diplomatic asylum should determine whether the fugitive is a common criminal who should not be granted asylum or a refugee who deserves asylum.

However, Canada has opposed any attempt at reform. The Canadian government has said it fears reform would result in excessively rigid or excessively ambiguous rules. And if attempt at reform failed, according to officials, Canada's limited humanitarian concept of temporary refuge would be defeated. The government maintains the present situation permits flexibility and pragmatism.[12]

The Australian government has called this argument unpersuasive.[13] States that now tolerate a grant of temporary refuge on humanitarian grounds will not cease to tolerate such a grant simply because an international attempt to improve the law failed.

The present law of diplomatic asylum is itself ambiguous. The law's ambiguity creates risks, not flexibility. Unnecessary human suffering and loss of life can result when diplomatic asylum is refused. Where asylum is granted, diplomatic friction can occur between the granting state and the territorial state due to a lack of understanding about conditions for granting asylum and its consequences.

Other countries' objections to international law reform are no more persuasive than Canada's. The U.S. take the position that, rather than attempt to improve the law of diplomatic asylum, states should be urged to eliminate within their own frontiers all infringements of human rights. Unfortunately, this is only a pious hope.[14]

According to another argument, if the law of diplomatic asylum is extended, territorial states may be embarrassed by those seeking asylum. However, asylum is not granted unquestioningly. Acceptance of the principle of asylum does not mean states will abuse asylum or accord it lightly. In any event, human rights must take priority over a potential for state embarrassment. The protection of refugees is more important than a violating state's reaction to a grant of asylum. If countries were unwilling to offer refuge to any persons whose home country was embarrassed by such a condemnation, we would not have a single refugee protection system in the world today.

Opponents claim that more relaxed standards for granting diplomatic asylum would infringe on the sovereignty of territorial states. That is true of every rule of international law. The real question is not whether diplomatic asylum involves a limitation of state sovereignty, but whether the limitation is unacceptable.

As well, it has been argued that diplomatic asylum is inconsistent with the status and functions of diplomatic missions — namely to promote friendly relations. But the real question is whether the grant of asylum is an appropriate use of diplomatic premises. A country can grant diplomatic asylum and still maintain friendly relations with the territorial state.

Canada need not wait for changes in international law to extend its right to grant diplomatic asylum. A number of conventions governing diplomatic asylum have already been developed in Latin America.[15] If Canada negotiated accession to these conventions, Canada would have a greater right in Latin America to grant diplomatic asylum than now. Under the Convention on Diplomatic Asylum, signed at Caracas in 1954, asylum may not be granted for persons charged with, on trial for, or convicted of common offences. But according to the Convention, the granting state determines whether the offence is common or political. As well, the territorial state must provide safe passage from the country upon the request of the signatory granting state.

The Chilean coup of 1973 illustrated the importance of these conventions. After the coup the Pinochet government granted safe conduct to refugees who had been given diplomatic asylum in foreign missions, including the Canadian embassy. But in mid-December, 1973, the Chilean government announced it would grant safe conduct only from the missions of countries who had signed the various conventions to which Chile was a party. Non-signatory countries such as Canada had to try to arrange for asylum of refugees in missions of signatory countries, which then arranged for the Chileans to be taken out of the country.[16]

Canada took the position that granting asylum in Iran to U.S. diplomatic personnel in 1979 fell within general international rights respecting asylum. In addition, the Americans granted asylum had special status as members of the diplomatic corps.[17] Nevertheless, to be consistent with its previously articulated legal position on diplomatic asylum, Canada would have been obliged to hand over the American hostages on request from

Iran. Further, Iran would not have been obliged to accede to a Canadian request for safe conduct for the hostages. And should Iranian officials have removed the American hostages from the Canadian embassy in Iran, it is uncertain in the stated view of the Canadian government whether the government of Iran would have been debarred at international law from doing so. If Canada is not prepared to admit these consequences of its previously stated position on diplomatic asylum, then, if for no other reason, Canada should review generally its position on asylum.

Firstly, Canadian consular instructions should be amended to invite granting of diplomatic asylum in accordance with local usage and subject to the acquiescence of the local state. Secondly, Canada should join efforts to improve the international law of diplomatic asylum. Lastly, Canada should attempt to negotiate accession to the existing conventions on diplomatic asylum.

PART TWO

CANADA AND THE WORLD'S REFUGEES

Chapter 6

CANADA'S OLD AND NEW REFUGEE DETERMINATION SYSTEMS

The old refugee determination system in place from April 10, 1978 to December 31, 1988 was complex and filled with unnecessary steps. A backlog developed because of the complexity. Yet the new system is almost equally complex.

THE OLD REFUGEE DETERMINATION PROCESS

An analysis of the old system shows the evident need for reform to simplify the multi-step system and cut down the delays which provide an incentive to abuse.

Under the old determination procedure, a refugee claimant was faced with the system's intricacies as soon as he arrived in Canada. A refugee had to decide upon his arrival, without access to counsel, whether to claim refugee status immediately or attempt to obtain visitor status and make an inland refugee claim at a later date. If he claimed refugee status immediately, and his port of entry was not his ultimate destination, he might have to travel frequently between the port of entry and his destination to process his claim. A refugee claimant was not entitled to have his claim processed by the Immigration office nearest his destination.*

IN-STATUS OR OUT-OF-STATUS?

Under the old law, if the claimant entered as a visitor, he faced a conundrum: whether to make his claim in-status or out-of-status. As explained in Chapter 4, an in-status claim was made while a claimant was still a visitor in Canada. The claimant retained his visitor status while his claim was being determined. An out-of-status claimant lost his visitor's status or never had it in the first place, and could only stay in Canada pending determination of his claim.

Only out-of-status refugee claims were recognized by law at an immigration inquiry, where someone was reported for violating the Immigration Act. Many refugees had come to Canada with no intent or desire to break Canadian law.

The Department of Immigration, not wanting to force refugee claimants into Immigration Act violations simply in order to make their claims, allowed in-status claims to be made. Since the Act did not provide for these claims, there were no statutory criteria outlining when such claims were allowed to be made.

THE CLAIMS PROCESS[1]

A claimant making an out-of-status claim would normally wait until the day after his visitor status expired and appear voluntarily at the local Immigration office. An Immigration officer would schedule an inquiry, at which time an adjudicator would determine whether the claimant had indeed overstayed. Once the adjudicator decided that the claimant did overstay, he adjourned the inquiry to allow for the refugee claim to be made. This mandatory inquiry — even though the claimant did not

---

* This particular problem continues, even under the new law.

contest his overstay — could add months of delay to the refugee-status determination process.[†]

After the inquiry before an adjudicator was adjourned, the refugee examination was scheduled. At the refugee exam, the examining officer questioned the claimant on the nature of his claim to discern whether the claim was valid, even though the examiner had no prior knowledge of the claim. Examining officers often insisted that the claimant's counsel could question his client only at the end of the exam, after the examining officer had led the claimant to give what might have been a confused, elliptical statement. Witnesses were not allowed to testify at the examination in support of the claim, although, depending on the case, witnesses' testimony could bolster the claim.

A transcript of the claim was then sent to the claimant and his counsel and to the Refugee Status Advisory Committee (RSAC) in Ottawa for consideration. The claimant could not correct any errors in the transcript before the transcript was sent, but his counsel could forward to Ottawa written submissions and affidavit evidence of others. Later, that procedure was changed to allow thirty days for correction of the transcript before it went to Ottawa.

The RSAC did not consider the transcripts of claims its officials believed to be manifestly unfounded. The RSAC had no guidelines under which to operate, and did not hear the claimant before advising the Minister on the claim. It also did

---

[†] In 1981, as a result of a Federal Court of Appeal decision, adjudicators began making decisions on disposition of out-of-status claims before the adjournment for the refugee claim. An adjudicator has the power to choose between a deportation order and a departure notice. A deportation order permanently bars entry into Canada, except by consent of the Minister of Immigration. A departure notice simply restores the status quo. The person can leave voluntarily and can return provided he meets normal immigration criteria. But no refugee claimant would willingly leave the country. If he did, his claim would never be heard. The disposition of claims at this stage meant every refugee claimant got a deportation order. The adjudicator's early disposition of claims was a temporary aberration in the determination proceedings. In 1982, the Federal Court of Appeal reversed itself and returned the deport-depart decision to the end of the proceedings where it belonged.

not present the claimant with objections to his claim and give him an opportunity to respond. Committee members could examine information other than that submitted by the claimant. If found to be necessary, the examination would be reconvened so the claimant could comment on this additional information.

The RSAC advised the Minister, who ultimately determined refugee status. Several departmental officials had also been delegated power to decide claims. The Minister did not expound on why he rejected a claim until Fernando Molina successfully challenged that practice in the late 1970s.[2]

THE IMMIGRATION APPEAL BOARD

A refugee claimant refused by the Minister at the RSAC stage could apply to the Immigration Appeal Board (IAB) for a redetermination. The IAB could grant an oral hearing at that time. But more often it would disallow the request without a hearing and without an opportunity for the claimant to rebut the Board's objections to the claim.

While the RSAC could consider information in addition to that submitted by the claimant, the IAB was restricted by law to examine only the transcript of the claim and material submitted by the claimant. While the RSAC was a specialized body knowledgeable about the political and social conditions of the countries from which claimants sought refuge, the IAB was not. In an application to the RSAC, the claimant needed to say little about home country conditions. In an application to the IAB, the claimant was well-advised to detail any home country conditions that led him to flee.

At the Immigration Appeal Board level, at the stage of application of a hearing, any doubt had to be resolved against the claimant. The Federal Court of Appeal ruled March 23, 1979 in the case of *Salvatierra v the Minister of Employment and Immigration*,[3] that claimants did not have the benefit of the doubt in IAB decisions on whether to grant an oral hearing.

At this stage, the inquiry before the adjudicator would be reconvened. If the claimant had been refused by the minister and the IAB, the adjudicator would issue an exclusion order for port of entry cases, or a deportation or departure notice for inland cases.

FURTHER APPEALS

A person refused by the IAB could apply to the Federal Court of Appeal to set aside the Board's decision. It was here, for the first time, that the claimant was entitled to appear in person before someone deciding his case, and had an opportunity to answer apparent objections to his claim. However, the Federal Court of Appeal could not hear evidence or determine the claimant to be a refugee. It could only set aside the IAB's decision based on a failure of the IAB decision in law, fact, or natural justice. The Federal Court of Appeal could also refer the matter back to the IAB for reconsideration if these errors were made.

From the Federal Court of Appeal, the claimant could go to the Supreme Court of Canada if granted leave to appeal. Like the Federal Court of Canada, the Supreme Court of Canada could not hear evidence or find the claimant to be a refugee. The Supreme Court could only set aside the original decision or send the matter back to the IAB.

The refugee claim process ended for the claimant as it began, with a dilemma. If the claimant wanted to stay in Canada until his Federal Court of Appeal case was heard, he would be ordered deported as not willing to leave. If the claimant willingly left before his Federal Court of Appeal case was heard, and got a departure notice, he had in effect abandoned his claim. If he won at the Federal Court of Appeal the matter would be sent back to the IAB. If the IAB then determined him to be a refugee, the claimant was not entitled to re-enter Canada. A refugee lawfully in Canada is entitled to remain, but a refugee outside of Canada is not entitled to enter.

A claimant ordered removed could apply to the Federal Court of Appeal a second time to have the removal order shelved. Departmental policy was to stay execution of removal orders pending applications to the Federal Court of Appeal to set aside negative refugee determinations where, in their opinion, the applications were not frivolous.

If the claimant won on his first application to the Federal Court of Appeal (i.e., to set aside the Immigration Appeal Board determination), he would automatically win on his second application (i.e., to set aside the adjudicator's disposition to order a removal). Suppose a claimant was rejected by the Minister and IAB as a refugee and subsequently ordered deported by the adjudicator. The claimant then applied to the Federal Court of Appeal to set aside the IAB decision. Suppose the Court set aside the IAB decision. Once that was done it was as if the claimant's rejection as a refugee had never happened. The decision by the adjudicator to deport was without jurisdiction because his power to deport was founded on the IAB decision. And that was gone with the Court's ruling. Once the Immigration Appeal Board determination was set aside, then the adjudicator was without jurisdiction to proceed.

MINISTER'S PERMITS

There was one final twist. Departmental policy was to give a Minister's Permit to someone recognized as a refugee not already given refuge by another country. Once given a Permit, the refugee would be processed in Canada for landing. The granting of a Minister's Permit was fundamental to the claimant's success in remaining in Canada as a refugee. Without a Minister's Permit, a refugee is unlawfully in Canada and cannot remain here. Without a Permit, he is entitled only to the right not to be returned to a country where his life or freedom could be threatened.[4]

REFUGEE BACKLOG

By the time the new legislation took effect January 1, 1989, the backlog of refugee claimants had reached 85,000 cases. Given the complexities, it is understandable a backlog in Canada's refugee determination system developed. Yet it is unfair to blame the backlog on the complexity of the old system alone. Adding to the problem was the government's reluctance to impose visa requirements, an influx of Central American refugees, and a Minister's Permit system for citizens of eighteen countries.

Reluctance to Impose Visa Requirements

In 1987 and 1988, a good deal of abuse was generated by citizens of Turkey, Brazil and Portugal, who were not required to obtain visas at Canadian posts abroad before entering Canada as visitors. The Canadian government was reluctant to impose visa requirements because they are an inconvenience to genuine visitors. By waffling on the visa question, the government sacrificed the integrity of the refugee determination system, and helped to create a backlog that made the system unworkable. Eventually, abuse became so intolerable that visa requirements were imposed, despite the inconvenience to visitors. By then it was too late. A huge backlog created an incentive to abuse for false refugee claimants from elsewhere. In the end, on account of government's slow response, genuine visitors were inconvenienced and the refugee system undermined.

Influx of Central American Refugees

Another factor leading to the refugee backlog was an influx of Central American refugees caused by a change in U.S. law. In 1987, employer sanctions were introduced in the U.S. aimed at employers who knowingly hired undocumented foreigners without authorization. Consequently, many undocumented Central Americans lost their jobs in the U.S. and fled to Canada.

But, unlike the U.S., Canada still maintained a fair refugee determination procedure for Salvadorans and Guatemalans.[§] Canada too has employer sanctions. However, under the old Canadian law, Central Americans could claim refugee status without fear of forcible return, and obtain work permits provided they had no other means of support. Employer sanctions did not apply for those refugee claimants who were given permission to work.

In the past, Canada has reacted in a humanitarian way when faced with a temporary influx of refugees. Canada opened its doors to Asians rejected by Ugandan president Idi Amin, ethnic

---

[§] As explained in Chapter 11, the U.S. determination procedure is controlled by the State Department, which refuses to criticize regimes it supports by alleging they persecute their citizens. Thus, Central Americans are reluctant to claim refugee status in the U.S., knowing it is likely they will be forcibly returned to their countries of persecution. Employer sanctions reinforce this discrimination by denying underground illegals hope for work.

Chinese evicted from Vietnam, and supporters of Allende fleeing persecution from the Pinochet government in Chile. In principle, the persecution suffered by Central Americans justified a similar humanitarian approach, not an excuse for Canada to change its system and close its borders to genuine refugees.

Minister's Permits

In 1986 and 1987, Canadians were inundated with sensational headlines and stories about the landing on Canada's shoreline of the Tamils and the Sikhs. On August 11, 1986 fishermen picked up 155 Sri Lankan Tamils cast adrift in two lifeboats off the Coast of Newfoundland. The Tamils travelled to Canada from the West German port of Hamburg aboard the Honduran registered freighter *Aurigae*. At first, the Tamils said they had come directly from Sri Lanka. Most people believed the Tamil boat people abused the Canadian system. Yet Bill C-55 was not necessary to stop a recurrence of that abuse.

Many Canadians were offended by the government's response to the Tamils. The Tamils were received with open arms and given Minister's Permits despite the fact they lied, without any investigation of whether they were refugees. However, the granting of Minister's Permits to Tamils was not an inherent part of the system, but a temporary anomaly government created to lay down a fast track.

In May, 1986, the government decided it would end delays in the system that were creating an incentive to abuse. It introduced a Minister's Permit system, the third reason for large influxes of refugees and the subsequent backlog. Minister's Permits, which were issued to persons from eighteen main refugee-producing countries, removed their claims from the system and exempted them from having to claim refugee status. They remained in Canada on temporary hold with these permits. The government also granted an "amnesty" to those claimants who had arrived in Canada before May 21, 1986, and who had made a refugee claim. If such a person had successfully established himself, or was likely to establish himself successfully, or if he should be allowed to stay for humanitarian reasons, he was granted landing. The "amnesty" was an administrative adjustment to deplete the backlog.

With all these people cleared out of the system, the theory was that any new refugee claimant who came to Canada could have his claim disposed of quickly, even with the cumbersome multi-step refugee determination system then in operation. There would be no delays and no incentive for people to come to Canada to claim refugee status just for the time it would buy them, and the chance, for awhile, to earn higher incomes in Canada than they could back home. However, this so-called fast-track system was quickly derailed because of abusive claimants flooding the system from countries whose citizens were not eligible for Minister's Permits.

Unscrupulous consultants misrepresented the state of affairs in Canada to anyone interested who could afford their "expertise." For personal profit, they advertised in foreign papers, promising a future in Canada for the right price. They claimed Canada needed people for jobs, and that a person could simply come to Canada and be admitted as a refugee. Portuguese citizens, for instance, were told by immigration consultants in Portugal to come to Canada posing as Jehovah Witnesses if they wanted quick refugee status.

However, neither the consultants nor the abusers themselves can take the entire blame. The government must share the blame for making abuse so easy, obvious, and free of penalty.

The problem was not so much that the Minister's Permit system initially attracted abusive claims. The list of eighteen countries whose citizens were given Minister's Permits was a properly chosen list. The problem was that the Minister's Permit system was designed to extract from the refugee determination process a number of probably genuine claims so that the process would be free to deal quickly with abusive claims that remained in the system. However, because of a delay in imposing visa requirements on Portugal and on Turkey, a flood of abusive claimants prevented the system from dealing quickly with these abusive claims.

Nevertheless, the Permit system continued in place, although it ceased to serve any purpose. The fast track the government had wanted to create had become helplessly slowed down. Claimants from the eighteen countries continued to be given Permits unthinkingly, even once the reason for doing so had disappeared.

The Permit system, along with the backlog in the refugee determination process, created a backlash against the abuse. The Minister's Permit system was designed to prevent abuse by allowing claimants from the listed countries to have their claims decided quickly. Instead it became a potential source of abuse. Whether claimants from those eighteen countries had any colour of claim or not, they would be given permits. Even for genuine refugees from the eighteen countries, a suspicion of abuse could not be dissipated. It was impossible for the government to say for certain the claimants were refugees, even if they were, because the claimants were removed from the determination system.

Tamils who came to Canada by boat in August, 1986 fall into this category. Sri Lanka was on the list of eighteen countries. Eventually it became known that the Tamils came to Canada from West Germany. Their claims of flight from Sri Lanka followed by the discovery of their departure from West Germany were played out in the press. But that story was not relevant to determinations of refugee status since those determinations did not take place.

On July 12, 1987, 174 Indian Sikhs waded to shore at dawn on Nova Scotia's south shore. They were brought to the coast by a Chilean registered freighter *The Amelie*. The Sikhs were transferred to *The Amelie* the day the ship left Rotterdam in the Netherlands. They had come from West Germany, Belgium and the Netherlands. The Sikhs were not given Minister's Permits. India was not on the list of eighteen countries. In any case, by that time the list had been abolished. The Sikhs were treated as badly as the Tamils were treated generously. They were initially detained, denied access to counsel, and not brought before an adjudicator within the time period required by law.

Refugees arriving by boat off Canada's shores create a dramatic situation that attracts attention no matter how the government reacts. However, Canadians inevitably draw conclusions from the event based on government response. The government could have used the Sikh landing as an opportunity to highlight the problems in Europe, including disincentive schemes and the destruction of procedural safeguards that were driving refugee claimants from there to Canada. The Sikhs had come from Europe with complaints of their treatment there, just as the Tamils had complained of conditions in West Germany. Canada could have used the occasion to dramatize the need for more equitable sharing of the world's refugee problem, more international co-operation in maintaining procedural safeguards, and the elimination of disincentive schemes. The government could also have used the occasion to show the need for a speedier Canadian refugee determination system that would not provide an incentive for abuse. Instead, the government claimed there was an emergency demanding a general clampdown on refugees. In retrospect, we can see there was no emergency, just a couple of isolated incidents.

The conclusion that could have been drawn — should have been drawn — from the Tamil and Sikh incidents was the need to remove the deterrence and disincentive schemes driving refugees from Europe to Canada. Instead, the government invited Canadians to conclude there was a need to be tough with refugee claimants because they were abusers.

THE REFUGEE REFORM ACT — BILL C-55

In May, 1985, then Canadian Minister of State for Immigration Walter McLean announced the Conservative government's proposal for a major new refugee policy. Bill C-55, the Refugee Reform Bill, was formally introduced May 5, 1987, when it was given first reading in the House of Commons. Following the normal legislative process of second and third readings in the House, and Senate readings, the Governor-General gave royal assent to Bill C-55 in July, 1988, and it came into force January 1, 1989.

The government claimed the Bill was necessary to cut down on the rampant abuse of the refugee claims system. But it is unconscionable for a government to deny protection to genuine refugees in the name of a clampdown on abuse, especially when the abuse has been generated by government inaction. We saw a series of bungles in 1986 and 1987 that included a fast-track system which was destroyed by a delay in imposing a Portuguese visa requirement, a Minister's Permit system that invited abuse, and an administrative adjustment system that created expectations of further amnesties. With Bill C-55, the government moved away from unintended generosity toward unwarranted harshness. It had heard so much criticism of the abuse generated by its policies that it over-reacted by closing the doors more tightly than necessary, barring abusive claimants and genuine refugees alike.

The government's international position was compromised by the introduction of Bill C-55, the Refugee Reform Bill. The Bill did not provide a speedier system, but rather proposed closing down the system to refugee claimants. With the Bill, the government followed Europe's widespread disincentive schemes and destruction of procedural safeguards. So when the Sikhs arrived, the government could hardly complain about what the Europeans had done, since it was proposing the same remedy.

Bill C-55 violates the principle of universal access. As discussed in Chapter 18, according to the scheme of the Bill, not every refugee claimant has access to the Canadian refugee determination system. Claimants who have resided in countries listed by the Cabinet as safe third countries are denied access. Their claims cannot be considered by the Canadian authorities.

The denial of universal access is contrary to the UN Refugee Convention which Canada has signed. This Convention obligates each member to protect refugees who fall under the refugee definition and not forcibly return refugees to countries of danger. Universal access is just a facet of the right to protection. If a genuine refugee never gets to make his claim, then he never gets a chance to receive protection. Raphael Girard, head of refugee policy in the Department of Immigration and the Bill's architect, said before the House of Commons Committee that if there is a system "accessible to virtually everybody if they make a certain claim or request, then there is a strong tendency for them to use it regardless of the justification for that request...whether they are refugees or not."

Girard's attitude that everyone is an abuser or potential abuser of the refugee claims system exaggerates the danger of abuse beyond all reasonable bounds. Though abuse and the threat of abuse exists, not every single person who comes to Canada is dishonest. Neither does every person who wants to stay in Canada have a "strong tendency" to make a refugee claim.

Girard errs in his conclusion that access must be denied because of this tendency to make a refugee claim. He argues that because any system of universal access will attract such a high number of abusers, Canada must never again establish a system of universal access. The end of delays in determination are necessary to avoid abuse, but not the abolition of universal access. A universal access system that provides speedy determination would remove the incentive for abuse.

Many refugees from other countries came to Canada in search of protection because of Canada's fair determination process. Canada could remedy the world-wide lowering of standards by working internationally to have other countries develop fair refugee determination systems. Making the Canadian system unfair is no solution. Yet that is what Bill C-55 did. Designing a system that is both fair and speedy is not an impossibility. Chapter 8 outlines such a system.

This domino effect on fairness has led to comparisons with the voyage of the *St. Louis*. Jews on board the ship *St. Louis* fleeing Nazi Germany were refused by country after country, and each refusal made the next more likely. Today, refugees go from country to country seeking fair determination of their claims, but as their numbers increase the unfairness increases. Canada, one of the last to maintain a fair system, felt compelled by the unfairness elsewhere to destroy its own system.

REFUGEE DETERMINATION — THE NEW SYSTEM

Bill C-55's refugee determination process is as complex and multi-step as the system it replaced. A person first goes through an immigration inquiry to determine if he has violated the Immigration Act. Next the claimant appears at the initial hearing before a two-person panel, including an Immigration adjudicator and Refugee Board Member. The panelists determine whether the person is eligible to make a claim for refugee status. If one panelist approves the claim, the claimant goes on to the next stage. If both members reject the claim, the person is ordered deported or given a departure notice.**

Those refugees who pass the eligibility screening then go into the next stage: a credible-basis hearing. Again the case is heard by two panelists — an Immigration Department adjudicator and Refugee Board member. If one of the two accepts the claim, the claimant will be passed on to the full hearing.

After the credible-basis hearing, where the claimant succeeds, the adjudicator alone determines whether to issue a *conditional departure notice* (a notice that would allow a claimant to return once he left Canada provided he met normal immigration criteria) or a *conditional deportation order* (an order that would ban re-entry to Canada for life, except with the consent of the Minister). A conditional deportation order is more likely to be issued than a conditional departure notice because refugee claimants would be reluctant to agree to a departure notice after succeeding in establishing a credible-basis. Their claim is based on fear of persecution, and it would be inconsistent for a refugee to state he wished to return voluntarily to his home country. The decision is conditional because it takes effect only if the claimant fails at the full hearing. If at least one panelist accepts the claim, the claimant is passed on to the full hearing.

** If a "safe third country" list is drawn up, the safe third country rule would be applied at this time. If the claimant came from a designated safe third country, he would fail that hearing and be held ineligible. The government would then try to remove the claimant to the third country from which he came. If present experience is any guide, third countries would refuse to take the claimant back. Canada may send some refugees into orbit, forcing them to wander from country to country seeking refuge. The government estimates that if a safe third country list were implemented, fifty per cent of refugee claimants who come to Canada would fail eligibility screening without consideration of their claims. The community of non-governmental organizations estimates as many as ninety per cent of refugee claimants would be rejected at eligibility screening under the safe third country system.

If the claimant makes it to the full hearing, two Refugee Board members examine the claim. If at least one panelist accepts the claim, the claimant succeeds. He can and must apply for landed immigrant status. If both panelists reject the claim, the claimant may then apply for leave to appeal[††] to the Federal Court of Appeal if he wishes to remain in Canada. Because of the myriad of legal problems created by Bill C-55, many applications for leave to appeal will inevitably be allowed during the first couple of years under the new legislation.

Because of the controversial and problematic nature of the new legislation, issues arising on applications for leave granted by the Federal Court of Appeal will be common to a spectrum of refugee cases. Once leave is granted in one of the cases on a point of law, leave will be granted in all cases on that point, until the point is decided.

Moreover, the appeal mechanism before the Federal Court of Appeal is a drawn out multi-step mechanism. Once leave is granted, the delay between the granting of leave and the hearing of the appeal is lengthy. A one-year delay is considered short. A multi-year delay is not unusual.

The new legislation contains execution provisions against those who have failed the eligibility and credible-basis hearings, requiring the claimants to leave before the appeal is heard. Claimants who have passed credible-basis screening and are waiting for appeals before the Federal Court of Appeal (after leave has been granted from a refusal at a full hearing) can stay in Canada.

If they lose at the Federal Court of Appeal, claimants may appeal to the Supreme Court of Canada. While the legislation cuts off access to the Supreme Court when leave is denied to the Federal Court of Appeal, access remains where the Federal Court of Appeal grants leave. Access to the Supreme Court of Canada is also with leave. Given the problems of the new laws, the Court will likely grant leave in at least one refugee case. And once one case has been granted leave, all cases on that issue will

---

†† Leave to appeal is discretionary permission to appeal given by the court which hears the appeal.

have to wait the determination of that case. We will be caught up in a multi-year delay until that case is decided.

The new legislation creates delays, very much like the delays under the old legislation. Large numbers of people who may not be declared refugees will remain in Canada for years, waiting for their claims to be determined.

The new legislation marks a return to the pre-war and Second World War days when Jews fleeing the Holocaust were denied entry to Canada. Abuse control is the only purpose for Bill C-55, according to the government. But, in fact, denying protection to genuine refugees who might be or might have been protected elsewhere is another motivation. The government could have taken a number of steps to control abuse through prompt prosecution of unscrupulous immigration consultants, and speedy imposition of visa requirements for people from countries generating abuse. Instead, it chose to ignore the problems until they got out of hand.

If, in fact, the government's main concern with the new legislation was to remove abuse and not deny protection, it could have shortened the lengthy, complex refugee determination process. The government did not have to choose between the former cumbersome system and Bill C-55, with its lack of procedural protections. Reports by Gunther Plaut, Ed Ratushny, Jim Hawkes, and the Gerry Robinson task force proposed simpler refugee determination systems that maintained protection for refugees.

Improving opportunities for family reunification is another step government could have taken to control abuse. Close relatives prevented from reuniting with their families through normal immigration channels are more likely to abuse the system. Brothers and sisters of Canadians cannot come here unless they meet economic criteria. For years, up until July 8, 1988, unmarried children over 21 of parents in Canada could not be sponsored to come here unless they too met economic criteria. Government-set immigration levels could not be reached because it was difficult to meet the high standards. If immigration criteria were relaxed to allow family reunification, an incentive to abuse the refugee determination system would also disappear.

The government's priority is controlling abuse, not protecting refugees. Yet the protection of genuine refugees is more important than rejection of abusers. Consider what is at stake. When we protect refugees, we protect them from death, torture, cruelty, danger, imprisonment. We must strike a balance between the suffering of refugees on one side, and the losses Canada as a nation may face on the other side by not rejecting all abusers. When we admit abusers, all we have done is to admit an immigrant to Canada who does not meet normal economic and family immigration criteria. In any case, the addition of new people to Canada expands the economy. A system 100 percent free of any possible abuse is also going to reject many genuine refugees, and deny them the benefit of doubt in its zeal to remove abusers.

Chapter 7

ORAL HEARINGS FOR REFUGEE CLAIMANTS

The new refugee system has oral hearings for refugee claimants. There are many procedural failings in the new system as set out in the following chapter, but the absence of oral hearings is not one of them.

Oral hearings were not included in the new system by government choice. They were forced on the government by a Supreme Court of Canada interpretation of the Constitution. Before the Supreme Court decision, a refugee claimant under the old system never had an opportunity to appear before the person deciding his claim.

A refugee claimant could go through the whole process of inquiries and examinations, determinations and redeterminations, applications and appeals, without getting the chance to speak directly to anyone deciding or giving advice about his claim. He might never even get a chance to hear the objections to his claim.

As detailed in the preceding chapter, an official of the government and counsel for the claimant questioned the refugee claimant on his claim. A typed version of the questions and answers were sent to the Refugee Status Advisory Committee in Ottawa to read. The Committee read the transcript and advised the Minister of Immigration on disposition of the claim. If the Minister rejected the claim, the transcript was then sent to the Immigration Appeal Board along with a written decision by the RSAC. If the IAB subsequently rejected the claim, the claimant's only recourse was legal appeals. There were no more hearings.

The battle over oral hearings described in this chapter is instructive because it shows that procedural protection for refugees does not come willingly from government. Because denial of oral hearings is an omission of a procedural safeguard no longer open to government as the result of the Supreme Court ruling, other procedural safeguards omissions have sprung up to take its place.

For the claimant, the result may be the same. It is not enough for a procedure to be fair in only one respect for an accurate decision to be made. It must be fair in every respect.

The battle to restore the procedural safeguards taken away by the new law may be as long and arduous as the battle to institute oral hearings into the refugee determination process. The history of this battle over oral hearings indicates what is in store for those who intend to continue to struggle for a full range of procedural protection.

REASONS FOR REFUSAL — THE MOLINA CASE

In the late 1970s, refugees launched a number of court cases questioning Canada's refugee determination process. The challenges relied on the common law duty of fairness, the Bill of Rights and eventually, when it came into effect, the Canadian Charter of Rights and Freedoms.

Fernando Molina arrived in Canada from Chile in April, 1977 and applied for refugee status, claiming he was imprisoned and tortured by Chilean authorities before he fled. Molina, then 39, had left behind a wife, daughter and two sons. The Canadian government rejected Molina's refugee claim without giving reasons, in February, 1978. At the deportation proceedings Molina entered new evidence about his claim to refugee status, resulting in an adjournment of proceedings. Ottawa looked at the new testimony and upheld its original decision that Molina was not a refugee.

At this point, the new 1978 Immigration Act came into effect. Deportation proceedings were begun again for Molina under the new statute. Because of variations between the old and new legislation, Molina was able to claim refugee status for a third time, and the proceedings were adjourned once again.

I wrote to the Government asking for reasons for the first two refusals. I wanted Molina to have the opportunity to respond to the Department's objections. But the Department refused, claiming that its reasons were "restricted to use within the Department."

I then filed a Statement of Claim on behalf of Molina asking the Court to order the government to reveal its reasons. Molina also asked the Court to order the government to give him an opportunity to respond, once the reasons were revealed.

The government launched its own motion, asking the Court to strike out Molina's claim before it could be heard. The government argued that Molina had no reasonable cause of action and therefore his claim should not be heard in Court. In a judgement dated August 24, 1979, Mr. Justice Rhodes Smith dismissed the government motion.[1] He ruled that Molina's Statement of Claim did disclose a reasonable cause of action and could be heard in Court.

As well, Smith said Molina had a right to be heard on his refugee claim. That right to be heard, "it might at least be argued, includes a fair opportunity to answer anything contrary to his interest, and a right to make submissions with regard to the material on which the tribunal proposes to base its decision." Smith's decision did not mean Molina had won his case. He could, however, continue to fight his case, which Smith had ruled was plausible.

However, before the case came to trial, the government voluntarily handed over its reasons for refusal — apparently for the first time in any refugee claimant case in Canada. Shortly thereafter, in November, 1979, then Minister of Immigration Ronald Atkey announced a change in government policy: henceforth every refugee claimant who was refused would be given reasons for the refusal.

Molina had gone into his third examination in June, 1978 without the reasons for the two previous refusals in hand. He was unable, at this third examination, to respond to the objections to his claim that the Minister had raised. A transcript of this examination was duly prepared and sent to Ottawa. Over a year later, the Minister provided the reasons for the two previous refusals. On Molina's behalf, I sent a letter to the RSAC responding to the reasons. But before the answer came back, a policy change intervened.

Canada imposed a visa requirement on Chile on December 21, 1979, which meant that a person could not come to Canada without first receiving a visitor's visa issued abroad. In April, 1982, the government announced that it would review all cases of Chileans who came to Canada before January 1, 1980. Often in the past when the government made entry into Canada more restrictive through visa imposition, it gave refugee claimants backlogged in the old system some sort of benefit through an amnesty or administrative review. The avenue down which these people came — claiming refugee status at a Canadian port of entry — is closed off once a visa requirement is imposed. So the government saw no reason not to grant to the pre-visa requirement arrivals landing across the board.

Molina applied under the administrative review programme and was granted a Minister's Permit. Once it was clear he was allowed to stay, Molina wanted to bring his family to Canada as soon as possible. As he told *Maclean's* magazine in August, 1982, "The uncertainty of the past five years is driving me crazy." However, the Department would not allow his family to come to Canada until he was a landed immigrant and legally in a position to sponsor them.

But Molina could not be landed immediately because, according to the law, a person could be given a permanent resident status visa only outside Canada. A Cabinet-approved law of exception was necessary to give Molina landed status from within Canada.

He remained without his family until March 8, 1983. A November, 1982 government instruction said that Chileans who arrived here before January 1, 1980 could have their families come to Canada before landing procedures were completed. Molina applied under this policy. The family arrived in March, after a six-year separation.

THE SAMUEL BREMPONG CASE

Samuel Brempong came to Canada in February, 1977 from Ghana. At the time a military government headed by General Ignatius Acheampong was in power, following a coup in January, 1972. The 1977 Amnesty International (AI) report expressed concern about political trials and political imprisonments in Ghana. AI cited the case of three Ghanaians who received prison sentences of five to eight years of hard labour for circulating a pamphlet critical of the government. AI was also concerned about the use of the death penalty in Ghana. Military tribunals, immune from challenges in Court, were used to try civilians.

Brempong claimed refugee status in March, 1979 and was informed September 13 of that year that the Minister of Immigration had rejected his refugee claim. No reasons were given. I wrote to the Minister on behalf of Brempong, asking for reasons. Brempong meanwhile applied to the Immigration Appeal Board (IAB) for a redetermination of his claim, and he began court action.

I asked the Court to order the IAB not to consider Brempong's application for redetermination of his claim to refugee status until Brempong received reasons from the Minister and had a chance to respond to the Minister's objections to the IAB. In a judgement handed down in February, 1980, Mr. Justice Rhodes Smith ordered the IAB to wait until Brempong had received reasons and had an opportunity to respond to them to the IAB.[2]

Brempong then challenged the Minister's rejection of his refugee claim in the Federal Court of Appeal. The challenge was lost on a technicality of jurisdiction: the Court said the claim's rejection should be considered by the IAB for redetermination and not dealt with in the Federal Court of Appeal. The Court held it had no jurisdiction to hear the challenge, but expressed its opinion on the issues of fairness that Brempong's case had raised in the Trial Division.[3]

Mr. Justice Urie, who gave judgement for the Federal Court of Appeal, said, "With respect, I have grave doubts as to the propriety of requiring the Minister to give such reasons", (i.e., reasons for the determination that a person is not a refugee). These doubts, however, had no effect on the course of events. The Minister had already decided to give reasons as a matter of policy, had given reasons to Brempong, and had decided not to appeal the judgement of Mr. Justice Rhodes Smith.

The Court of Appeal's statement was too late to affect government policy on giving reasons, but it was indicative of what was to come. This judgement was one of several that showed a reluctance to apply the doctrine of fairness to the matter of refugee determination.

I wrote to then Minister of Immigration John Roberts in October, 1983 asking him to grant Sam Brempong and his wife Dorothy Taabea permanent residence within Canada. Brempong was working as a presser, and his employer wrote a glowing letter of reference. The couple had two children born in Canada, and two had been left behind in Ghana. An assistant to the Minister replied in January, 1984 that the Department was prepared to take special measures to allow the Brempongs to remain in Canada. The Brempongs were granted landed immigrant status from within Canada. All legal proceedings ceased.

THE MENSAH CASE

Once the claimants were given reasons for refusal by the Minister, they were able to respond to those reasons in their written applications for redetermination made to the Immigration Appeal Board. However, requiring the Minister to give reasons was not the only problem refugee claimants had to overcome. Claimants still did not have oral hearings. Nor did they have the right to answer objections of the person or persons deciding their claims.

Molina was in an unusual situation because he ended up making three refugee claims that the Minister had to decide. Molina was able to respond to the reasons for the first two refusals in his third claim.

The typical claimant made only one claim to the Minister and, if refused, one application to the IAB. Once the claimant was given the Minister's reasons for refusal, he could respond to these reasons only at the next stage, in his application for redetermination to the Immigration Appeal Board.

But the claimant could not respond to apparent objections to his claim the Minister might have before the Minister decided. And the claimant could not respond to apparent objections to his claim the Board might have before the Board decided. The Board might reject the claim for totally different reasons than the Minister. The claimant might have answered in his application to the IAB all of the Minister's objections satisfactorily. He might also have had responses to the Board's objections that would satisfy all their concerns. But the claimant never got a chance to answer those objections until it was too late. His next recourse was to apply for leave to appeal at the Federal Court of Appeal — at which time he could respond in his application to the reasons given by the IAB.

An oral hearing was needed. At the very least, there was a need for claimants to have a right to answer apparent objections to their claim by the Minister before the Minister decided, and raised by the Board, before the Board decided. That was a point I argued in the case of Jim Mensah.

Jim Mensah, then 25, came to Canada from Ghana in May, 1978. He claimed refugee status at an immigration inquiry held to determine if he was in violation of the Immigration Act. The inquiry was adjourned to allow for an examination of his claim, which took place in Winnipeg in January, 1979. By the time I became involved in his case, the Minister had determined Mensah was not a refugee. The IAB had refused to allow an oral hearing and had also found Mensah not to be a refugee. Mensah's then lawyer had filed a motion in the Federal Court of Appeal to set aside the determination of the IAB.

I argued Mensah's case before the Federal Court of Appeal. I argued that the Minister's determination was void because he had failed, before making his determination, to allow Mensah to respond to the Minister's objections to the refugee claim. However, in a March, 1981 judgement, Mr. Justice Pratte held that Parliament did not intend to subject the Minister to the procedural duty of fairness invoked by Mensah.[4]

Jim Mensah married a Canadian woman and applied for his permanent residency on the basis of his marriage. He was issued a Minister's Permit in April, 1981 and processed for landing from within Canada. The Department discontinued all immigration proceedings against him.

THE EDUARDO SARAOS CASE

Eduardo Saraos came to Canada on his own from Santiago, Chile, in October, 1979, fleeing persecution. At the time he was 32 years old, married with three children, aged four, two and one. He could only afford a ticket for himself so he left his family at his parents' house in Chile. Saraos himself was the one in immediate danger.

He came to this country before a visa requirement was imposed on Chile, and told an immigration officer when he arrived at the airport in Toronto that he wanted to claim refugee status. The Immigration Department began exclusion proceedings against him. As a refugee claimant, he was not a genuine visitor because he did not intend to leave. As someone who wanted to stay, he needed, but did not have, a landed immigrant visa.

At the immigration inquiry into his alleged violation of the Immigration Act, Saraos claimed refugee status. The inquiry, held in October, 1979 in Toronto, was adjourned for his refugee claim. Saraos' refugee claim examination was held in Winnipeg in November, 1979. I began acting for Saraos at that time. A transcript of his claim was sent, in due course, to Ottawa.

The Minister wrote back in July, 1980, rejecting Saraos' claim on the grounds that he did not believe Saraos' fear of persecution was credible. The Minister wrote that part of the evidence provided by Saraos was "incompatible" with another part of the evidence. However, neither the Minister nor the Refugee Status Advisory Committee had heard or seen Saraos, asked him any questions, judged his demeanour, nor given him any chance to explain what the Minister saw as an inconsistency. Examining officer Garry Komar made no recommendation on the claim.

Saraos applied to the IAB for a redetermination. The IAB denied the application, without a hearing, without posing any questions, and without giving him an opportunity to respond to their concerns.

Saraos then went to the Federal Court of Appeal alleging lack of fairness. I argued that the Minister was obliged before dismissing a refugee claim to inform the claimant of the reasons and to give him an opportunity to respond. I also argued that the IAB's decision erred in law, because the Board denied Saraos a hearing and denied him the benefit of the doubt.

The Court rejected all of these arguments,[5] claiming the issues raised were not worthy of consideration. A technical question on the admissibility of evidence was judged the "only one of the many arguments raised on behalf of the applicant that deserved consideration". But Mr. Justice Pratte decided against Saraos on this issue.

The Court also made some general statements about the refugee determination process. Mr. Justice Pratte said the Minister may decide a refugee case based on *any* material obtained from *any* source, without giving the claimant a chance to respond to that evidence. In the case of Saraos, I had no reason to believe extraneous evidence was used in determining his refugee claim. But, according to the Court, even if such extraneous evidence had been a determining factor, the decision could still not be challenged.

Saraos asked me to take his case to the Supreme Court of Canada. I applied for leave to appeal, arguing that fairness was denied and that this lack of fairness violated the law. However, Supreme Court Justices Estey, Martland, and Ritchie dismissed the leave application.[6]

After failing at the Supreme Court of Canada, Saraos went to France to seek refugee status and join a family member.

POLICY INITIATIVES FOR ORAL HEARINGS

Litigation was not the only avenue I followed in an attempt to bring more fairness into the refugee determination process. As well as relying on the court system to rectify any legal inequities in the operation of the refugee claims process, I also attempted to change government policy. If there were a focussed study on positive modifications to the determination process, the government would have a model for instituting fairness in the system.

In September, 1980, then Minister of Immigration Lloyd Axworthy established a Task Force on Immigration Practices and Procedures. As a member of the Task Force, I wrote a report on the refugee status determination process. The conclusions represented the consensus of all five lawyers on the Task Force, which included chairman Gerry Robinson of Vancouver and members Carter Hoppe of Toronto, Ed Ratushny of Ottawa, and Manon Vennat of Montreal. The report, released by the government in November, 1981, proposed three alternative measures to provide oral hearings for refugee claimants:

- a refugee claimant should be entitled to a hearing in every case where the Refugee Status Advisory Committee is not prepared to make a positive recommendation on the basis of the transcript;
- the Immigration Act should be reworded to permit oral hearings at the Immigration Appeal Board for all but frivolous applications;
- an entirely new determination process should be legislated to create one central tribunal which would hear and determine claims.

The Task Force said that apparent fairness existed when an applicant had a full opportunity to present his case, without restraint or challenge, and the Minister or his designate subsequently decided based on that information.

However, the existing refugee determination process was not fair, the report stated. Without an oral hearing and an opportunity to respond and clarify points, the claimant was at the mercy of the Senior Immigration Officer conducting an examination. If the officer did not take the initiative to explore and resolve apparent discrepancies in the case during the examination, the claimant may never have a chance to explain what to him was obvious, but to the decision-maker crucial. An interview transcript showing apparent contradictions, misrepresentations or the concealment of material facts may have at that time led to a claim's rejection. For example, a claimant may have said he quit his job for one reason and later provided a different reason. Both reasons may have been valid, and inconsequential to his claim anyway. But the examination would not be reconvened to pursue such matters, even where the Senior Immigration Officer had failed to do so on the original examination.

Senior Immigration Officers were faced with a real dilemma. On one hand, they were instructed not to cross-examine a refugee, and thereby set up an adversarial atmosphere in which a refugee would be reticent to speak freely and provide a full account of his case. On the other hand, if Immigration Officers refrained from asking probing questions, the claimant may not have a chance to meet objections to his claim. A claimant was treated unfairly, if, without ever having the chance to answer objections raised, a subsequent determination found he was not telling the truth. A person whose credibility was challenged by Immigration should have been warned and given the opportunity to explain, the Task Force recommended.

Similarly if a claimant considered the government's application of the refugee definition to be incorrect, he or his counsel should have the chance to make representations in support of another interpretation. Relying exclusively upon the transcript process totally removed the "give and take" of oral argument and oral presentation of evidence which the Canadian system of adjudication has long viewed as important.

GOVERNMENT RESPONSE

Axworthy announced his government's response to the report of the Task Force on Immigration Practices and Procedures at a symposium, held in Toronto in February, 1982. He accepted the recommendation calling for refugee definition criteria and credibility assessment guidelines for the RSAC. "Henceforth, the Committee [the RSAC] is to be governed in its deliberations by two overriding presumptions: First, the applicant is presumed to be telling the truth unless there is clear evidence to the contrary; and second, the benefit of the doubt must always be resolved in favour of the applicant. This pertains both to the application of the [refugee definition] criteria as well as to the assessment of credibility."

When the Immigration Act of the time was being considered in Parliamentary Committee, refugee determination had been discussed only in the context of removals procedures, Axworthy told the symposium, leading some people to perceive a refugee claim simply as a device to beat the Immigration Act. Like any law, he insisted, the refugee determination process is sometimes abused. "However, there is an unacceptable risk in operating on the presumption that claimants generally are seeking to avoid normal immigration procedures," Axworthy said. "A legitimate claim could be prejudiced by what was described by the Task Force as 'crystallized patterns of scepticism.' Changing this attitude is even more important than clarifying each and every aspect of the definition or of credibility."

As well, he endorsed the need for the RSAC to be independent from government. Axworthy told delegates he would exercise his right to appoint the Immigration or External Affairs Officers to serve on the Refugee Status Advisory Committee. "In the future, departmental appointees will be required to serve full time and be free of departmental responsibilities during the term of their appointment."

POLICY ON ORAL HEARINGS

A number of issues were left out of Axworthy's speech, including the question of oral hearings. Axworthy asked the symposium to discuss these additional issues, postponing implementation to a later date. The Toronto symposium was held only two weeks before the Canadian Charter of Rights and Freedoms took effect April 17, 1982.

The Charter has profoundly affected the refugee determination process and totally changed the nature of the debate. For instance, the Singh case, decided April 4, 1985, relied on the Charter's guarantee of fairness to require oral hearings for refugee claimants. The Charter argument can be raised to buttress other positions concerning fairness or individual rights.

After a year's deliberation about the Task Force recommendations, Axworthy announced a pilot project that would grant oral hearings to claimants who wanted them in Montreal and Toronto. An RSAC member would be present at the examination under oath and could conduct his own interview with the claimant after the initial interview required by law was completed. The RSAC member present would make a recommendation to the RSAC.

The claimant could choose whether or not to participate in this pilot project. But the project was optional only in Toronto and Montreal, not in Winnipeg.

AYIKU AND WILSON

Pat Ayiku and his wife Catherine Wilson came to Canada from Ghana and claimed refugee status in Winnipeg at an inquiry in November, 1984. When the inquiry was adjourned for their refugee claim, they told me they wanted an oral hearing for their claim. I wrote the Minister of Immigration, by then Flora MacDonald, to request an oral hearing be allowed for the couple. The Minister refused.

On behalf of the couple, I asked the Court to order the government to hold an oral hearing. By the time of the court judgement, Ayiku and Wilson had already had their refugee examination without an oral hearing. I amended the request to the court to require the examinations to be redone so that Ayiku and Wilson could have an oral hearing. In a judgement dated February, 1985, Mr. Justice Strayer denied my request.[7] I argued that the Charter required an oral hearing. Mr. Justice Strayer referred to the cases of Brempong, Mensah and Saraos in the Federal Court of Appeal.

> These cases, while recognizing that there is some requirement of fairness in the Section 45 process [the refugee determination process], indicate that the specific content of fairness depends on the particular circumstances, and the implication is that the content

is not very great. It appears to me that, Subsection 45 (1) being quite explicit as to how the Committee is to use the transcript of the examination, it is not possible to imply that fairness demands an oral hearing by a member of the Committee for the claimant.

The Charter's equality provisions did not come into effect until April 17, 1985. Mr. Justice Strayer pointed out that his February, 1985 decision might be different after April 17

> Conceivably, it might be arguable after April 17, 1985, when section 15 of the Canadian Charter of Rights and Freedoms comes into effect, granting equality "before and under the law" and the "equal benefit of the law" that this kind of regional disparity [oral hearing in Montreal and Toronto, but not Winnipeg] though hallowed by tradition is constitutionally impermissible.

Harbhajan Singh's case would be decided in the Supreme Court of Canada two months later in the opposite way on the issue of fairness, making it unnecessary to pursue the suggestion of Mr. Justice Strayer about equality.

Like Molina, Brempong, and Mensah before him, and many others, Ayiku got to stay in Canada, not because he was recognized as a refugee, but because of an administrative measures exception. In July, 1986, the government announced an administrative review programme allowing any refugee claimant who had claimed before May 21, 1986 to stay in Canada if he had successfully established himself here. Ayiku qualified under the programme. So he and his wife Catherine Wilson were processed for landing from within Canada.

IMPLICATIONS OF THESE CASES — CONTROL

These cases raised a number of important legal issues, and also represent a fair sample of what happened. Refugee claimants were rarely recognized as refugees. Although they had every appearance of being refugees, an unfair determination system made it extremely difficult to convince the decision-makers.

Why officials would go to such great lengths to deny claimants refugee status and then allow them to stay anyway was superficially puzzling. However, the underlying explanation for the operation of the old laws was the same as for the scheme of the new law: control. Officials were reluctant to have a functioning, effective refugee claims system because it meant refugees could choose Canada. Officials were quite content to let claimants stay here on a discretionary basis because it allowed the government to choose among the refugees.

MORE REPORTS

Axworthy asked Task Force member Ed Ratushny to prepare a detailed report on the implementation of oral hearings, to be used as a basis for public comment before legislative change. The report Ratushny prepared focussed on alternative forms of change, rather than the need for change.

By the time Ratushny's report was completed and ready for release, John Roberts had replaced Lloyd Axworthy as Minister of Immigration. Roberts released the report in May, 1984, and announced the commissioning of yet another report, by Gunther Plaut. Roberts did not indicate publicly why the Plaut report was necessary in light of the Ratushny Report and the Task Force report. On the surface, Plaut was being asked to do the very thing Ratushny and the Task Force had just done.

I can only speculate that the Plaut report was commissioned because the Department of Immigration didn't like what the two previous reports had proposed. Although both the Task Force and Ratushny submitted a range of options, the Department found none of the alternatives acceptable. I had heard civil servants use the term "workable." The Department, it seems, felt no "workable" system had been devised.

Cabinet did not have a firm policy direction for the refugee determination process: it commissioned reports because it was casting about for a policy. The bureaucracy, on the other hand, had a policy that refugees should not be able to come to Canada on their own to claim status, but should be selected from abroad. At that point, however, the Immigration Department could not sell its policy to Cabinet. Instead the Department simply objected to all the policies proposed by others. Eventually the government changed, and the bureaucracy found a government receptive to its "closing the door" policy.

A few years later, when Bill C-55 came out, we would see what the Department meant by "workable". It meant denial of access to the system for all but a small percentage of refugee claimants. At this time, however, the Department was still simply objecting to every option in the Task Force and Ratushny reports rather than proposing any new system of its own.

Plaut's study was released April, 1985 after the government had changed from Liberal to Conservative and Flora MacDonald had become the new Immigration Minister. Plaut recommended three useful options for change. But Plaut's models were no more "workable" to the Department than the proposals of Ratushny and the Task Force. The three reports were considered helpful by the public at large — certainly by anyone concerned with refugees — and by non-governmental groups trying to raise consciousness and focus discussion on the determination system. Within the Department, however, the Plaut report, like those before, fell on deaf ears.

THE HARBHAJAN SINGH CASE

After the Charter came into effect, the issue of oral hearings came up again in the courts, in the case of Harbhajan Singh and six others. All seven had claimed refugee status and been refused by the Minister. They had also been refused by the Board without oral hearings. The Federal Court of Appeal had dismissed their applications to set aside the decisions of the Immigration Appeal Board without reasons. Their applications for leave to appeal to the Supreme Court of Canada were last ditch efforts to seek protection from Canada.

C.D.L. Coveney was legal counsel for Satnam Singh. Ian Scott, Q.C. represented Harbhajan Singh, Sadhu Singh Thandi, Paramjit Singh Mann, Kewal Singh, Charemjit Singh Gill, and Indrani. Mendel Green, Q.C., Barbara Jackman and Donald Chiasson were legal counsel for the intervenants, the Federation of Canadian Sikh Societies and the Canadian Council of Churches.

The Charter guarantees the right to life, liberty and security of the person, and the right not to be deprived of these rights, except in accordance with the principles of fundamental justice. In a broad sense fundamental justice refers to basic or essential rights. The principles of fundamental justice include, for example, the right to a fair trial, the right to be considered innocent before proven guilty and the right of an accused to hear charges against him.

Counsel for Singh argued that this Charter guarantee was violated when a refugee claim was denied without an oral hearing, and the Supreme Court of Canada agreed. The Supreme Court granted leave to appeal on the seven refugee cases in February, 1984, on the question of whether the refugee claims procedure met the Charter requirement of fundamental justice. The appeal was heard beginning April 30, 1984.

Counsel for the appellants and intervenants argued that the refugee claims procedure violated the principles of fundamental justice, because claimants are not granted an oral hearing, as of right, before any tribunal that determines whether they are refugees, and because claimants are not advised of the case against them and given an opportunity to respond.

The Minister's counsel said the refugee claims system itself complies with fundamental justice despite the absence of an oral hearing. Counsel for the Minister argued that, at the level of Immigration Appeal Board application for redetermination, claimants have no case against them and therefore are not required to have an opportunity to meet their case. The claimant puts in his own case. At the IAB level, if the claim does not go to an oral hearing, the Minister does not respond. The process, at this stage, is not adversarial. Counsel argued that the fairness of the prior Ministerial determination was not before the Court, since all the cases were appeals from reviews of IAB determinations.

Counsel for the Minister also argued the system was a reasonable limit on the Charter guarantee of fundamental justice, and fell within the Charter exception. Counsel said to require the IAB to conduct a full oral hearing of refugee cases unlikely to succeed, even if unopposed, would place a pointless burden on the Board's resources.

After the arguments were heard, the Court requested written arguments on the Bill of Rights. According to the Bill of Rights, no law of Canada shall be construed or applied so as to deprive a person of the right to a fair hearing in accordance with the principles of fundamental justice.

When the Supreme Court decision came down on April 4, 1985, three judges decided on the basis of the Charter and three judges decided on the basis of the Bill of Rights. All agreed an oral hearing was required.[8] The court panel consisted of seven judges, but one judge, Ritchie J., did not participate in the judgement.

Madame Justice Bertha Wilson, who gave judgement for the judges who relied on the Charter, made an acerbic comment about the way the Court of Appeal had previously applied the notion of fairness to refugee claimants. She referred to a statement by Justice Pratte in the Mensah case: "Parliament did not intend to subject either the Minister or the Refugee Status Advisory Committee to the procedural duty of fairness invoked by the applicant." Madame Justice Wilson said, "If Pratte J. intended, by this statement, to suggest that Parliament has excluded the duty of fairness articulated in this court's decisions in *Re Nicholson and Haldimand Norfolk-Regional Board of Commissioners of Police* [a 1978 case], I believe he must have been mistaken."

Justice Estey, the same judge who had decided against oral hearings in the Saraos case a few years earlier, now decided in favour of an oral hearing in the Harbhajan Singh case on the basis of the Bill of Rights. Yet the Bill of Rights was in effect when the Saraos case was argued.

When the Charter was entrenched, there was initially a good deal of uncertainty about what effect it could have. The Bill of Rights had been gutted by the courts, essentially becoming a meaningless document to serve as a last resort of desperate counsel. There was a fear that the Charter might suffer the same fate. I was concerned that the Bill of Rights would be an albatross around the neck of the Charter, since much of the Bill's wording was repeated in the Charter. If the Charter were interpreted like the Bill, it would mean little.

Fortunately, exactly the opposite happened. Instead of the Bill killing the Charter, the Charter resuscitated the Bill, giving it a quasi-constitutional status it never had when it stood alone. The Harbhajan Singh case was a graphic illustration of that legal trend.

The Supreme Court decision was too late to help Saraos, but for those caught in the system, everything changed. They finally had a right to oral hearings before the IAB. No legislative change was necessary.

Unfortunately, as this book explains later, Bill C-55 was soon to cut off access to the very Court that was responsible for finding the previous refugee determination process unconstitutional. The system had become fair, not because of government initiative, but because the Supreme Court of Canada upheld the Charter's guarantee of fundamental justice and required oral hearings. The new system has oral hearings but infringes on refugees' rights in other ways. Yet it may be free from challenge in the Supreme Court of Canada.

Chapter 8

BILL C-55: REFUGEE MISTAKES

The test of any legal system is how it handles mistakes. Are mistakes easy or hard to make? Once made, are they simple or difficult to correct? Are they likely to be disastrous or inconsequential?

The consequences of a judgement may be severe in criminal law. If a mistake is made on a murder charge, for instance, an innocent person may be deprived of liberty for the rest of his life. The criminal law system is hedged in with safeguards to prevent any such errors in judgement from taking place.

A person is presumed innocent until proven guilty and the Crown prosecution must demonstrate the guilt of the accused beyond a reasonable doubt. Elaborate rules allow into court only reliable evidence, and a preliminary inquiry presents the accused with the case against him. A person convicted of any crime may appeal the Court's decision to a higher court on issues of fact as well as law.

Criminal law operates according to the maxim: it is better ten guilty people go free than one innocent person be punished. The overriding concern is that the innocent are acquitted.

Our criminal law system is successful if it avoids convicting the innocent, and if any slip-ups are easily rectified. By the same test, the new refugee determination system established by Bill C-55 is an abysmal failure: mistakes are easy to make and virtually impossible to correct. And a mistake once made can be catastrophic. If a genuine refugee seeking protection is found not to be a refugee and sent back erroneously to the country he fled, he may be killed or tortured.

CATASTROPHE FROM MISTAKES

Under the new legislation, mistakes will be catastrophic once made for two reasons:

- the deport/depart decision is made at the beginning;
- the B-1 list has been abolished.

Conditional Orders

An adjudicator decides at the beginning of the inquiry whether to issue a deportation order or a departure notice. The decision will take effect only at the end of the refugee determination process. The end of the process may be years down the road, years after the original deport/depart decision is made. The decision sits in suspended animation, a conditional order only, waiting to take effect once the process ends. If the person is recognized as a refugee, the conditional order does not take effect. But, if the person is determined not to be a refugee, the earlier deport/depart decision comes into play.

Once this conditional deport/depart decision is made, it cannot be changed. The circumstances that lead to the decision being made may themselves have changed drastically. Yet the decision remains what it was.

A departure notice is a notice that the claimant will depart Canada by a certain day, for example, thirty days after he has been finally determined not to be a refugee. A deportation order is an order that the claimant will be deported from Canada. In practice, a departure notice means the person can return to Canada at any time provided he meets normal immigration criteria. A deportation order means a bar from Canada for life. Unless the Minister of Immigration consents to his return by way of exception, the person cannot legally return to Canada.

How does one get a departure notice, rather than a deportation order? The decision is made by the adjudicator, not by the claimant. But a prerequisite is that the person is willing and able to leave — not immediately, but after the claimant has been determined to be a refugee. If the claimant says he is willing and able to leave Canada should his claim fail, the adjudicator may issue a departure notice. If the claimant says that he is not willing or not able to leave Canada, then the adjudicator is sure to issue a deportation order.

In theory, a person ordered deported may be allowed to leave voluntarily and select the country of departure. In practice, those ordered deported are systematically returned to the home country.

At the beginning of the refugee determination process, a claimant is unlikely to say he is willing to leave Canada voluntarily, because that would undercut his claim. It would be inconsistent for a refugee claimant to agree to leave, since his claim is based on fear of persecution. Nor, even if he is willing, is he likely at this point to be able to arrange entry to a third country at some uncertain date in the future.

Further, the person may not be able to leave even if he is willing. He may not have the funds. His return ticket may have expired by the time his claim is determined. At the conclusion of the refugee determination process, a claimant who has exhausted his legal resources in Canada may be willing to leave voluntarily to a third country in order to avoid being deported back to his home country. He may have accumulated sufficient funds to leave during his stay in Canada, but never gets a chance to show that he can depart Canada on his own funds.

Some claimants removed will be abusive claimants who, under any system, would be deported back home. But others will be real refugees, rejected in error by the Canadian system because of its lack of procedural safeguards. Others still will be people fleeing generalized violence rather than individualized persecution — not legally refugees, but not abusers either. These people should have the chance to depart voluntarily to a third country, but they won't have that alternative.

Under the old system, an adjudicator decided whether to issue a deportation order or a departure notice after a refugee claim was finally determined. The deport/depart decision was moved to the beginning from the end of the process because the Department feared that reconvening the inquiry to decide deport/depart — after the refugee decision was finally made — would create an additional delay.

However, because a deportation order is more likely at the beginning than at the end; and a deportation order is more likely under the new system than under the old, disaster from a mistake is more likely under the new system than under the old. As elsewhere in the process, fairness and common sense have given way to the insistence on speed.

Abolition of the B-1 List

Catastrophe from a mistake is also more likely under the new system because of the abolition of the list of countries to which Canada does not deport. At one time, Canada considered it inhumane to deport anyone to a set of listed countries where repression was extremely severe or the breakdown of law and order was excessively widespread. Originally, the list was kept secret. When the government announced the May 21, 1986 administrative adjustment, it also made public a B-1 list, or Annex B-1 to the administrative adjustment announcement. The list was comprised of eighteen countries to which Canada would not deport, and whose citizens would be given Minister's Permits in Canada if they claimed refugee status.

When the Minister's Permit policy was put in place (see Chapter 6) the non-deportation policy continued in operation. The Minister's Permit fast-track system soon became clogged due to a delay in imposing visa requirements on countries generating abusive claimants. But the B-1 list remained in effect until February, 1987, when the government ceased granting Minister's Permits to claimants from listed countries. Although the non-deportation policy had been in place long before the Minister's Permits plan, the government abandoned this policy at the same time.

Once the non-deportation list was repealed, there was no policy to let people at our borders who have fled generalized violence stay in Canada.* Initially, the government's revocation of the non-deportation list and the Minister's Permits did not cause much concern because there was a growing backlog of refugee claimants and few people were actually deported. The policy became significant only when the new law came into effect and there was no unending backlog to provide at least temporary protection to these people fleeing generalized persecution. In the legislation's first six months of operation, from January 1 to June 30 1989, 295 refugee claimants failed their credible-basis hearing and were thus subject to deportation. Of the 295, 151 refugee claimants were deported.

Ironically, while the Immigration Department is sending claimants back to countries of danger, another government body, the Canadian International Development Agency (CIDA), refuses to send Canadians to these same countries. CIDA has its own B-1 list of countries too dangerous for Canadian aid and development workers. CIDA will not finance projects requiring Canadians to be sent to areas of danger such as El Salvador. Yet the Immigration Department is willing to send claimants to these countries.

---

* There is a policy which allows Canadians with relatives in danger abroad to bring their extended family members over to Canada, according to the *Immigration Manual.*[1] The relatives must reside or have resided in zones of conflict or be directly affected by adverse natural disasters such as floods and earthquakes, or human domestic events like revolutions and wars. They must be in personal danger and may have lost homes and jobs directly to those events, ranging from civil war to sectoral violence. Special programmes are in effect for El Salvador, Guatemala, Iran, Lebanon and Sri Lanka. To be eligible, refugees must demonstrate they have a reasonable ability to settle in Canada with the assistance of a guarantor. However, the policy is relevant only to claims made outside Canada and not inside Canada or at a port of entry. Thus, a person from one of the five listed countries would be allowed entry if he applied outside Canada, but deported back to danger if he applied from inside Canada. A Canadian relative can bring over a foreign relative in danger, but if the foreign relative is already here, the Canadian cannot keep him here.

If the refugee determination system were error-free, and everybody in danger were protected, then a non-deportation policy would be unnecessary. But the system is not error-free. In fact, the new refugee claims system is more likely to lead to mistakes with serious consequences than the old system. Thus, it is incumbent upon legislators to devise a system incorporating every precaution to compensate for these mistakes, including a list of countries to which rejected claimants will not be deported.

REASONS FOR ERROR

Under the new legislation mistakes will be easy to make for eight reasons:

1. The claimant is denied access to counsel at the original refugee interview;
2. The decision not to claim refugee status is irrevocable;
3. The law promotes a hurry-up atmosphere;
4. A designated counsel is foisted on the refugee claimant;
5. The burden of proof is imposed on the claimant;
6. The proceedings are adversarial in nature;
7. Credibility screening is based on the disposition of other cases from the claimant's country of origin;
8. Immigration adjudicators are involved in the refugee decisions.

1. Denial of Access to Counsel

An immigration officer interviews a refugee claimant upon arrival at a port of entry about the substance of his claim. Counsel is not present. Yet the interviewing officer's notes are used for cross-examining the claimant at the credible-basis hearing. Any discrepancy between the interviewing officer's notes and the claimant's story at the hearing can be used to fail the client on the credible-basis test.[†]

Refugee claimants are not legally obliged to take part in these initial refugee interviews. However, claimants will want

---

[†] Originally, the problem was made more acute because the interviewing officer's notes were unavailable to the claimant prior to his credible-basis

to participate in the initial interview in order to try to convince the case presenting officer that their claim has a credible-basis, so that the case presenting officer will concede that it does at the hearing. That concession would be binding on the tribunal hearing the claim.[3] But claimants may be imprecise in telling their stories and omit relevant details if they partake in the initial interview without access to counsel.

2. The Irrevocability of the Decision Not to Claim Refugee Status

When a person arrives at a Canadian port of entry without proper documentation he is sent to an immigration trial as soon as possible and asked if he wants to claim refugee status. This trial is his only opportunity to claim refugee status in those proceedings,[4] even though the person may be confused or frightened, and may not have had a chance to consult counsel. The person may believe he should try entering Canada as a visitor and claim refugee status later. He may be suspicious of Canadian government officials, having learned to fear authority in his own country. He may be uncertain whether his testimony will be kept confidential from his own government.

If the person does not claim refugee status, he will not get another chance. The claims system is permanently closed to him. According to the new law, "no such claim by that person shall thereafter be received or considered."

3. Hurry-Up Atmosphere of the Law

In this area of law, like the highway, speed kills. Claimants are not benefitted by a process so slow that it seems interminable.

---

hearing. The interviewing officer may have mischaracterized, misunderstood or mistranscribed the claimant. The claimant did not have a chance to anticipate, prepare for or correct any error until it was put to him in cross-examination at his hearing. On request, the Department of Immigration now provides the immigration officer's notes to the claimant prior to his credible-basis hearing. I challenged in court the practice of keeping notes from a refugee claimant. I represented Omar Ruz from Chile in a challenge against the government's refusal to release notes. In February, 1989, Mr. Justice Leonard Martin of the Federal Court gave me the order I sought[2] and the Department produced the immigration officer's notes on the interview with Ruz. Ruz, a photojournalist who was jailed and beaten for photographing demonstrations against the Chilean government, was eventually granted refugee status in April, 1989.

That was a major problem with the old law. The new legislation is an over-reaction to the inordinate delays in the old law. Claimants may be given little time to find counsel, and cases are often dealt with hastily.

A programme delivery strategy prepared by the Executive Director of Immigration, Joe Bissett, dated December 22, 1988, outlines the rushed manner for applying the law. The first priority is removing ineligible or non-credible-basis claimants from Canada. Processing eligible and presumed-credible refugee claimants is a last priority.

The government's attempts to deter refugee claimants from seeking status in Canada seems to be working. Statistics already show a drop in refugee claims since the new legislation took effect. From January 1 to June 30, 1989, 5,057 persons claimed refugee status compared to approximately 7,000 during the same six-month period in 1988. As of June 30, 1989, 4,574 cases of the 5,057 claimants completed the credible-basis stage while 483 claimants were granted short adjournments or postponements.§

According to Bissett's strategy, the way to get "the word" around about the new Canadian policy is to physically remove illegal migrants from Canada. The new refugee determination system's purpose is "to make quick final decisions." Removing ineligible non-credible refugee claimants quickly — not making accurate decisions — is described by Bissett as the new law's cornerstone.

---

§ Of the 4,574 completed cases, 4,106 passed credible-basis hearing and were referred to a full hearing, 295 were rejected as not having a credible-basis, and another 169 claims were withdrawn or abandoned by the claimants. Four claimants were found to be ineligible. The 295 rejected claimants were subject to removal from Canada. As of June 30, 1989, 2,149 cases — out of 4,106 referred to full hearing — were completed. Eighteen claims were withdrawn, 318 had decisions pending, and 1,813 claimants had their decisions rendered. Of the 1,813, 1,607 claimants received favourable decisions, while 206 were rejected. Overall, 1,607 claimants (76 percent) were granted refugee status and 505 (24 percent) failed refugee status.

Of the approximate 7,000 claims made during 1988, 1,607 have been granted refugee status, 207 were denied refugee status, 18 claims were abandoned, and the remaining claimants are still being processed.

Because mistakes are virtually impossible to correct once made, claimants' lawyers must be not only good, but also better prepared than for any other case in their careers. Yet claimant and counsel are faced with pressure from the Department, adjudicator and Refugee Board member to have the case heard quickly to dispel any impression of system abuse. If counsel and claimant succumb to this pressure, mistakes will be easily made.

4. The Right to Counsel of Choice is Denied

According to the new law, a person who makes a claim at a port of entry has a right to a counsel of his choice. But in practice, this right is severely limited by time requirements under the law. Counsel must be "ready and able" to proceed at a time fixed by the adjudicator,[5] which could be immediately. Further, if a claimant is ordered removed, counsel has only seventy-two hours to file an application for leave to set aside the order of the screening panel.** Most experienced immigration lawyers in private practice are not in a position to prepare a case without notice or an appeal on three day's notice.

If a lawyer of choice cannot be found on such short notice, the new law provides for a designated lawyer to represent the port of entry refugee claimant. The new law even allows the lawyer to be imposed on the claimant after a negative decision at the credible-basis or eligibility stage. If no lawyer of the claimant's choice is available to take instructions within twenty-four hours, then a lawyer must, by law, be forced on the claimant.

Further, when a port of entry claimant has retained a private counsel who is not ready to proceed at the adjudicator's pace, the Act gives the adjudicator the power to dismiss the private lawyer and replace that lawyer with designated counsel. Losing counsel who is in the midst of preparing a case, and starting

---

** Claimants who have spent some time in the United States don't even have seventy-two hours to appeal. The law allows for them to be returned "as soon as is reasonably practicable." Preparing the documents immediately for an appeal is an impossibility. Especially for people coming from the U.S., effective access to Canadian courts is denied.[6]

again from scratch with a new lawyer who is totally unprepared, is a recipe for error.

It is unsatisfactory to foist designated counsel on any litigant. It is particularly unsatisfactory to foist counsel on refugee claimants who may distrust government actions as politicized or corrupt. A refugee claimant thrown into a hearing shortly after arrival with only designated counsel to assist him is bound to feel disadvantaged.

Contrary to the old refugee determination process, the new law has adversarial proceedings. At the initial credible-basis hearing, the representative of the Minister of Employment and Immigration is given an opportunity to present evidence, cross-examine witnesses and make representations.[7] A refugee claimant is now faced with a hearing in which a representative of the Minister argues against him and a designated counsel, paid for by the Minister, argues for him. The claimant will inevitably feel that he is not being represented in as vigorous and forthright a manner as would be the case with a lawyer he chose.

Ironically, if a designated counsel succeeds in guiding his client through the credible-basis hearing and the client develops confidence in the lawyer, there is no guarantee the claimant will be able to retain the same lawyer for the second stage in the process, the full hearing. Designated counsel is counsel paid by the government of Canada. At the full hearing stage, the law does not allow for designation. Payment of the lawyer by the government of Canada ceases. If the claimant is not able to afford to retain the designated counsel privately, legal aid may not be willing to retain the lawyer or the lawyer may not be willing to work at legal aid rates. So the claimant is left with discontinuity of legal assistance through the process, another potential source of error.

Who is designated to represent refugee claimants? In some cases, they are lawyers with no previous refugee law experience or even little experience with the law. A designated counsel list is drawn up according to agreements between the federal government and each province. In British Columbia, Alberta and Quebec, the accounting firm of Peat Marwick has been responsible for drawing up the designated counsel list. In

Ontario, Legal Aid provides the list of designated counsel. In some provinces, Legal Aid will not designate counsel because it wants refugees to have competent representation not based on a moment's notice. Also, if there is no federal-provincial agreement, and no provincially designated list, the adjudicator selects a lawyer from his own designated counsel list. The Refugee Board provides designated lawyers with some training, albeit an unbalanced form of preparation. A discussion of all constitutional pitfalls in the law is conveniently omitted. It is hard to be confident that every one of these designated lawyers in every case will be error-free.

5. Burden of Proof

When refugee claimants come to Canada, they normally do not arrive with witnesses, documents, or evidence to support their claims. All they have is their personal story. Unless refugee claimants are given the benefit of doubt, their claims will be virtually impossible to establish.

The United Nations High Commission for Refugees (UNHCR) executive committee, which sets guidelines for the determination of refugee status, recommended that claimants be given the benefit of the doubt. Canada is a member of the UNHCR executive committee. Yet Canada's new law places the burden of proof on the refugee claimant.[8] The burden of proof includes the burden of presenting evidence and the burden of persuasion.

Ideally, the burden of presenting evidence should be shared by the claimant and the examiner. Examiners should use all means at their disposal to produce evidence in support of the claim. But under the new law, the claimant alone has the burden of persuading the examiner of his claim. That means any doubt is resolved against the claimant. The claimant is not given the benefit of the doubt.††

The Department and the Board both say the claimant has the benefit of the doubt. However, the law contradicts this. When the law was going through Parliament, the government rejected

---

†† Similarly, under the past Immigration Act, the Federal Court of Appeal ruled that the claimant did not have the benefit of the doubt, and that if there was any doubt, it must be resolved against the claimant.[9]

amendments stating clearly that claimants have the benefit of the doubt.

6. Adversarial Proceedings

At the credible-basis hearing, the Minister's representative, the case presenting officer, has the power to cross-examine witnesses and make representations. Unless the case presenting officer concedes, he argues that the claimant is not a refugee, and often goes to inordinate lengths to discover minor discrepancies between the claimant's written statement and the claimant's oral statement, or among parts of the oral statement. Some lawyers even advise claimants not to make oral statements to eradicate opportunities for the officer to find minor discrepancies, that may be used as a basis for denying a claim.

The spirit of the hearings has become exactly the opposite of what is recommended by the United Nations High Commission for Refugees handbook. The handbook says hearings should be co-operative attempts by the investigators to elicit all the relevant information. Every step possible should be taken to win over the refugee's confidence so that he will tell the whole story.

Instead, we see systematic and concerted attacks on claimants by the representatives of the Minister. Claimants try to protect themselves by saying as little as possible. But saying little has its own dangers. A reticent claimant may fail to persuade the screening panel. The written statement may not be sufficiently convincing.

One consequence of the adversarial nature of the system is the degeneration of credible-basis hearings into credibility hearings. Credible-basis hearings are meant to determine whether the claims are manifestly unfounded. The French term in the statute on the hearings is "minimum de fondent", a minimum of foundation. Yet the presence of a cross-examining case presenting officer and an adjudicator who bring an Immigration Department scepticism to bear results in close questioning of claimants about minor discrepancies in components of their claim.

The credible-basis hearing should be used for the purpose of determining whether the basis of the claim is credible, not whether the claimant is credible. If it is manifest that the claimant is lying, then the claim is without foundation. But a determination that the claimant is lying on the balance of probabilities properly belongs in the full hearing, not the screening hearing.

The adversarial nature of the screening hearing, the presence of a case presenting officer and adjudicator who bring an immigration perspective to refugee determination, and the perversion of the credible-basis test into a credibility test means these screening hearings are harder for claimants to get through than full hearings. It is not unusual for these credible-basis hearings to go on for days. The difficulty of screening hearings for claimants increases the likelihood of error.

7. Judging a Case Based on Past Cases

Under the new law, one ground for determining credible-basis is the disposition of other claims by persons who alleged fear of persecution in the claimant's country of origin.[10]

Although the details of these cases are confidential, the rejection and acceptance rate of claimants from each country is available. At the screening stage, decision-makers are told by statute to suspect claimants from a country with a high rejection rate. Thus, the case is not decided on its merits, but on the outcome of other cases, without knowledge of the reasons for previous conclusions or possible differences between these cases and the case before the tribunal.

This practice negates the principle of benefit of the doubt. An apparently credible claim is put in doubt just because other claims from the country of the claimant have been rejected.

8. The Involvement of Immigration Adjudicators in Refugee Decisions

The immigration adjudicators who determine refugee cases may be independent of the Minister of Immigration, but they are certainly not independent from the perspective and concerns of the Immigration Department. The same adjudicators also enforce the Immigration Act. They are not expert in refugee law or country conditions. Nor, given their other duties, can they be expected to be. Adjudicators will inevitably bring immigration considerations to bear on refugee determinations.

Generally, adjudicators have a duty to apply the Immigration Act so that it works. Yet refugees represent, in a sense, a loophole in the Immigration Act. Refugees, once recognized as such, are allowed to stay in Canada even though they do not meet normal immigration criteria.

The adjudicator may see the claimant as a violator of the Immigration Act. Refugee claimants may be viewed by adjudicators as a threat to the immigration system's integrity. This inherent scepticism is bound to have an impact on individual refugee determinations.

At the credible-basis screening stage, the refugee claim is heard by two panelists, an adjudicator and a Refugee Board member. The claim must be unanimously rejected for the claimant to fail the screening test. If the Refugee Board member thinks the claim is credible, the claimant goes on to a full hearing, whether or not the adjudicator agrees.

However, a certain collegiality is bound to develop between adjudicators and Refugee Board members. It is unlikely Refugee Board members and adjudicators will diverge consistently over time across Canada. Those participating are unlikely to want to raise doubts about the system, which would be fostered by persistent disagreement.

Rapport between the decision-makers may be advantageous to refugees if adjudicators defer to the decisions of Refugee Board Members. However, refugees may also be disadvantaged by this closeness if, instead, Refugee Board members adopt the immigration perspective of adjudicators.

CORRECTING MISTAKES

Mistakes are virtually impossible to correct for three reasons:

1. there is no appeal on the merits;
2. appeals are heard only by leave;
3. claimants are removed before the appeal is heard.

1. No Appeal on the Facts of a Rejection

The right to appeal a rejected refugee claim on the merits of the determination is a principle accepted internationally by the

UNHCR executive committee, of which Canada is a member. Canada's new law denies this principle.

The right of appeal is necessary in order to correct mistakes. Without appeal, genuine refugees can be returned to situations of danger without recourse.

Under the new law, a claimant may be granted an appeal, but only under certain limited conditions. These include an error of law or jurisdiction. They also include an error of fact made in "a perverse or capricious manner" or without regard to the material before the decision-maker.[11] However, they do not include an error of fact where the decision-maker comes to a wrong determination after considering the facts presented. This is important because most refugee decisions turn on questions of fact, human rights conditions, interpretation of evidence, or credibility, and misjudgements predominantly involve errors in the appreciation of the facts presented.

2. Appeals Heard Only By Way of Leave or Permission

In the Federal Court Trial Division or Federal Court of Appeal, refugee claimants require leave of the Federal Court to gain access regarding any matters, even technical matters, arising within Canada under the Immigration Act.

Requiring leave distinguishes in-land immigration cases, or claims made inside Canada, from all other cases. Anyone else filing an application in the Federal Court with respect to any matter arising under any other Act does not need leave.

A denial of equal access directly contravenes the Refugee Convention, which provides that a refugee is to have free access to the courts of law in all signatory countries.[12] This provision is one of few in the Convention applying to refugee claimants. Obviously, free access to the courts would be meaningless if applied only to refugees which have already been recognized as such. The UN High Commission for Refugees confirms this provision applies to claimants.

Allowing appeals only by leave denies a person the right to appeal. A person who can get to court only with leave essentially has his right to go to court removed. Even for errors of law or process, the court could still deny leave. When leave is refused, typically reasons are not given. A request for leave is not made through an oral hearing, but is simply a written application.

The new law also explicitly cuts off access to the Supreme Court of Canada. The Refugee Reform Act (Bill C-55) does not allow appeal to the Supreme Court if the lower Federal Court of Appeal first denies the refugee claimant leave to appeal.[13] The past refugee determination process, it must be noted, was the result of a decision of the Supreme Court of Canada requiring oral hearings and holding that the legislated process which did not require oral hearings was unconstitutional.[14]

There is only one circumstance in which the claimant may gain access to the Supreme Court. When a claimant is granted leave by the Federal Court of Appeal and then loses his appeal, the claimant may apply for leave to the Supreme Court of Canada. In practice, this possibility may mean little. If the government has won at the Federal Court of Appeal level after leave to appeal is granted, the government can cut off access to the Supreme Court of Canada simply by issuing a Minister's Permit to the person concerned. The person then has no reason to go to the Supreme Court of Canada, since his personal problems are resolved. The Federal Court of Appeal will not grant leave to appeal on the same issue again, since it has already decided the issue. The Supreme Court of Canada will never get a chance to examine the issue.

A Minister's Permit would not likely be issued solely to cut off access to the Supreme Court of Canada. Under the new law as under the old, Minister's Permits will be issued when the facts of the case warrant their issuance.

However, good faith behaviour on the part of the department, when the result is issuance of a Minister's Permit, leads to problems with the new law. The Supreme Court never gets to decide the issue, in that case or any other.

3. Removal Before an Appeal is Heard

Formally in law, when a case is under appeal, no interim change in the state of affairs can take place that would render the appeal meaningless. For instance, when Canada still had the death penalty, the courts did not authorize an execution before an appeal. Yet, under the new refugee law, a refugee claimant whose case is rejected at the initial credible-basis hearing is forcibly returned to the country of claimed danger before the leave application and subsequent appeal. In the meantime, he may be tortured, imprisoned, or even killed.

SECOND CREDIBLE-BASIS DETERMINATION ADDED

A last minute amendment to the Refugee Reform Act, then in Bill form, reveals the petty spirit the government has brought to the refugee determination process. Originally the new law called for only one credible-basis determination at the screening stage, but an amendment put before third reading included two credible-basis determinations: one at the screening stage and a second at the full hearing level.[15]

In principle, a credible-basis screening system is not objectionable. As a right, however, credible-basis screening should be subject to appeal on fact and law. After such an appeal, there is nothing wrong in principle with requiring the person leave Canada while all further appeals are exhausted.

The government's amendment, in effect, allows only the government to appeal a credible-basis determination. The person concerned cannot appeal except by leave to the court. If a claimant is found to be incredible at the screening level, he never gets a full hearing. If a claimant is found to be credible at the screening level, the Minister may present evidence at the full hearing of the claim to show the claimant is not credible. Allowing no appeal as of right on credible-basis is bad enough. Giving an appeal to the Minister but not the claimant makes the system even worse.

A person who is determined to have a credible-basis for a refugee claim, though not actually a refugee, can remain in Canada while his application for leave to appeal is being considered. If, however, a person is determined not to have credible-basis at either stage, he must leave within seventy-two hours, whether or not his application for leave is decided in that time.[16]

THE CARRION CASE

The new system has no right of appeal. Claimants have no second chance. The old system had a right of redetermination which gave claimants a second chance. The first chance was a decision by the Minister and the second a decision by the Immigration Appeal Board. In this respect, the old system was better than the new.

When the new law came into effect, it denied a second chance not only to new claimants who arrived after January 1, 1989, but also to claimants who had started their refugee claims in the old refugee determination system, and who had not yet received an initial decision from the Minister. These claimants had to begin their claims again under the new system. The effect was to make the second chance disappear for claimants under the new law and claimants under the old law alike. Marco Carrion decided to challenge in court the loss of his second chance.

Carrion, 26 and single, came to Canada from Chile in August, 1988. After his visitor status expired, Carrion told an immigration officer he wanted to claim refugee status. At the inquiry, the adjudicator found that Carrion had overstayed and adjourned his inquiry for examination of his refugee claim.

No examination was scheduled, and none was in sight. Department staff had stopped scheduling claims because they were busy training for the new law. I went to court on behalf of Carrion to ask the court to order the government to schedule a refugee claim for Carrion. The Court issued the order with government consent. Carrion's refugee examination was held November 22, 1988.[17]

Given the backlog, it was unlikely the Minister would decide on his claim before the legislation ran out December 31, 1988. The new legislation swept up everybody in the old system in Carrion's position: he would have to start his refugee claim all over again in the new system. Under the old system Carrion had two chances to establish he was a refugee — a determination and a redetermination. The new system gave him only one chance with no appeal on the merits, and no redetermination. As well, the new system gives the Department two chances to establish Carrion is not a refugee — at the credible-basis screening and at the full hearing.

If Carrion actually got a decision from the Minister under the old Act before the new Act came into effect, he would get his first chance to claim refugee status under the old Act, and the Minister would decide on his claim. If he failed, he would move into the new system, and get his second chance to claim refugee status under the new Act.

I asked the court to order the Minister to decide Carrion's claim before the new Act came into effect. I argued that if the Minister could not decide before December 31, 1988, then the operation of the new Act should be postponed for Carrion until the Minister decided. Once Carrion had made his refugee claim, his right to determination and redetermination was vested. I argued he had a substantive or legal right to a redetermination, not just a procedural right. When Carrion had his right to redetermination taken away by the new Immigration Act, I argued, the deprivation was a violation of the Charter. It was fundamentally unjust for Carrion to lose his vested right to a second chance to claim refugee status retroactively.

The right to a second chance is a meaningful right. Immigration Appeal Board statistics showed that under the old system, in its last year of operation, about nine percent of claimants determined by the Minister not to be refugees were determined by the Board to be refugees. The Minister had erred and the Board corrected errors in favour of the claimants. If Carrion got a Ministerial determination denying him refugee status, the second time around he could respond to the Minister's objections to his claim. In losing his second chance, Carrion lost the opportunity to rebut the reasons the decision-maker might have to his claim. He might be refused in error and not have a chance to correct the mistake until it was too late.

Mr. Justice Muldoon of the Federal Court Trial Division disagreed with this line of argument. The right to a second chance in the old Act, Muldoon ruled, was not a substantive right, but a mere procedure. According to the Charter, Carrion was entitled to an oral hearing. He was getting that oral hearing under the new legislation. Because of that oral hearing, Carrion stood "in no jeopardy of being denied any substantive right."[18]

COMPASSIONATE AND HUMANITARIAN GROUNDS

Department officials justify the system, with all its difficulties in correcting mistakes, by pointing to their power to make exceptions on compassionate and humanitarian grounds. The Department has the discretion to allow anyone to stay on compassionate and humanitarian grounds.

The system began January 1, 1989 without any compassionate and humanitarian guidelines. Some officers began applying draft guidelines circulated at the end of January. Others decided to wait until the draft was eventually finalized at the end of February, 1989.

The guidelines provide for a humanitarian and compassionate review at both the beginning and the end of the refugee claims process. The initial review is very narrow. Defecting athletes from Eastern Europe and claimants with immediate family members in Canada are the sorts of people who qualify for special treatment at the initial review. The Department also conducts a final review as a result of which rejected claimants may be allowed to stay, or may at the end of the process have their removal orders temporarily suspended.

Those allowed to stay on compassionate and humanitarian grounds at the final review include not only defecting athletes and those with a Canadian spouse, but also persons who would face unduly harsh or inhumane treatment in the country they fled. There must be strong evidence that the person will face a life-threatening situation in his homeland as a direct result of political or social conditions there.

Temporary suspension of removal orders will be granted to persons likely to be at risk because of natural disasters, civil strife, or political disturbance. The removal will be carried out once the risks have subsided.

That Canada's refugee system could operate for any period of time without special considerations of those in life-threatening situations is shocking. People who met these criteria in early

1989 were not eligible to stay simply because there was a gap in the system — a delay between the implementation of the new law and the implementation of humanitarian guidelines.

As well, the review on humanitarian grounds after the inquiry and before removal is unlikely to succeed. To find a claimant is in danger back home on humanitarian grounds, after he has been rejected as having no credible-basis for his claim, undercuts the whole government-stated programme delivery strategy. The strategy states that removal of non-credible refugee claimants is the new law's cornerstone. Thus, letting rejected credible-basis claimants stay in Canada on humanitarian grounds means the Department's strategy has failed.

THE BHATTIA AND ABDI CASES

We expected to see one mistake after another under the new system, and that is exactly what is happening. Indeed, the very first decision made under the new system appears wrong.

Chhinder Pal Bhattia of India was the first person to fail credible-basis screening under the new system. He arrived in Canada January 1, 1989, and was told January 6, 1989 by a two-member panel that he did not qualify as a refugee.

Amnesty International believed that Bhattia would be detained, held without trial, and possibly tortured on return to India. Amnesty intervened in the case and asked the Minister of Immigration to halt the deportation. Amnesty International intervenes in only three to four refugee cases a year. However, Immigration Minister Barbara McDougall ignored the AI request and refused to halt Bhattia's deportation. It was the first time in ten years a Canadian Immigration Minister had ignored an Amnesty International request.

Bhattia applied for leave to appeal to the Federal Court of Appeal and then asked for a stay of execution of the deportation order until the leave application was decided. The Federal Court of Appeal denied the application to stay deportation proceedings.

The Government deported Bhattia back to India January 21, 1989. AI sent representatives to New Delhi and Bombay airports in an attempt to meet him, but Indian security officials blocked these efforts. Bhattia's family in India has not been able to confirm his whereabouts.

In another case, Abdi Moalin Aden from Somalia was rejected after a full hearing. In his claim, Abdi stated that he was arrested and tortured, that his father and brother were involved in opposition to the government, and that both had disappeared.

On April 20, 1989 Abdi was deported from Canada to Belgrade, Yugoslavia. He was given no ticket beyond that destination. The Yugoslavs imprisoned Abdi and beat him, not believing his story about what the Canadian authorities had done. Abdi went in orbit from Belgrade: he was deported in turn to Dubai, Cairo, and finally Mogadishu in Somalia.

At the airport in Somalia, police were waiting for Abdi. They knew he was coming because Canadian officials took him to the Somali embassy in Ottawa to get a passport after he had failed his hearing. Abdi was detained on arrival in Somali.

REFORM

What reforms should be introduced to improve the present system? Immigration adjudicators should have no part in refugee determination. The Act should state the claimant has the benefit of the doubt. Disposition of other cases from the country the claimant fled should not be a basis for determining credible-basis. A decision not to claim refugee status should be revocable.

There must be an opportunity to appeal from errors of fact as well as errors of law. Appeal and access to the Federal Court Trial Division must be by right and not by leave. The claimant must be allowed to remain in Canada pending appeals — where the claim is manifestly unfounded, for at least one level of appeal, and where the claim has foundation, for all appeals. The Act should not impose designated counsel on the claimant. The deport/depart decision should be made at the end of the whole process rather than at the beginning. If all these changes were made, the Act would be a viable Act. If all these changes were made, the Act would be a very different Act.

Given the system we have, what is the simplest way to reform it and remove its failings? The most obvious step is to remove the credible-basis hearing. For most cases, that can be done without any legislative or regulatory change. The Immigration Act already gives the government the power to remove these hearings simply by consenting to their not taking place.

In order to consent, the representative of the Immigration Minister has to believe that the claim has a credible-basis. Representatives cannot exercise the power systematically without examining the case's facts. But the Minister's representatives can exercise the power to consent more readily than they have to date.

A claimant is presumed to be telling the truth, unless there is some reason to believe he is lying. A claimant is to be given the benefit of the doubt. The credibility of a claimant should not be doubted unless it is manifestly obvious he is lying or clearly fraudulent. Evidence or testimony should not be rejected as incredible as long as it may be plausible. A claim may have a credible-basis, even if the claimant is not credible, as long as other evidence supports the claim.

These are all appropriate principles for applying the credible-basis test. It is often because these principles are neglected that the Minister's representative refuses to consent, and a screening panel rejects a claim as having no credible-basis. If these principles were applied systematically by the Minister's representative when deciding whether to consent, few credible-basis hearings would occur under the present system, even without legislative change.

The second change that should be made is to provide for an appeal on the merits of a claim. Again, this can be done administratively as a part of the post-inquiry pre-removal review. Now the Department reviews the cases on humanitarian grounds before deciding whether to remove the claimant. The Department could set up a system to allow for a review of any rejected claim on the merits, where the claimant wishes to appeal. The Department would remove only those who failed the appeal.

The combination of these two reforms should involve no additional administrative costs. Now, the number of cases contested at credible-basis is roughly equal to the number of cases that are rejected at the full hearing step. If there were no credible-basis hearings, the resources saved by the removal of that step could simply be transferred to a new appeal process. Even if every rejected claimant appealed, there would be no net cost to the system.

Ideally, the removal of credible-basis and the addition of an appeal should have a statutory basis. Legislative reform would mean there would be enforceable rights to the procedures established. If the rights were abused or taken away arbitrarily, claimants could seek the protection of the courts. But the changes do not have to await new legislation. They can and should happen now.

Canada's refugee determination system inspires little confidence. It is possible that so many mistakes will be made, people will eventually give up all hope in the system. Real refugees seeking protection in Canada will evade authorities rather than submit themselves to a deadly game of Russian roulette. Similarly, those concerned with protecting refugees will adopt extra-legal rather than legal strategies — a Canadian sanctuary movement is possible (see Chapter 16). We need a refugee determination system that is less prone to mistakes, not only to protect refugees, important as that is, but also to maintain the confidence of Canadians in their own legal system.

Chapter 9

A WAR MEASURES ACT FOR REFUGEES

Over the past two years, the refugee cause in Canada has been dealt one blow after another. First came the government announcement in February, 1987 requiring Central American refugees to wait in the U.S. until their inquiries could be scheduled. As well, Canada's list of countries to which refugees are not deported was abandoned, and transit visas were required for persons from countries for which visitor's visas were imposed.

Next was the Refugee Reform Act, denying the right to counsel of choice, denying the right to appeal, denying the benefit of the doubt to refugee claimants, refusing access to refugees who come from a government-deemed safe country, and imposing a decision-maker who is not independent from immigration considerations.

Lastly, the government introduced draconian legislation with Bill C-84. Bill C-84, The Refugee Deterrents and Detention Bill, followed close on the heels of Bill C-55, the Refugee Reform Bill. They were meant to be complementary, but they are very different in form and spirit. The Refugee Reform Bill articulated a long-held Department of Immigration belief that refugees should be selected from abroad and not allowed to come to Canada on their own to seek protection. However one might view the policy option, the Bill reflected a clear and firmly held point of view. The Refugee Deterrents and Detention Bill reflected no such position: it left an impression of panic. The Act gives government the power to detain refugees for seven days without review, and to keep undocumented refugees in detention indefinitely. The Act was an exaggerated and hysterical over-reaction to the landing of 174 Sikhs in Nova Scotia in July, 1987. The Refugee Deterrents and Detention Act is akin to the War Measures Act, invoked during the 1970 FLQ crisis and used to imprison hundreds of innocent Canadians.

The behaviour of the government in proposing this bill resembled its behaviour during the Second World War when it interned Japanese Canadians. Canadians today reject and regret the internment of Japanese Canadians under the War Measures Act, and the government is paying compensation to these Canadians. Canadians will one day equally regret Bill C-84 and the detentions that result from it.

Public concern over abuse of the refugee claims system is warranted. Government, however, allowed abuse to continue by maintaining for much too long a drawn out, cumbersome refugee system. In the old system, one person heard the refugee claim, a second advised on the claim after reading a transcript of the claim, and a third person decided on the claim, taking months to accomplish what a single person could accomplish in days.

Instead of removing delays, which created an obvious incentive for abuse, the government came up with an extreme and irrational response. It is as if government reacted to the public's concerns about crime by sending out vigilante squads to shoot and kill on the spot every alleged or suspected criminal.

People truly interested in stopping crime do not favour such a response, just as people concerned about refugees do not want real refugees turned away.

Government hysteria surrounding the Bill was apparent by the speedy drafting of C-84, and the emergency recall of Parliament in the summer of 1987 to deal with it. It is also apparent in the Act's contents. Under this legislation detention without judicial or quasi-judicial review is allowed for seven days; airlines can be required to hold passports, in violation of international standards; and government was temporarily given the power to turn back boatloads of refugees in Canadian waters. The Act allows the government to label persons as security risks without a refugee determination; criminalizes help to refugees; and permits search by force without a warrant of any place, including homes, looking for any evidence that a person plans to help refugees come to Canada.

WORDS AND ACTIONS

A measure of the government's panic over C-84 can be seen in the difference between what the government said it would do and what it actually has done. Then Immigration Minister Benoit Bouchard issued a press release on July 30, 1987 stating the government would implement emergency measures to prevent a repeat of the Sikh landing in Nova Scotia. However, most of these measures were never taken.

To be sure, Bill C-84 should not have included everything government set out to do in the July 30 press release. Dropping some of the original proposals was welcomed. But the dramatic shift from July 30 to August 11, when Bill C-84 received first reading, shows how determined government was to do "something" without knowing precisely what it wanted to accomplish.

Bouchard said in his press release that any person considered a security risk will be removed from Canada before his appeal to the Federal Court is heard. In fact, Bill C-84 allowed for a review by the Federal Court before removal. He also said people who can be admitted to a safe third country will be returned to that country. The safe country concept had already been put in C-55, and was not part of C-84.

Moreover, many provisions in Bill C-84 were not mentioned by the government on July 30, 1987. The expanded powers of search and seizure, power to require airlines to hold passports, power to turn back boat loads of refugees on the high seas or Canadian territorial waters, and the new offence of helping refugees were nowhere hinted at in Bouchard's press release. Only government's power to place refugees without documents under detention indefinitely, and to deny access to the refugee determination process for people deemed security threats were included in both the July 30 announcement and Bill C-84.

The government said penalties for smugglers and their accomplices would substantially increase. Yet the Bill did not increase penalties for this existing offence. Instead, it contained new offences. As well, the government said a person who cannot prove a credible-basis for a refugee claim will be removed from Canada, although the subject was not mentioned in C-84.

The government also said a person who can prove a credible-basis for a refugee claim, but who is found not to be a refugee, will be removed from Canada if their appeal to the Federal Court fails, presumably before any appeal to the Supreme Court of Canada. Again, there was nothing in Bill C-84 to this effect.

THE DETENTION PROVISION

A significant component of the Refugee Deterrents and Detention Act is the detention provision. Under the old law, immigration adjudicators decided whether refugee claimants would be detained, and the Security Intelligence and Review Committee (SIRC) resolved whether a refugee claimant should be deported as a security risk. Both immigration adjudicators and SIRC are independent from government. The Act takes away decision-making powers from independent immigration adjudicators on detention, and gives authority to government bureaucrats.

The old law required a detained person be brought before an adjudicator within forty-eight hours. If the adjudicator ordered detention to continue, he had to review the case every seven days. The adjudicator could keep a person detained only if he believed the person was a danger to the public or would otherwise not appear for immigration proceedings. The Refugee Deterrents and Detention Act allows for detention simply because Immigration may not know who the person is. Detention can continue for seven days, at which time the person must be brought before an adjudicator.[1]

Although the adjudicator must review the detention after seven days and every seven days thereafter, the adjudicator need only be satisfied that the Department is making reasonable efforts to identify the person. As long as he concludes the Department is making reasonable efforts, detention can continue indefinitely. An adjudicator cannot order a detainee's release even if he believes he knows who the person is and disagrees with the government about identification.

This detention provision reflects the harsh treatment of persons without documents. But real refugees often destroy their travel documents *en route*, arriving in an asylum country without travel papers. They hope to avoid possible return to their country of origin or to a third transit country, where they faced harsh living conditions, an unfair refugee determination procedure, or a denial of protection.

Guatemalan and Salvadoran refugees in the U.S. routinely destroy their identity documents because of American policy to return these refugees to their home countries. Salvadorans and Guatemalans caught by U.S. authorities without documents often pose as Mexicans in hopes of being deported there rather than to the countries of persecution they have fled. These Central Americans who now come to Canada face the possibility of indefinite detention until the Department decides they have been properly identified.

A WAR MEASURES ACT FOR REFUGEES

The Refugee Deterrents and Detention Act's exaggerated detention provisions must be compared with steps taken under the War Measures Act during the 1970 FLQ crisis. At that time, Cabinet passed the Public Order Regulations allowing detention without charge for twenty-one days. The Regulations were later replaced by the Public Order Act which allowed for detention without charge for a maximum of seven days. The Criminal Code of Canada says that a person must be charged within twenty-four hours of detention. Mr. Justice David McDonald, head of the Commission of Inquiry Concerning Certain Activities of the RCMP, recommended in August, 1981 that the War Measures Act be amended to prohibit detention without charge beyond seven days.

Even in case of war, invasion or rebellion, it is impossible to justify detention without court appearance beyond a maximum of seven days. So how can the government justify this practice for refugees when there is no national emergency threatening the security of the nation?

As a signatory to the Refugee Convention, Canada cannot impose penalties on refugees because they enter Canada or are present without authorization, provided they come directly from the country of persecution and present themselves without delay to the authorities.[2] According to the Convention, countries also cannot apply unnecessary restrictions to the movement of refugees on account of their illegal entry or presence.[3] As well, the Canadian Charter of Rights and Freedoms guarantees everyone freedom from arbitrary detention.[4] All of these provisions are violated by the new refugee detention provisions.

The provision in the Act about indefinite detention will have the greatest impact on refugees. Church groups may or may not be prosecuted, and new boat loads may or may not arrive by sea, but the continued arrival of undocumented refugees is certain. The government has denied rumours in the past that large detention centres are being built in Toronto and Montreal. Regardless, the government may need to build detention centres to handle the volume of detainees unless the rule of indefinite detention is struck down by the courts as a violation of the Charter.

Already hotels are being used in part as detention centres. In downtown Montreal, for instance, the Maritime Hotel has been partitioned off to house detainees. Barred windows and locked doors seal off the detention floors from the rest of the hotel. In hotels, claimants are not offered workshops or educational activities. Recreation may be confined to a fenced-off parking lot.

AIRLINES AS IMMIGRATION POLICE
The Immigration Act, even before the recent amendments, required airlines to ensure that immigrants and visitors who need a visa have one. The penalty for violating the requirement has been increased from $1,000 to $5,000, and the violation has been changed to a strict liability offence.* Airlines can be found guilty whether or not they knowingly commit an offence.

The government has also been granted the power to require airlines to hold passports and to hand them over directly to Immigration officials, and to demand that airlines provide documentary evidence to establish the identity of a person coming to Canada.[6] Airline personnel become immigration police — a distinct and separate violation of international standards. At a meeting in May, 1988 the Executive Committee of the United Nations High Commission for Refugees found that imposing sanctions of this sort on transport companies violates the Refugee Convention. Canada initiated this informal meeting, and should not contradict its conclusions now.

The Refugee Deterrents and Detention Act also gave the Minister of Immigration temporary power, until July 1, 1989 to turn back ships carrying refugees within twelve miles of Canadian waters,[7] using force if necessary. While the Minister of Immigration promised not to turn away any genuine refugee, it is impossible to conduct a proper refugee determination on the high seas. Once a ship is turned away, the government would never know whether those on board were real refugees or not.

Fortunately, the power to turn away ships expired July 1, 1989, and during that time no ships were turned back. But the turn-away provision should never have been included in the first place.

---

* A strict liability offence is an offence where no intent is required. It is not necessary for the prosecution to prove that the accused intended to commit the act. All the prosecution has to prove is that the act was committed. Even if the act was committed carelessly, inadvertently, or unintentionally, the accused must be found guilty.[5]

Jean Pierre Hocke, the UN High Commissioner for Refugees, protested the turn-away provision in the Bill. He said it "would risk exposing bona fide asylum-seekers and refugees to forcible return to countries where their lives or freedoms would be threatened." A few years ago, when the Thais were doing the same thing to Vietnamese boat people, Canada protested and asked the Thais to stop. Now Canada has passed legislation to do the same thing.

SECURITY PROVISIONS

The Act's security provisions pose problems for real refugees. Under the Act, a person who is considered a security risk has no access to the refugee determination process, whether or not he may be a refugee.[8] Because the refugee determination is never made, he may be removed to his country of origin.

Previously, a security risk could claim refugee status before being removed. Once a person was recognized as a refugee, the government was hesitant to return him to his country of persecution. Under the old law, the Security Intelligence and Review Committee (SIRC) reviewed any government decision to deport a person as a security risk and concluded whether the person was a security risk. Now responsibility has been handed over to the Federal Court, which decides only whether the government's determination of a person as a security risk is reasonable.[9]

The August, 1981 McDonald Commission — the Commission of Inquiry Concerning Certain Activities of the RCMP — recommended against using the Federal Court for screening the security aspects of deportation cases. The Commission recommended instead a specialized security tribunal comprised of experts in security matters. Until the Refugee Deterrents and Detention Act took effect, a tribunal was in place to hear security appeals, the SIRC, set up largely because of the McDonald Commission. The tribunal remains in place doing security work, but this part of its jurisdiction has disappeared.

Real refugees are almost always viewed as security threats by their home governments. An expert tribunal aware of political situations in foreign countries is more knowledgeable than a "tribunal of first impression" like the Federal Court, i.e., a tribunal that learns of each situation for the first time when a case comes before it. A tribunal of first impression is much more likely to defer to government allegations of security threats.

CRIMINALIZATION OF REFUGEE ASSISTANCE
Criminalizing help to refugees is the part of the Refugee Deterrents and Detention Act with the broadest sweep. Church groups, lawyers, immigrant aid societies — anyone who helps a person without documents come to Canada — may be in violation of the law. The provisions are not restricted to help for gain: voluntary and charitable aid are subject to penalty as well.

The offence of helping up to nine refugees arrive in Canada carries a maximum punishment of five years in prison and a $10,000 fine.[10] The offence of helping ten or more refugees carries a maximum penalty of ten years in prison and a $500,000 fine.[11] Ironically, in 1987 Canada was awarded the Nansen medal for helping refugees. Now, the very effort which warranted the award has been declared criminal.

A similar provision under U.S. law is far less drastic than its Canadian counterpart. Helping a refugee come to the U.S. is not an offence as long as you direct the refugee to report to Immigration and Naturalization Service (INS) officials. It is only illegal to offer assistance in evading detection by authorities.

Under the Canadian Act, even assisting refugees to report to the authorities is a crime. As long as a person without documents is aided in coming to Canada, the offence is committed, regardless of whether the person reports to Immigration officials immediately.

Normally, the law sets out an offence and penalizes those who commit or assist in committing the offence. However, in this case, it is not an offence to come to Canada, but it is an offence to assist refugees to come to Canada.

Even without the Refugee Deterrents and Detention Act, the law states that every person who knowingly contravenes the Immigration Act or its regulations, or knowingly induces, aids or abets any person to contravene the Act, is guilty of an offence. Then Immigration Minister Benoit Bouchard said Bill C-84 created no new offence, and that church groups aiding refugees could have been prosecuted under the old law. However, there are important differences. The new law adds the offence of "organizing" refugees to come to Canada. And it penalizes "aiding or abetting a person not in possession of a valid and subsisting visa, passport or travel document" whether or not you know the refugee lacks documents. As well, to aid the "coming into Canada" of persons without documents is a new offence created under the Refugee Deterrents and Detention Act. The Immigration Act before C-84 penalized only someone who aided in the destruction of a document, not someone who aided a person coming into Canada. Now, a person arriving in Canada without documents can be recognized as a refugee, allowed to stay and not be charged with any offence. However, the person who helped him come can be convicted for assisting and be given up to five years in prison and a $10,000 fine.

Parliament enacted a law with this offence because Canada's unworkable refugee system created an incentive for abuse. Reforming the system was the obvious solution. Instead the law created the power to penalize anyone who tells refugees about the law, or helps them get access to it.

The entire refugee support system in Canada is affected by the new law. Refugee assistance groups, church groups and lawyers who help refugees get access to the system are now contravening the law. Although the government has said it will not prosecute church groups, theoretically any individual or group involved in assisting refugees could be charged at any time in accordance with the new legislation. The new offences serve to intimidate claimants and those who help them.

SMUGGLING

The offence of helping refugees come to Canada was not necessary to deal with the problem of refugee smuggling. There are a number of offences which were part of the Immigration Act before Bill C-84 was passed which are adequate to address the refugee smuggling problem.

The Immigration Act already contained the offence of coming to Canada at a place other than a port of entry and failing to report to an immigration officer.[12] It was already unlawful to enter Canada by use of false or improperly obtained documents or aid any person to contravene the Act or its regulations.[13] It was also an offence to knowingly make a false representation leading a person to seek admission to Canada,[14] or to disseminate false information, knowing that information to be false, for the purpose of inducing immigration into Canada.[15] With all of these offences already available under the Immigration Act, the Refugee Deterrents and Detention Act's additional offences were not needed.

SEARCH WITHOUT WARRANT

The Refugee Deterrents and Detention Act provides for search without warrant in urgent circumstances.[16] If a delay would result in loss or destruction of anything liable to seizure, search without warrant is allowed. Force is permissible to complete the search even in private homes, including knocking down doors, breaking open windows, and coming through floors, ceilings and walls.[17] The Act allows search without warrant, not just for illegal immigrants, not just for refugees themselves, but also, for any evidence of helping ten or more refugees, including mere scraps of paper.

In contrast, the Narcotic Control Act prohibits home searches without a warrant, and provides for search without warrant, other than in private homes, only for narcotics.

Normally, under Canada's Criminal Code, when documents are seized from a lawyer, they must be sealed and taken to court, and a judge must decide whether the documents are confidential due to solicitor-client privilege. The Refugee Deterrents and Detention Act provides no such protection: all documents seized from someone alleged to be aiding or abetting refugees can be used in court.

Under the Canada Customs Act a search can normally be made only after a police officer swears an oath before a justice of the peace that goods liable to forfeiture are in a building. The search must take place between sunrise and sunset.[†] The search is for goods, not just pieces of paper which might show a contravention of the Act. Again, the Refugee Deterrents and Detention Act does not provide comparable protection.

PROPOSED WARRANT PROVISIONS

Bill C-84's first draft even allowed for a warrant to be issued when there are reasonable grounds to believe evidence *may* be found that a person wanted to help ten or more refugees come to Canada. These powers of search violated the Charter. The Criminal Code, by contrast, allows a warrant to be issued only when reasonable grounds are present to believe evidence *will* be found about the commission of an offence. In other words, a person who "may" be helping refugees would have had a greater risk of state intrusion than a person believed, on reasonable grounds, to have committed murder.

At issue was the choice of the word "may" as opposed to "will." The Bill allowed for a search warrant to be issued on the basis of a mere possibility evidence of an offence may be found.

The Supreme Court of Canada had already ruled in September, 1984, in the case of *Hunter v Southam*,[18] that granting a search warrant on mere possibility of finding evidence violates the Charter. The Court called "may" a very low standard which would allow intrusion into someone's home on the basis of suspicion and authorize wide-ranging fishing expeditions. The balance of justice would be tipped strongly in favour of the state and give the individual the right to resist only the most flagrant intrusions.

Fortunately, by final draft of Bill C-84, the government had accepted a Senate amendment to grant a power to search only where evidence "will", not merely "may", be found of refugee smuggling.[19]

Instead of dealing with a real emergency, the international breakdown of burden-sharing of refugees, the Canadian government is trying to send away from our shores innocents who

---

[†] No oath is required if a justice of the peace does not live in the area or within five miles.

need protection. The government has put more effort into passing legislation to keep out genuine refugees who the government believes can be protected elsewhere and penalizing those who help them, than it has into protecting real refugees from persecution and death they face in their home countries. The efforts of the government would have been better devoted to seeking improvements in the refugee system in Canada and world-wide to provide fair refugee determination procedures.

The legislation only exacerbates the refugee system's problems by creating a need for detention centres, and by intimidating refugee claimants and those who assist them. Refugees are threatened with passport seizure by airlines, while church groups are threatened with prosecution and midnight searches of their homes for scraps of paper. The new legislation has been challenged in the courts on the ground that it quashes Canadians' civil liberties. Only if the court challenge succeeds will refugee activists once again be able to feel safe in helping genuine refugees fleeing persecution come to Canada.

Chapter 10

SENATE RESPONSE TO THE REFUGEE BILLS

The proposed changes by the Senate to Bills C-55 and C-84 that were rejected highlight the problem with the current law. The changes the Senate proposed that were accepted show how far the government wanted to go before the Senate intervened.

The Senate proposed many amendments to C-55, the Refugee Reform Bill, but neither rejected the government's basic proposal out of hand, nor replaced one system with another.[1] What is glaring about the Senate's actions is what it ignored and did not amend. Although the few Senate amendments accepted by government changed the face of Bill C-55 for the better, the new legislation continued to deny first asylum as an option for Canada, to rebuff protection of refugees and to quash their rights.

SAFE THIRD COUNTRY

The Senate proposed that the Chairman of the Immigration and Refugee Board rather than Cabinet be responsible for drawing up the safe third country list, the list of countries to which Canada would send back refugees.* When determining a safe country, the Senate submitted, the decision-maker should regard not only the country's policies and practices with respect to Convention refugee claims, but also its human rights record.

According to the Senate version, a person would be sent back to a safe country not merely if he was allowed to return, as the House would have it, but only if the country was willing to receive him or if the claimant had a right to have the merits of his claim determined in that country. The Senate was trying to prevent the possibility of refugees in orbit: refugees forced to travel from country to country in search of protection.

Senate amendments would have removed some of the problems with the safe third country proposal, but several difficulties inherent in the concept endured. No mention was made of living conditions, deterrence schemes, and detention in so-called safe countries. Hazardous living conditions, government-generated deterrence schemes, and systematic detention can make countries unsafe for refugees. No Senate provision dealt with a shift in safety from the time the safe country determination is made to the time the refugee determination is made. One must question what will happen to a person sent to a country where he is personally unsafe even though others generally are safe.

The government rejected the Senate proposal that the Refugee Division of the new Immigration and Refugee Board draw up the list of safe countries. It was prepared to allow a consultative committee to advise the government on a safe country list privately. The government did accept the Senate suggestion to consider a country's human rights record when determining whether or not it was a safe country. But only the government, not an independent person or body, could look into the country's human rights record.

---

* See Chapter 18 for a discussion of the safe third country concept.

As well, the government rejected the Senate's proposal that a refugee should be returned to a third country only if the country is willing to receive him or to determine his refugee claim on the merits. The government insisted that a refugee must only be allowed to return. To the government, the fact that a person might be evicted immediately after his return did not matter.

Gone also was the proposed requirement of an individual test. It is not necessary, according to the government, that the *individual* be allowed to return. It is enough if the laws or practices of the third country allow *all claimants* (or claimants of a particular class of person of which the claimant is a member) to return. It does not matter if the individual is an anomaly within his class, and would not be allowed to return. The claimant could be evicted, and put into orbit, bouncing around the world from country to country until one destination returns him to the country of danger he originally fled.

APPEAL PROVISIONS

In addition to the safe third country concept, Bill C-55 also proposed a denial of appeal to claimants to deter refugees from seeking first asylum in Canada. The government advocated appeal only by leave on points of law and jurisdiction, but not on fact.

As well, a claimant from a safe country or one who failed the full credible-basis screening could not remain in Canada during the appeal. He would be ejected within twenty-four hours of his rejection and could not return to Canada even if leave to appeal was granted. The claimant could return only if the appeal succeeded in his absence.

Essentially, the Senate maintained this scheme too, although it did propose an appeal on grounds of fact, or the merits of the claim, as well as law. It also recommended the removal time be prolonged from twenty-four hours to seventy-two hours.

The government rejected out of hand granting an appeal of a refugee determination on the merits of the claim. But it accepted the Senate suggestion of a seventy-two-hour delay instead of a twenty-four-hour delay.

SECURITY RISKS

The Senate capitulated to the government provisions in Bills C-55 and C-84 to deny security risks the right to claim refugee status. The same proposal was in both Bills. Although C-55 was introduced into the House of Commons first, Bill C-84 got to the Senate first. When the proposal got to the Senate in Bill C-84, the Senate rejected it. By the time C-55 got to the Senate, the Senate had abandoned its objections. Senators accepted the government proposal, asking only that the Minister of Immigration, and not a bureaucrat, personally deny a security risk the opportunity to claim refugee status.

The government snapped up Senate approval of the government proposal to exclude security risks from the refugee determination process. Accepting the Senate's request to have the Minister personally decide on the exclusion was an easy concession for the government to make.

SECOND CHANCE

Senate reform, while essentially approving Bill C-55, picked away at the edges. According to the Bill, a refugee had to claim refugee status at his first opportunity or he would never have another chance. The Senate wanted an adjudicator to allow a second chance to claim if the claimant could establish he had failed to claim originally due to a misunderstanding of the nature or consequences of the law or from a well-founded fear for himself or his family. The government rejected giving claimants a second chance to claim on the grounds such a possibility would provide an incentive for abuse.

COUNSEL OF CHOICE

Refugee claimants were denied the right to counsel of choice under a provision in Bill C-55, which held that unless private counsel was ready and able to proceed, designated counsel would be foisted on refugee claimants. The Senate suggested private counsel ought to be ready and able to proceed within a reasonable period of time, not immediately.

The implication of the government proposal was that private counsel had to be ready and able to proceed immediately. By suggesting that private counsel had to be ready and able to provide within a reasonable period of time, the Senate mitigated the government proposal but did not remove it. In other non-immigration proceedings, if the lawyer of choice is not ready and able to proceed within a reasonable time, the client may choose to change lawyers. If the delay is an abuse of the court process, the court has power to intervene and direct the matter to proceed. But replacing the lawyer of choice by a designated lawyer so that matters proceed expeditiously is unheard of in all other forms of litigation.

The government rejected giving the claimant's counsel a reasonable period of time to proceed before the adjudicator foisted designated counsel on the claimant. The government did not just reject the Senate proposal, but amended the original proposal to make it even more unfair to claimants. Previously, both private counsel for the claimant and designated counsel for the claimant were subject to the same requirement: they had to be ready and able to proceed immediately. In this second proposal, designated counsel needed to be ready and able to proceed within a reasonable period of time.[2] Private counsel still had to proceed immediately.

As a result, a double standard was imposed. Lawyers of choice had to be ready and able to proceed more quickly than designated counsel. The Senate proposal, in a sense, was accepted but turned on its head. What the Senate wanted to give to the claimant's chosen lawyer, the government took away and instead gave to the lawyer it wanted to force on the claimant.

IMMIGRATION ACT APPEALS

Although C-55 was meant to be a refugee bill, the government used the Bill to attack immigration generally. The Bill proposed cutting off access to the Federal Court Trial Division as of right for anyone litigating any matter under the Immigration Act, as well as for refugee claimants. Since no apparent abuse of the Federal Court Trial Division had taken place, the government seemingly included this provision to avoid any independent outside assessment of its own behaviour in immigration matters. Government proposed to shut down access to the Federal Court as of right on immigration matters such as excess of jurisdiction, denial of natural justice, error of law on the face of the record, and denial of fairness. The Senate found this proposal repugnant and proposed abolishing this restriction in its entirety.

The government went part way in accepting the Senate proposal about denial of access as of right to the Federal Court. Originally, the government wanted total denial of access, while the Senate wanted complete access. In the second proposal, the government supported partial access or access as of right "with respect to a decision of a visa officer" made at visa offices abroad.[3] However, the government continued to deny access as of right to all decisions made at Canadian immigration offices within Canada.

Why should claimants have easier access to the courts for decisions made outside Canada than for decisions made inside? The government of Canada would make it easier for its officials here to violate the law than for its officials abroad.

This government proposal highlights the paranoia behind the drafting of Bill C-55. The government apparently feared that if the illegality of internal decisions can be challenged as of right, the right will become an avenue of abuse. However, real rights should not be sacrificed because of imaginary dangers. When and if abuse occurs, Parliament then could examine whether the right of access to the courts should be circumscribed. If we abandon rights for fear of potential abuse, we will soon lose all of our rights.

THREAT TO INDEPENDENCE OF THE BOARD

One Senate proposal dealt with an issue I had litigated in the Federal Court. In the case of Harvinder Singh Sethi, I argued that Bill C-55 threatened the independence of the Immigration Appeal Board by terminating the Board, denying severance pay, and holding out the possibility that the fired Board members might be reappointed to the new Immigration and Refugee Board. Refugee Status Advisory Committee members were in the same situation.

From the time the Bill was announced in August, 1987, until rehiring took effect in December, 1988, the implicit threat to Board members cast a pall over the IAB decisions and amounted to an attack on the Board's independence. Whether Board members continued to act independently or not in this context of mass firing, the situation created a perception of bias and lack of independence.

In its report on Bill C-55, the Senate wrote:

> There is an important matter of principle at stake... that the very reason for establishing quasi-judicial boards and tribunals is to vest important decisions with expert decision-makers independent of government control. In that manner, the necessary impartiality is achieved. For this reason, the Committee recommends...that the terms of the current Immigration Appeal Board members continue under the new board.

In a submission to Parliament on Bill C-55, the Canadian Bar Association wrote,

> It is contrary to well-established Canadian tradition to fire by reorganization all of the members of an independent tribunal appointed by a former government. Independence of thought and action is not likely to be encouraged in a climate of job insecurity.

The Senate removed the government's "no right to compensation" provision in Bill C-55 in order to restore the individual's legal rights. According to common law, however, members of the IAB (and the RSAC) had no right to compensation.[†] While the Senate's intentions were laudable, they were not sufficient to remove the government's power to deny compensation. A just compensation provision would have had to be inserted. The government rejected the Senate proposal that IAB (and RSAC) members be continued under the new Board. It did accept that the "no right to compensation" provision be removed.

[†] In the 1930s, the matter was litigated all the way to the Privy Council by a Mr. Reilly who was trying to get compensation for being terminated when the Pensions Appeals Board was abolished. He had lost his member status in mid-term but failed at every level of court to receive compensation.[4]

With this provision, however, the Senate fell into a trap and the government closed the trap door. Because this provision to deny compensation to Board and Committee members is only a statement of the already existing law, as developed by the courts, removal of the provision does not enhance rights. Obviously, the Senate wanted to give terminated members a right to just compensation. Senators assumed once the "no right to compensation" provision was removed from C-55, Board and Committee members would have a right to compensation. And equally clearly, the government wished not to be obliged to give those terminated compensation. When the Senate made a mistake of law — not realizing the provision was just declaratory of common law — the government was quick to pick up the error and take advantage of it. The government removed the "no right to compensation" provision as requested, and was still not obligated to provide compensation.

THE SETHI CASE
Harvinder Singh Sethi came to Canada from the United States on May 25, 1985. Sethi, 23 and single at the time, was a citizen of India. The Immigration Department arrested him just inside the Canadian border near Emerson, Manitoba.

At an inquiry, the adjudicator found Sethi to have eluded examination. He claimed refugee status. The Minister of Immigration informed Sethi in March, 1986 that he did not consider him to be a refugee. Sethi applied for a redetermination to the Immigration Appeal Board.

I appeared on behalf of Sethi at his scheduled hearing before the Board in September, 1987, and asked them not to hear the case. I argued that because the government was threatening to fire the Board under Bill C-55 — introduced in Parliament on May 5, 1987 — Sethi could not have a fair hearing.

As long as the threat continued, I argued, the Board should adjourn and not hear Sethi's case. Once the new law came into effect, Sethi would move into the new system or he could carry on under the old if the government relented on the mass firings.

The Board ruled there was no reasonable apprehension of bias — no reasonable appearance that they were not independent from government. However, the IAB did grant an adjournment to allow me to raise the matter before the Federal Court.

In March, 1988 Madame Justice Barbara Reed set aside the Immigration Appeal Board's decision.[5] She ordered that the Board not hear Sethi's claim for as long as reasonable apprehension of bias existed.

In her judgement, Justice Reed said:

> The present Board members have been put in a position where they have every reason to think that their immediate financial future is unsettled and in the hands of the government. That same government is opposing the applicant's [Sethi's] claim for refugee status, the question which is before the Board.
>
> The question is whether the facts are such that a reasonably well informed person would have a reasonable apprehension that the members of the Board, in the present circumstances, might be likely to please the government, by favouring its position over that of the person opposing the government. I think such exists.

Operations of the Immigration Appeal Board were effectively shut down across the country for immigrants being deported, as well as for refugees. Anyone who wanted an appeal could waive the objection of reasonable bias and an appeal would proceed. But anyone who did not want the Board to hear his case could raise the objection of reasonable apprehension of bias and the Board would have to adjourn.

The government immediately appealed the decision and attempted to have the appeal heard as quickly as possible. At an appeal heard in June, 1988, Madame Justice Reed's judgement was reversed.[6] Mr. Justice Mahoney reasoned the government did not want Board members to decide in its favour unfairly. Members of the Board "would not think that such conduct [deciding in favour of the Government unfairly] would, in fact, please the government." However, as I argued when applying for leave to the Supreme Court of Canada, the government is in a poor position to judge what is fair and unfair, because it is an interested party. What may seem fair to the government would seem unfair to an independent outside observer.

The Federal Court of Appeal overturned Reed's judgement as well, because of the "chilling effect" it would have on the democratic process. The Court said, "Judges ought not to intervene" in the legislative process.

However, on leave to appeal, I argued that the democratic process includes the independence of the courts, as well as debates in Parliament. By emphasizing the chilling effect on government, the Court had ignored the chilling effect on the courts. When independence of the courts is weakened, democracy too is weakened.

A contrary decision by the Court might in the future inhibit governments from proposing a mass firing of judges. Governments would think twice about proposing mass firings of judges if it meant that all pending cases where the government was a party could not be heard. But the public interest is not at stake in removing that inhibition. In a democracy, a government should be inhibited from firing its judges. Making it easier for government to do it, or propose it, does not advance the cause of democracy.

Although the facts of the case applied to the IAB, I argued in the Supreme Court leave application that the issue was more general. The government of Canada could threaten to terminate all members and rehire the ones it liked in any federal administrative tribunal or statutory court, including the Federal Court and Supreme Court of Canada.

The purpose of these mass firings was, I submitted to the Court, greed for patronage. The government wished to replace friends of past governments with friends of the present government on boards and tribunals at an accelerated rate. Previous governments filled vacancies as they occurred rather than create openings through systematic terminations of administrative boards and tribunals in mid-term.

David Sgayias, counsel for the government, argued in a memorandum presented at a hearing on the leave application to the Supreme Court that "the questions in this case are now purely academic." He supplied to the Supreme Court of Canada an affidavit signed September 13, 1988 by Gordon Fairweather, then chairman of the IAB and present chairman of the Immigration and Refugee Board. Fairweather swore in the affidavit that on September 1, 1988 the Government had offered all members of the existing Immigration Appeal Board appointments to the new 115-person Immigration and Refugee Board. Of forty-seven old Board members offered positions, forty-one accepted appointment to the new Board. Thirty-five persons out of a total of forty-one were appointed for longer terms on the Immigration and Refugee Board than they had under the IAB, and six were appointed for shorter terms.

Sgayias said in his argument that because all of the Board members had been offered reappointment, the fear they would favour the government by rejecting Sethi's case in order to get a reappointment had subsided.

The government charged the issue I raised in my application for leave to the Supreme Court was moot, that is, not a live issue. Though no reasons were given, when hearing the motion for leave the Supreme Court judges considered only the question of mootness. Leave was denied.

Sethi lost his case legally, but won it practically. Because of the reappointments, he could have a redetermination of his claim heard by a secure panel of the Immigration Appeal Board.

IMPACT OF THE SENATE

Although Senate amendments to Bill C-55 retained the legislation's basic structure, the government, by and large, was not interested in the amendments. Nominally, two Senate recommendations were accepted without change and four with changes. Allowing immigration applicants abroad access as of right to the Federal Court was the only significant improvement between the government's first and second version of the Bill.

When presented with Bill C-55, the Senate was faced with two competing constitutional considerations. The Senate's Legal and Constitutional Affairs Committee, which examined the Bill, had a duty to reject a Bill that did not conform to the Constitution. And virtually the whole of the Bill was constitutionally questionable.

But the Senate also regards itself as a chamber of sober second thought, improving government legislation, but not setting government policy. Denying access by refugees to Canada as a country of first asylum may be unconstitutional, but the government chose the option. And the Senate felt it could not question that option.

SENATE REFORM TO C-84

Why the Senate felt so constrained with C-55 when it had not felt similarly impeded when amending Bill C-84 is difficult to understand. Senate reforms to the Refugee Detention and Deterrents Bill cut right to the heart of C-84. Twice the Senate sent the Bill back to the House of Commons, although the changes proposed the first time were a good deal more dramatic than those in the second round.

In the case of Bill C-55, Committee Chair Joan Neiman said in an interview that the Committee had decided to leave the major constitutional questions of the Bill for decision by the courts. She said, "We know there is an army of lawyers out there ready to take it whenever it passes into the Supreme Court." However, for Bill C-84, the Committee said "when major portions of a bill as it stands appear to be constitutionally defective, we, as legislators, must recommend change."

In C-84, the government repeated its C-55 proposal that people declared security threats should not be allowed to make refugee claims. The Senate at first argued that only after a decision on a refugee claim is made should the security risk to Canada be considered. If the person is a refugee, then the risk to security should be weighed against consequences to the person upon return to the country of persecution. Allowing security risks to make refugee claims made no sense to the government, and it rejected the Senate proposal.

Bill C-84 gave government the power to direct a ship carrying refugees to leave or stay out of Canadian waters. The Senate rejected this power, and recommended instead that government have the power to direct a ship to be escorted to the nearest port. The government insisted on maintaining the right to turn ships away, at least until six months after C-55 came into force.

Bill C-84 criminalized assistance by churches and others to help refugees come to Canada. The Senate threw that proposal out and replaced it with two offences, encouraging spurious refugee claims and smuggling refugees into Canada in a clandestine manner. Again, the government rejected the Senate proposal.

The Senate also proposed to gut the Bill's Draconian search provisions. It rejected Bill C-84 provisions giving government power to search on the mere possibility of finding evidence of smuggling refugees, and replaced it with a power to search only when finding evidence was probable. Gone was the power to search without a warrant simply to preserve evidence, when there was no danger to human life or safety. Gone was the power to break open doors and windows in furtherance of a search. The Senate added that searches could be done only by day unless a justice of the peace authorized search by night.

The government felt the majority of the Senate search-and-seizure proposals would seriously hamper immigration officers. In only one of two Senate proposals accepted outright, the government agreed the power to search could be used when the findings of the evidence were probable, not merely possible. The government was determined, however, to give no credit to the Senate for this change, and claimed its original proposal was the result of mistranslation.

INDEFINITE DETENTION AND SECURITY CASES

Bill C-84's most dramatic provision was the proposed indefinite detention of unidentified claimants with no substantive independent review. Under the Bill, claimants without identification could be detained up to twenty-eight days. After that time, an adjudicator would review every seven days whether the Department was making reasonable efforts to find out who the person is.

The Senate insisted on independent substantive review. Rather than the adjudicator restricted to determining only whether the government was making reasonable efforts to identify the detainee, the Senate proposed the adjudicator would actually decide whether he knew the person's identity and if so, order the person's release.

The government rejected the Senate suggestion and returned to limiting the adjudicator to assessing whether the
government was making reasonable efforts to determine the
detainee's identity.

The Senate also called for changes to the security cases. The
government wanted to be able to eject whomever it considered
to be a security risk, with review by the Federal Court restricted
to the question of whether issuance of a security certificate was
reasonable on the basis of information available to the government at the time. The Senate recommended the Federal Court
consider the reasonableness of the security certificate itself and
not just look at the original decision that the person was a
security risk.

For the second time, the government relented by giving to
the Federal Court power to determine the reasonableness of a
security certificate. The government did not insist on limiting
the Federal Court to examining whether the issuance of a
security certificate was reasonable on the basis of information
available to the government at the time.

SECOND LOOK AT C-84
When Bill C-84 went back to the Senate a second time, the
Senate was more flexible than the first round, insisting on some
amendments, but not others. The Senate stood firm on the issue
of not turning ships around.

The Senate relented on the need for security risks to have the
chance to claim refugee status. But it said the Minister must
make the exclusion decision personally.

The Senate refused to give in on criminalization of aid by
church groups to refugees. It wanted the groups to be protected.
The Senate also maintained its concerns about search and
seizure. It said there was no evidence other than the Minister's
statements to support the need for such provisions. However,
the Senate felt the Charter would provide sufficient protection,
and so dropped its proposed search-and-seizure amendments.

Giving the adjudicator a substantive power of review was
abandoned. Bill C-84 had proposed no review at all for twenty-

eight days, and the Senate had wanted a review within forty-eight hours. The government then proposed seven days, and the Senate accepted that proposal. It gave up on its other changes to detention review.

The Senate oscillated between principle and politics. Originally with respect to C-84, it took a number of stands on principle. Yet, the second time round it took the position that it need not insist. Anything wrong with the Bill could be challenged in court as a violation of the Canadian Charter of Rights and Freedoms. On some issues, such as turning ships back, the Senate took a policy stand. On others, such as the no first asylum policy, the Senate deferred to the government from the start.

For people concerned about refugees, the issue is not so much whether the Senate had performed its constitutional role properly as whether it was helpful or harmful in considering the Bills. The Senate was helpful, but not as helpful as it could have been.

PART THREE

THE UNITED STATES REFUGEE SYSTEM

Chapter 11

THE U.S. REFUGEE DETERMINATION SYSTEM

The practical obstacles placed in the way of persons seeking asylum in the United States reflects that government's increasing disinclination to open its doors, especially to Central American refugees. Salvadoran and Guatemalan refugees have faced particular problems because of the American administration's friendly relationship with their governments. Their cases manifest all that is wrong with the American refugee determination system.

THE EL SALVADOR STORY

Two events stand out as significant in the flare-up of human rights abuses in El Salvador during the early 1980s.[1] One was the Nicaraguan revolution of July, 1979. The other was Ronald Reagan's election as President of the United States in November, 1980.

The Nicaraguan revolution both alarmed and emboldened the left-wing political opposition in El Salvador. Fearing a repeat of the Nicaraguan experience, military officers removed President General Carlos Humberto Romero in a coup of October 1979. The junta that succeeded Romero had little internal unity. Its civilian members had no control over the security forces.

The opposition organized a series of demonstrations and strikes, and occupations of ministries and embassies, which were suppressed by the military. In response, various guerilla groups set up a united command structure in October, 1980.

Reagan's election prompted the guerillas to launch an offensive against the Salvadoran government in January, 1981, because they feared Reagan would allocate massive military aid to government forces. But their offensive was unsuccessful and lead to murderous retaliation by government militia. Figures compiled by the Legal Aid Office of the Archdiocese of El Salvador show an estimated 1,000 civilians were killed in 1979, 10,000 in 1980, 13,500 in 1981 and 6,000 in 1982. Evidence indicated the overwhelming majority of murders were committed by the government security forces or officially sanctioned para-military groups.

The killing of civilians by Salvadoran military, security and para-military forces took the form of disappearances and death squad killings. Armed forces indiscriminately attacked civilian populations in conflict zones or guerilla-controlled zones by air and ground attacks, shelling and bombardment. Air force activity was accompanied by ground sweeps to burn remaining structures and to shoot persons who had not already fled.

Torture, arbitrary detention and denial of fair trial by the government authorities were commonplace in El Salvador. Many civilians killed were found mutilated. Few torture victims survived. In January, 1982, the number of politically detained was estimated at 1,800. At trial, confessions elicited by torture were admissible in evidence. The right to appeal was limited.

Death squad killings and disappearances have abated from the peak of 1981, but they have not been eliminated. In 1985, the army and death squads were linked to 1,740 of the killings and disappearances, and the guerillas were linked to another 173. Overwhelmingly, civilians were the targets.

The civil war and human rights violations in El Salvador have led to massive refugee movements. By mid-1984, the number of internal refugees — people who fled their homes but not the country — had climbed to 500,000. Another 750,000 refugees had fled El Salvador, many to the United States.

THE GUATEMALA STORY

Guatemala is a unique human rights violator. In no other country have human rights been violated so regularly over such a prolonged period of time. Disappearances, death squads, and extra-judicial killings are used systematically against insurgents and their supporters, in fact, against any form of political or social opposition.

Human rights violations have taken place whether the government has been democratic or military, in the face of what on paper appears to be a liberal constitution and an independent judiciary.

Even though the violators may not be under the direct command of the government, they are officially tolerated and given logistical support. They are given a free hand to use force as they see fit, and deliberately placed beyond the control of the law enforcement apparatus.

Death squads and disappearances have been a fixture of Guatemalan life for decades. In 1979, there were over 2,000 disappearances and extra-judicial executions. From July, 1978, when Lucas Garcia took power, until February, 1981, Amnesty International estimated some 5,000 Guatemalans were seized and killed. In 1981, AI estimated a minimum of 4,500 were killed. However, obtaining reliable, comprehensive figures on political violence is difficult in Guatemala because the country lacks a domestic human rights monitoring organization to collect such information.

The Rios Montt government, which came to power in 1982, imposed a "scorched earth policy" — burning food and lodging of civilians, forcibly removing civilian populations from areas of guerilla activity and killing all those who attempted to resist or flee relocation, including women and children.

The current democratically elected government under Vinicio Cerezo is plagued by contraventions of human rights. Politically motivated killings and disappearances continue. The military continues to administer the countryside, while only the cities are run by the civilian government. The government has been unable to prosecute the military even for the worst crimes. There continue to be temporary camps and "model villages" — forced resettlement camps of those moved out of guerilla-held areas. People in these villages are effectively detained and may not leave without permission.

The massacres and forced displacements have led to a massive refugee population. According to the Guatemalan Conference of Bishops, an estimated one million people had been displaced by the conflict in April, 1982. Approximately 100,000 refugees fled to the state of Chiapas, Mexico by 1983.

MEXICAN IMPEDIMENTS

Salvadoran and Guatemalan refugees in Mexico are faced with a barrage of impediments when they try to gain refugee status in the U.S. These people are regularly turned away at American ports of entry or denied status inland. They are told to apply for refugee status through the U.S. embassy in Mexico, even though in practice they are not allowed entry to the U.S. as refugees through the embassy. Legally, it is possible for refugees to be processed through this channel, but in practice Central American refugees are always in danger of being sent back to the countries they fled before an application filed at the U.S. embassy is even processed. Since Mexico has not signed the Refugee Convention, it is not obliged to respect the Convention and has returned Central American refugees to their countries of origin.

Refugees from Guatemala and El Salvador poured into Mexico in the late 1970s and early 1980s because of government and military sanctioned persecution of these countries' citizens. Mexico in turn sent many refugees back to Guatemala.

Those not forced back to their home countries set up camps just across the border inside Mexico. The Guatemalan army viewed the camps as potential support for the guerrillas and engaged in cross border raids on the camps. Subsequently, the Mexican government forced refugees to relocate their camps away from the Guatemalan border further into Mexico to discourage the military raids. Refugees who did not want to relocate were arrested. Mexican authorities also had crops burned, medical supplies cut off, and canoes used for transportation destroyed. Refugees refusing to move lived on the edge of starvation. Access was denied to service organizations, the UNHCR, the press and international human rights organizations. The Mexican government's policy of reprisals was an attempt to pressure dissidents to move.

In 1981, deportations from Mexico to Guatemala were massive and systematic: an estimated 3,000 refugees were deported. In 1982, deportations continued on a smaller scale.

At one point, the government of Mexico charged refugees were coming for economic reasons. However, Central American refugees deported back from Mexico to Guatemala have been detained, tortured and interrogated by Guatemalan authorities as possible opposition group members, solely because they have been deported from Mexico.

U.S. REFUGEE POLICY

Central Americans encounter difficulties in being recognized as refugees both outside and within the United States. However, the refugee determination process for claims made at a U.S. embassy abroad are even more problematic than those made at a port of entry or inland.

In the regulations, no information regarding the requirements of the determination process is set out. Approval or denial is made by the Immigration and Naturalization Service (INS) officer in charge abroad and no appeal is allowed on denial of a claim. The decision-maker is not independent from the INS. As well, the requirement of due process and the right to counsel at refugee claims interviews are denied. Observers may be present at refugee interviews, but they are not allowed to participate.

A refugee may be denied entry to the U.S. solely for economic reasons: claimants who will not be "productive" will be refused, in accordance with the INS examination handbook. Refugees physically capable of working, who have a period of unexplained unemployment on their record and are being supported by relief or unemployment payments, are subject to refusal. By contrast, a refugee in the U.S. or at a port of entry cannot be deported or excluded from the U.S. for these reasons.

The INS officer in Mexico may also deny a refugee admission to the U.S. because he considers the refugee not to be of good character. Persons with recent or frequent arrests — not necessarily convictions — even for minor offences may be rejected. A refugee in the U.S. or at a port of entry can be deported or excluded only if he was convicted of a particularly serious crime, not on account of arrests for petty offences.

A person may be a refugee yet be denied entry to the U.S. by the INS in Mexico for medical reasons, including retardation, insanity, psychopathy, drug addiction, chronic alcoholism, affliction with a dangerous contagious disease, and any physical defect, disease or disability that may affect his ability to earn a living. A person medically inadmissible may be allowed entry to the U.S. on waiver by the Attorney General; however a refugee outside the U.S. has no entitlement to a waiver. By contrast, again, a refugee in the U.S. or at a port of entry cannot be deported or excluded for medical reasons.

A refugee application made outside the U.S. will not be approved unless there is an acceptable sponsor such as a responsible person or organization. The sponsor must guarantee the refugee's transportation to the place of resettlement. Again, a refugee in the U.S. or at a port of entry can be approved for asylum whether or not a sponsor has come forward.

Even more onerous than these general restrictions are the numerical limitations and priorities facing Central American refugees. Under the Immigration and Nationality Act, the President is awarded power to determine how many refugees may be admitted to the U.S. each year. He is free to allocate as he wishes that total among various groups of refugees around the world.

The President has used that power to assign very small numbers to Latin America. In 1980, out of a total determination of 231,700 refugees, Latin America (excluding Cuba) was allotted 1,000 refugees. In 1981, out of a total of 217,000, Latin America (including Cuba) was allotted 4,000. In 1983, out of a total of 90,000, Latin America and the Caribbean were allotted 2,000. In 1984, out of a total of 72,000, 1000 were from Latin America and the Caribbean. In 1985, out of a total of 70,000, Latin America and the Caribbean were allotted 3,000.

A Salvadoran in Mexico can meet the refugee definition, overcome all obstacles, and still not be admitted to the U.S. as a refugee because the ceiling for Latin Americans has been reached. However, a Central American refugee claimant already *in* the U.S. will not be denied protection simply because too many others from his region have been recognized as refugees.

A refugee may fall within numerical limits and yet not be admitted to the U.S. because he is in one of the Attorney General's lower-designated processing priority categories. The first priority are refugees in immediate danger of loss of life and for whom there appears to be no alternative to resettlement in the U.S., and refugees of compelling concern to the U.S., such as former political prisoners and dissidents. The second priority is former U.S. government employees. The third priority is refugees with close relatives in the U.S. The fourth priority is refugees with other ties to the U.S., such as former employment by U.S. foundations. The fifth priority is more distant relatives of persons in the U.S.

Central Americans in Mexico likely do not meet any of these priorities because the U.S. does not consider them to be in immediate danger of loss of life. Because people with ties to the U.S. are more likely to be persecuted by regimes the U.S. opposes than by regimes the U.S. supports, the fourth priority shows how a theoretically neutral refugee definition can be subverted to favour refugees from regimes the U.S. opposes.

Under international law, the U.S. is obliged to provide protection to those in the U.S. or at a port of entry and cannot expel or return these refugees to a country where their lives or freedom would be threatened. A refugee in the U.S. who can be returned only to a country of danger and no other has, in effect, a right to remain in the U.S. However, there is no comparable right to enter for refugees outside the U.S. The only U.S. obligation is to co-operate in sharing the burden of the world's refugees.

INCENTIVE FOR ILLEGAL ENTRY

Due to the many disadvantages of applying for protection at an American post abroad, it is not surprising that a refugee would seek to apply within the U.S. or at a port of entry. Garry Rehbein, an INS shift supervisor at the Nogales, Arizona port of entry, has said that Central Americans who ask for asylum are told as a matter of policy to apply at the U.S. Consulate in Mexico. But for American officials to suggest a Central American refugee need not come to the U.S. to apply for protection, and to advise him to simply apply in Mexico, is misleading.

American law grants foreigners a right to claim refugee status at a border point and imposes on the Attorney General a duty to establish procedures for foreigners wanting to do so. Regulations approved by the Attorney General give jurisdiction over asylum applications to the district director at the port of entry.

The district director has the right to commence exclusion proceedings against the alien even after an asylum application is made. Once exclusion proceedings commence, jurisdiction over the asylum application shifts from the district director to an immigration judge. Unless the director requests otherwise, the refugee must then submit his asylum application to the immigration judge.

An immigration judge alone has the power at a hearing to bar entry to a foreigner at a port of entry except for security cases, in which the immigration officer also has power to keep foreigners out of the U.S. The immigration judge decides whether the foreigner is excludable. At the exclusion hearing, the foreigner has the right to make an asylum application.

For Salvadorans and Guatemalans appearing at American ports of entry, none of these rules are followed. Asylum-seekers are not allowed to make asylum claims through the district director. They are not referred to exclusion proceedings where they can make asylum claims before an immigration judge.

They are barred entry, without any semblance of compliance with the procedures set out in American law.

Moreover, Mexican officials are alerted to the presence of Central Americans who have sought asylum at a U.S. border point. American officials detain Central Americans at border points and turn them over to Mexican officials, who in turn forcibly return them to Guatemala. This practice amounts to American participation in refoulement (forced return). Mexican and American officials are both guilty of sending refugees back to a country where their lives or freedom may be threatened. Mexico is not, however, a signatory to the UN Refugee Conventions which forbids this practice. The United States is.

VOLUNTARY DEPARTURE FORMS

An undocumented foreigner would serve his own interests better by leaving the U.S. voluntarily at his own expense than by waiting to be deported. A deported foreigner is excludable from the U.S. for five years after deportation, unless the Attorney General consents to readmission. But an undocumented foreigner who departs the U.S. voluntarily at his own expense is in the same position as other foreigners applying for admission who have never before resided illegally in the U.S.

The INS has developed voluntary departure forms for undocumented foreigners to sign. By signing the forms, the foreigners undertake to leave the U.S. voluntarily. A foreigner in the U.S. has a right to make a refugee claim. But by signing the voluntary departure form, the claimant waives this right.

A foreigner also has the right not to be deported unless he goes before an immigration judge to determine his deportability. The foreigner waives this right as well, and is subject to removal by the INS immediately after signing the form, without a hearing, appeal or judicial review.

INS agents have been involved in coercing Salvadoran and Guatemalan refugees into signing these so-called voluntary departure forms. Once signed, refugees are removed to their country of origin. INS agents tell refugees to sign the forms without explaining what they say, or they inform refugees they must sign the forms. Those who refuse and say they want to claim political asylum are told that political asylum will be denied, and they will have to remain in jail for a long period of time while the denial is being processed. On occasion, refugees are warned that any information on their refugee claim would be given to their home government authorities. INS agents also allegedly advise refugees they will be sent back home whether they sign the form or not.

Refugees are not instructed of their right to make a refugee claim, call a lawyer, place a bond to get out of custody, or go before an immigration judge to ask for their release. Every scrap of paper they carry is confiscated, making it nearly impossible for them to get in touch with their U.S. contacts for assistance.

Refugees who make their claims at the border are denied the opportunity to consult with counsel until after the voluntary departure form is signed. Once counsel is contacted, the INS refuses to recognize counsel is acting for a refugee until counsel files a formal notice of representation. Counsel is not allowed to revoke a refugee's voluntary departure agreement until he has personally interviewed the refugee. In the meantime, before the notice is filed and the interview between counsel and refugee can take place, in many cases the refugee is removed to the country of origin on the basis of the signed voluntary departure form.

As well, refugees are not permitted to keep the signed voluntary departure forms. The cumulation of these factors means the forms are not voluntary. Most refugees have no idea signing of the forms was intended to be voluntary.

Disproportionately large numbers of Salvadorans and Guatemalans who came to the U.S. to seek refuge have signed voluntary departure forms when detained by the INS before contact with counsel. An estimated eighty to ninety percent of detained refugees from these countries sign the forms.

Tactics of coercion employed by INS agents are not limited to any particular geographic area in the U.S. or to the conduct of a few INS agents. There are not just a few isolated incidents of INS misconduct, but a consistent pattern of misbehaviour.

A group of Salvadorans launched a class action in the U.S. asking the Court to prohibit the INS from using coercion to obtain their signatures on voluntary departure forms. They also asked the court to require the INS to advise Salvadorans of their right to apply for political asylum and their right to a deportation hearing before requesting them to depart voluntarily.

In June, 1982, Judge Kenyon of the Central District Court of California made the order requested. The judge concluded the INS routinely gives incomplete, misleading and even false advice to Salvadorans regarding their legal rights. He held that widespread acceptance of voluntary departure is due in large part to the coercive effect of the practices and procedures employed by the INS and the unfamiliarity of most Salvadorans with their rights under immigration laws.

The injunction in that case was temporary. For six years, it was not made permanent nor was it appealed. According to a judge of the United States Court of Appeals, the government was in no hurry to have the injunction set aside because it was not obeying the injunction.

The injunction, which was finally made permanent in April, 1988, enjoins the coerced signing of voluntary departure forms, and it requires the INS to notify Salvadoran detainees of their right to political asylum and their right to representation by counsel in deportation proceedings.

In his reasons for the 1988 judgement, District Judge Kenyon said that since the preliminary temporary injunction was granted INS agents continued to discourage class members (Salvadorans) from pursuing asylum claims, while counselling them to accept voluntary departure. The order of the Court "was not diligently respected nor were agents disciplined for failing to adhere to its terms."

The INS has also been involved in high-pressure methods to get children to sign voluntary departure forms. Three Salvadoran children, aged 16, 13 and 12, brought a court action to ask the court to order the INS to stop coercing children when informing them of the availability of voluntary departure. Children were deprived of access to their parents, even by telephone, until the forms were signed. The Salvadoran children's court order request was granted.

THE BURDEN OF PROOF

A refugee in the U.S. can avoid forcible return to the country he fled if he is granted asylum or his deportation is withheld. The U.S. Attorney-General has the power to grant asylum in his discretion to an asylum-seeker, provided the refugee meets the Convention refugee definition. Withholding deportation is not discretionary. If the person's life or freedom would be threatened, for listed reasons, deportation must be withheld.

The burden of proof is on the asylum-seeker to show he meets the refugee definition. Similarly, a refugee claimant applying for a U.S. deportation order to be withheld has the burden of showing that upon return to his home country he would be subject to persecution on account of race, religion or political opinion. The asylum-seeker must not only provide evidence to support his claim, but also persuade the immigration judge that he is in fact a refugee. The INS has made the burden impossibly heavy by insisting on independent proof or corroboration.

For applications to withhold deportation, U.S. courts have imposed a clear probability test. Factual support, concrete evidence, or some documentary evidence is required. Unless the applicant can show he would be more likely than not be subject to persecution upon deportation back to his country of origin, deportation will not be withheld.

As well, the INS has asked for corroborative evidence to satisfy the clear probability standard in applications for deportation to be stayed. In December, 1984, the U.S. Court of Appeals held in the case of *Bolanos-Hernadez v. INS* that specific corroborative evidence was not necessary. Until the Bolanos case, the Attorney-General, the INS and Immigration Court decided claims on the basis of whether specific corroborative evidence had been presented. But a refugee claimant seeking asylum is unlikely to arrive with extensive documentation or witnesses supporting his claim.

For refugee claims, as opposed to applications to withhold deportation, clear probability of persecution need not be established. The standard of proof required by the courts is that persecution is a "reasonable possibility".

While this standard is relatively generous, it was not articulated until March, 1987 by the U.S. Supreme Court in the case of the *INS v. Cardoza-Fonseca.* Until then, the INS position was that asylum applicants, like applicants for withholding deportation, had to meet the standard of clear probability.

Even for cases decided since *Cardoza-Fonseca,* and despite the Court's ruling, the previous high standard of corroborative evidence showing clear probability is still being imposed on Salvadoran and Guatemalan refugees.

In July, 1987, the U.S. administration announced that the Attorney-General had asked the INS to encourage Nicaraguans whose claims for asylum or withholding of deportation had been denied to reapply for another hearing. The administration was finally ready to concur with the standard set by the U.S. Supreme Court decision of reasonable probability rather than clear probability. However, the invitation was extended exclusively to Nicaraguans.

Presumably the shift from clear probability to reasonable possibility will have no influence in the determination of refugee claims from El Salvador and Guatemala. If the administration thought these claims would be decided differently in a new hearing, they would have invited reapplications for Salvadorans and Guatemalans as well.

Perry Rifkin, the INS director of Miami, explained the omission of Salvadorans by saying, "A Salvadoran claim is harder to prove. They don't have a dictator there."

In principle, not having a dictator or having a dictator should not change the standard of proof. Governments can be simultaneously democracies and gross and flagrant violators of human rights. The right to life and the right to be free from torture have been consistently violated in El Salvador and Guatemala in a gross and flagrant way, despite those countries' democratically elected governments.

When the U.S. administration says Salvadoran claims are harder to prove because the country is not ruled by a dictator, the administration is stating a policy, not a fact. The U.S. government policy is to make standards tougher on Salvadorans because the Government is supporting the existing regime, no matter how repressive, or how widespread the violence.

When two victims come to U.S. authorities with identical evidence of persecution, one from a democracy and the other from an autocratic dictatorship, the victim from the democracy is denied protection. The victim from the autocracy is granted asylum. The victim from the democracy has not proved his claim, while the victim from the autocracy has, although the evidence in both cases is the same.

THE U.S. AND HUMAN RIGHTS

United States law prohibits both development and security assistance to any government which consistently violates internationally recognized human rights. For fiscal years 1982 and 1983, U.S. law required the President to certify El Salvador was making a concerted and significant effort to comply with internationally recognized human rights before military assistance could be given. The President had to attest that El Salvador was achieving substantial control over its own armed forces, so as to bring an end to indiscriminate torture and murder of Salvadoran citizens by these forces.

In theory, these laws are supposed to create pressure for compliance with human rights standards. It is assumed the beneficiary wants the aid and the donor wants the human rights improvements. However, in the case of military aid, the donor may want to give the aid to support an ally. Where the donor is determined to give, the pressure for human rights compliance disappears.

The United States views the governments of El Salvador and Guatemala as friendly to U.S. interests, while the guerilla opposition in both countries is seen as hostile. The U.S. wishes to provide aid to keep the current governments of Guatemala and El Salvador in power, and keep their opponents out of power. In this context, the U.S. is tempted to minimize, discredit, and undercut recognition of human rights violations that would make supportive aid difficult or impossible.

Recognizing a large number of refugees from El Salvador and Guatemala directly contravenes U.S. foreign aid policy. Refugee recognition means acknowledging persecution. A high volume of refugee recognition means the home government is consistently violating human rights in a gross and flagrant manner. A government cannot credibly give aid based on human rights compliance and, at the same time, recognize a large volume of asylum-seekers as refugees.

In order to avoid tainting refugee recognition by foreign policy considerations, refugee determination should be made independently from foreign policy. But in the U.S., however, the State Department determines both foreign policy and, through the Bureau of Human Rights and Humanitarian Affairs (BHRHA), refugee cases.

The ultimate decision-maker on an asylum claim, an INS district director or an immigration judge, must first obtain an advisory opinion from the BHRHA before determining a refugee claim. The U.S. Court of Appeals has said these advisory opinions do both too little and too much. They provide little or nothing in the way of useful information about conditions in a foreign country. At the same time they recommend how the petitioner's request for asylum should be decided. There is a risk, according to the Court, that these advisory opinions will carry more weight than they deserve. These advisory opinions are inevitably influenced by foreign policy considerations, since the BHRHA will not undermine its State Department colleagues in their efforts to support the regimes of Guatemala and El Salvador.

COUNTRY REPORTS ON HUMAN RIGHTS PRACTICES

The State Department releases an annual volume titled *Country Reports on Human Rights Practices*. The reports are submitted to the Committee on Foreign Relations of the Senate and the Committee on Foreign Affairs of the U.S. House of Representatives. They are used by Congress to determine whether human rights requirements for foreign aid are met.

The reports on Guatemala and El Salvador have been more public relations briefs for those governments than fair and even-handed assessments. They attempt to defend the governments against charges of abuse by referring to murdered civilians as victims of opposition guerilla warfare.

The Watch Committees and the Lawyers Committee for Human Rights said the 1985 report on El Salvador was "not a serious attempt to assess the human rights situation in that country." Any reports of government-sponsored abuse are discredited by the U.S. State Department.

The Salvadoran press, a mouthpiece for the government and the Armed Forces, serves as the main source of information for the State Department's reports. The U.S. government rejects eyewitness accounts as politically-motivated, and obtains no information for its reports from human rights organizations or American journalists in El Salvador.

The State Department also relies on the Guatemalan press to prepare reports on that country. Although the Watch Committees and the Lawyers Committee consider the Guatemalan press to be more enterprising than the Salvadoran press, it is far from comprehensive and routinely censors itself to avoid criticizing the government.

The U.S. government *Report* does not attribute responsibility for Guatemalan disappearances, because the press does not. Guatemalan Armed Forces statements claiming that people have just "pretended" to disappear are quoted in the *Report* without criticism. By downplaying human rights violations in El Salvador and Guatemala, the State Department is also minimizing these violations for its refugee advisory opinions.

REJECTION RATES

Another manifestation of this conflict of interest is in rejection rates. Asylum-seekers from Guatemala and El Salvador are rejected at a much higher rate than asylum-seekers from countries with equal or lesser turmoil that the State Department does not support.

A U.S. government study revealed that Salvadorans are much more likely to be rejected in their asylum requests than other nationals, even when they present the same facts as other refugees. Even for Salvadorans described as being tortured, the rejection rate was ninety-six percent. For Poles the rate was twenty percent, and for Iranians thirty-six percent.

GENERALIZED VS. INDIVIDUALIZED PERSECUTION

Some elements of the refugee definition are routinely ignored by the U.S. government. INS policy insists that a refugee must be singled out for persecution or be politically active, or at least be seen by the home government to be politically active. But this is wrong in law. A person does not have to be singled out for persecution in order to be a refugee. Nor does a person need to have political opinions or be politically active. It is enough if those persecuting think he has a political opinion.

This artificial restriction of the refugee definition means genuine refugees are denied refugee status. The pool of refugee claimants viewed as abusive increases, and the problem of abusive claimants appears larger than it actually is.

These errors particularly affect refugees from countries such as El Salvador and Guatemala that are beset by civil war and a general breakdown of law and order. When law and order prevails it is easier to be singled out for persecution, but when extensive internal strife prevails there is general suffering from persecution and people with no political opinion are much more likely to be drawn into violent political disputes.

The Federal Court of Appeal ruled in favour of Bolanos-Hernandez on this question of generalized persecution. Bolanos, a Salvadoran, had his claim for asylum in the U.S. rejected by the Board of Immigration Appeals on the basis that the specific threat against Bolanos' life was merely representative of the general conditions in El Salvador. But the Court reasoned a specific threat to an individual's life or freedom is not lessened by the fact the individual resides in a country where lives and freedoms of a large number of persons are threatened. If anything, in the words of the Court, that may make the threat more serious and credible.

The U.S. government also argued that any persecution Bolanos might suffer would not be on account of his political opinion, because he was neutral. The Court held that choosing to remain neutral is no less a political decision than choosing to affiliate with a political faction.

Despite the Court's decision in December, 1984, the government continued to assert the position it argued in *Bolanos*. In October, 1985, Laura J. Dietrich, then Deputy Assistant Secretary of State wrote in a letter to the *New York Times* that refugee determination partly depends on the answer to the question: "How have you been singled out?"

In my opinion, a group approach rather than an individual approach to the refugee definition is sometimes necessary to protect those who fled the danger of their home country. By identifying groups of persons fleeing generalized violence who require asylum, the need for each person in the group to establish that he falls within the legal definition of a refugee disappears.

Recognizing this need, the U.S. has in the past granted temporary asylum or extended voluntary departure* to Yugoslavs, Lebanese and Ugandans. Ethiopians were issued a blanket grant of extended voluntary departure from 1978 to 1981. Since 1976, the INS has refused a blanket grant of extended voluntary departure to Lebanese asylum-seekers, but has encouraged its immigration officers to view individual requests sympathetically.

A temporary dispensation from removal was given to Nicaraguans in 1979. In April, 1986, the INS chief in Florida announced that he would not send any Nicaraguans back home. At least three-fourths of all asylum applications by Nicaraguans are made in Florida. Temporary deferment of enforced departure has been granted to Afghan nationals since December, 1980. A similar policy has been in effect for Poland since 1982.

Extended voluntary departure has been proposed for Salvadorans but never implemented. Senator Dennis DeConcini of Arizona and Representative Joe Moakley of Massachusetts introduced a bill in Congress to suspend deportation of Salvadorans in the U.S. Reagan administration officials testified

---

* Extended voluntary departure is a form of temporary humanitarian refuge. Foreigners in the U.S. without legal status may, with permission, depart the U.S. voluntarily. They suffer no penalty for their lack of status in the U.S. For members of groups granted extended voluntary departure, the period of time before which they must leave voluntarily to avoid penalty is extended.

against the bill, claiming it would "attract illegal immigrants and undermine immigration law."

DETENTION

In principle, a refugee claimant or asylum-seeker should not be detained unless he is likely to abscond or he is a danger to public safety. In practice, Central American refugee claimants in the U.S. are detained as a matter of course.

The Refugee Convention requires the U.S. not to impose penalties on refugees who enter or are present in the country without authorization, provided they have come directly from the country of persecution and present themselves without delay to the authorities. The U.S. also cannot apply unnecessary restrictions to refugees on account of their illegal entry or presence, according to the Convention.

Until 1981, the U.S. had a detention policy in line with the Refugee Convention. The general rule was that all foreigners would be released pending determination of their admissibility, except for those who were likely to abscond or whose freedom of movement would be adverse to national security or public safety. However, in July, 1981, the government adopted a policy of general detention. The purpose, according to the INS commissioner, was "to deter the continuing arrival of illegal undocumented foreigners to our shores."

A group of Haitian asylum-seekers challenged the 1981 policy in the courts on the ground of a failure to "provide notice of a proposed rule in the Federal Register, and afford an opportunity for interested persons to present their views." The Haitians asked the court to hold the new policy invalid since the procedures had not been followed, order a return to the old policy, and order their release. The U.S. Court of Appeals ruled the new policy invalid and granted the orders requested by the Haitians.

The government subsequently used the statutory rule-making procedures to set out its new policy. First the government published an interim rule that would continue to allow foreigners to be detained if their release was not in the "public interest". The "public interest" included prolonging detention because of likelihood of absconding or because freedom would be adverse to public safety. As well, "public interest" included detention as a deterrent to entry for others.

The United Nations High Commission for Refugees wrote to the U.S. objecting to the interim rule as a violation of the Refugee Convention. Nonetheless, in 1982, the government issued a rule in final form substantially unchanged from the interim rule.

Afghan refugee claimants challenged the "detention as deterrent" rule in the courts on the grounds it violated the Convention. Counsel argued detention of the refugees amounted to imposing a penalty on the Afghans by reason of their illegal entry. As well, counsel said detention was unnecessary because nothing indicated they would abscond or pose a threat to society.

The Court rejected the argument that the Convention's prohibition against penalties for illegal entry had been violated. The reason for the rejection was that the Afghans had travelled through Pakistan and India to get to the U.S. As well, the Afghans were not refugees, just refugee claimants. The Convention, the judge said, was meant to protect only those already recognized as refugees.

By international legal standards, however, the judge erred in both his reasons. A refugee who passes through a country of transit without any delay or a minimum of delay is considered to be coming directly from the country of persecution. "Coming directly" does not mean travelling non-stop, but rather refers to travelling to a country of asylum without undue delay. As well, the refugee is "coming directly" to the country of protection where the first receiving country — in the Afghans' case India and Pakistan — is shown to be a country of persecution.

Further, the judge was wrong to say the Afghans were merely claimants rather than refugees. Recognizing someone as a refugee does not make the person a refugee. It is a declaratory, not a constitutive act. A declaratory act recognizes someone to be what he is or always was. A constitutive act makes a person something he was not before. An asylum government cannot constitute someone to be a refugee, because he already is one.

Certain benefits of the Refugee Convention depend on recognition, but freedom from unnecessary detention must be available to bona fide refugees pending determination of their claims. This right would be useless if a person who appears to be a refugee could not claim the benefit of the provision from the outset.

Using detention to discourage refugee claims is a disguised form of expulsion. It violates the Convention's prohibitions against penalties for illegal presence and unnecessary detentions. Detention of asylum-seekers also contravenes the Convention's prohibition against refoulement or forced return.

Port of entry claimants are subject to different treatment from inland claimants in the area of detention. The result is a "Catch-22" for refugee claimants. A foreigner who is at the U.S. border, or considered to be at the border, can be detained simply "in the public interest" to discourage a refugee claim. A foreigner inland can be detained only as a threat to national security or as a poor bail risk, in particular if he is likely to abscond. In order to avoid detention at the border, the claimant may enter the U.S. illegally. He then creates a justification for detention inland since he will be considered likely to abscond.

In practice, many inland asylum-seekers who are subject to deportation proceedings are detained. The government has to allow release on a bond, but this can be set at a high amount. In contrast to criminal proceedings, where the courts will accept a percentage of cash or security on the bond, immigration proceedings require a deposit of the full amount of the bond.

TREATMENT OF DETAINEES — EL CENTRO
Refugees in detention are not criminals, but victims. Yet they are treated worse, granted fewer rights, and subject to higher security than convicted criminals in the U.S. prison system.

Poor treatment is aimed at deterring others from making claims, and discouraging or coercing the detainee from pursuing his claim. Overcrowding is commonplace. Accommodations are inadequate to house the increased volume of refugees in detention since the 1981 policy change in favour of general detention.

The U.S. prison system is being privatized, and detention facilities are contracted out to profit-making companies. Private institutions emphasize stricter security than government institutions and make no distinction between convicted criminals and refugees. A disproportionate number of recent refugees have been placed in the newer, private, high security institutions. Refugees are detained in a warehouse atmosphere, under conditions of forced inactivity, without work, training or education, including even English language instruction.

A hunger strike was organized to protest poor conditions at the foreigner detention centre in El Centro, California from May 27 to June 3, 1985. The centre held a number of Central American refugees. Although designed for 340 people, the facility housed nearly 500 people at the time of the strike.

Strikers complained of insanitary facilities, including inadequate and uncleaned showers, sinks, toilets and shaving facilities, and inadequate supplies of soap, shampoo and tooth paste. They also complained of improper and insufficient food. Their diet consisted mainly of starch. Dairy products, fruits and vegetables were provided rarely if at all.

Poor medical attention and health care were the rule. The INS estimated adequate medical facilities would demand a fifteen person medical staff, yet only one medical staff person serviced the whole facility. Aspirin was prescribed for virtually every ailment. Skin rashes, dental problems, and stomach problems went untreated.

A newspaper and the New Testament were the only reading materials. There was no law library and only one lawyer from the town of El Centro was available to inmates. Inmates who wanted to represent themselves were denied photocopying access and prohibited from using pencils or typewriters.

Inmates were locked out of their barracks all day and left to stand in a dirt yard in the summer, with little or no shade, despite temperatures as high as 100 degrees F. Administrators justified keeping out inmates by claiming there were not enough security guards. A few guards could more easily keep an eye on inmates standing outside than inside. There was a lack of recreation facilities. The playing field was an uneven dirt yard, without grass, containing pieces of glass.

Authorities imposed mail censorship, requiring all letters from and to lawyers to be read by the institution mail censor. As well, inmates were subject to solitary confinement without respect for due process. They would be punished without hearings. Refugees alleged physical abuse such as beating and hair-pulling. The administration did not provide shoes or clothing. If inmates wanted clean clothes they had to pay for laundering.

Once the strike began, there were widespread allegations of mistreatment of the strikers. Strikers were forced to sleep outside and denied access to their lawyers. Finally the strike leaders were transferred out of El Centro without notification to their families or lawyers.

Allegedly, on May 29, about fifty officers in riot gear attacked the strikers, kicking and beating them. Several strikers suffered injuries. The administration admitted strikers were forcibly moved from the exercise yard into an isolation area. After the forced move, all but seven of the strikers dropped out of the strike action. Rev. Alex Koski, a retired Lutheran Minister, posted $26,750 bail to free the seven remaining foreigners on strike from the detention centre. With their release, the strike ended.

THE LAREDO DETENTION CENTRE

The detention centre at Laredo, Texas is run on behalf of the Immigration and Naturalization Service by the private, profit-making Corrections Corporation of America. Mainly Central Americans are detained at Laredo.

Although intended for refugees, the Laredo detention centre is designed like a maximum security prison. It is surrounded by barbed wire, and it has electronic surveillance, electronic door locks, and guards with walkie-talkies. Cameras monitor all but the toilet areas. Microphones monitor all conversations except in the attorney room. Persons in detention are kept locked in their dormitories for twenty-four hours a day, except for one hour allowed in an outdoor barbed wire area for recreation. Some days inmates are not let out of their cells at all.

All inmates, including infants, are strip-searched on arrival and subjected to a pat-down search every eight hours. In the past inmates were also subjected to a strip-search, including a genital examination, after speaking with their lawyers or appearing in court. Strip-search after consultation with a lawyer was discontinued May 10, 1985 because of complaints, but strip-searching after court appearances continued.

The facility has three isolation cells, which have been used to punish children who disobey orders. Inmates do unpaid janitorial labour. In theory this is voluntary, but in practice it is the only way to get out of the cell for more than an hour. The usual minimal food portions are increased for people who do janitorial work.

Counselling facilities and educational advancements are blatantly lacking in Laredo, even for children. Aside from "voluntary" janitorial work, no work programme is in place.

Inmates have been restricted access to counsel. Paralegals have been denied permission to interview clients. Attorneys have been denied access during weekends.

Central American refugees have taken the mistreatment endured in detention centres to the courts. Two cases were each decided in favour of the refugee.

In *Nunez v. Boldin* the Court issued an injunction prohibiting the INS from failing to make available to detainees pens, pencils and paper. Confiscating addresses and phone numbers of lawyers, friends and relatives was prohibited, and the Court ordered the notes previously confiscated returned. Reading of counsel-detainee correspondence and scheduling of legal proceedings without notifying counsel were prohibited. The court forbade restricted visiting by attorneys and paralegals, and restricted access to self-help legal materials. Finally, the court ordered the INS to give detainees notice of their right to apply for political asylum.

MORE ON DETAINEE CONDITIONS

In *Orantes-Hernandez v. Smith* the Court examined conditions in INS detention centres in Pasadena, Los Angeles, Chula Vista and El Centro. District Judge Kenyon rejected the INS argument that "aliens are not entitled to the same rights as prisoners" and ordered the ban on written materials be lifted, particularly for those explaining foreigners' legal rights. The court found that it was unreasonable to limit visiting hours at El Centro and unreasonable and impermissible to deny telephone access for detainees at Chula Vista. The court held that paralegals must be allowed to interview detainees without an attorney present. Detainees could not be placed in solitary confinement without notice of charges, an opportunity to be heard, and a written statement of reasons for a decision to confine, provided confinement was for more than twenty-four hours.

The American Civil Liberties Union filed a complaint with the United Nations about the treatment in detention of asylum-seekers. The complaint was restricted to Cuban asylum seekers, but the problems are general. The complaint said detainees were subjected to cruel, inhuman and degrading treatment in violation of the Universal Declaration of Human Rights. Confinement of detainees allegedly failed to comply with the UN Minimum Standard for the Treatment of Prisoners. The specific allegations included overcrowded and unhealthful living conditions, lack of exercise, inadequate access to religious materials and personal property, and poor medical and psychiatric care. The complaint held that these transgressions amounted to a consistent pattern of gross human rights violations.

The United Nations system handles complaints of this sort on a confidential basis. What, if anything, the UN did with the complaint is not a matter of public record. However, the mere fact that the ACLU felt compelled to make such a complaint is a condemnation of how refugee claimants are treated in the U.S. determination process.

Chapter 12

THE U.S. SANCTUARY MOVEMENT AND SANCTUARY TRIAL

The American sanctuary movement was initiated in 1982 in response to the government's increasingly harsh policy toward refugees. Its mandate was to assist Central American refugees make their claims and protect them from exploitive immigrant smugglers or "coyotes". Two men emerged as important leaders of the movement, Jim Corbett, a retired Quaker rancher from Arizona, and the Reverend Mr. John Fife, Minister of the South Side United Presbyterian Church of Tucson, Arizona. Corbett was mobilized to action by a personal experience, Fife by a public event.[1]

JIM CORBETT'S STORY
On May 4, 1981 a friend of Corbett's picked up a Salvadoran refugee hitch-hiking in Nogales, Arizona. Just north of Nogales,

the refugee was seized by border patrol. Corbett tried to locate the Salvadoran the following day in order to offer assistance. He was quickly acquainted with the problems Central Americans faced on a day-to-day basis in the U.S. He began trying to help refugees systematically.

Corbett started visiting refugees held by Mexicans for deportation back to Guatemala and El Salvador at the Nogales Sonora Penitentiary in Mexico, just across the Arizona border. He sent refugees' letters back to Central America, telephoned relatives in the U.S., and distributed information about legal services in the U.S. and refugees' legal rights.

Corbett set up an apartment in his house where refugees could stay until their asylum applications were completed. From the start, he did not shy away from assisting those illegally in the U.S. He arranged for medical attention and helped refugees cross the Mexico-U.S. border through a fence.

JOHN FIFE'S STORY

The abandonment of 26 Salvadoran refugees by commercial smugglers in the desert in the summer of 1980 triggered John Fife's commitment to the Sanctuary movement. Half the group died of thirst and exposure. The survivors were arrested by the INS for deportation back to El Salvador as soon as they were well enough to move.

Jaded by the treatment refugees received in the U.S., immigration lawyers asked Fife for his help. Fife began a prayer vigil for the people of Central America. As government hardened its policy, the vigil gained momentum. Participants at the vigil from different churches decided the time had come to do more than merely pray.

In the spring of 1981, the group formed a task force, with Philip Willis Conger as director, under the Tucson Ecumenical Council. Sixty-five Protestant and Roman Catholic churches began systematically to raise money for bonds to free refugees in detention, and for paralegals to help refugees make their claims. Once refugees were freed on bond, the Council assisted them in settling, and contacting families and support groups. The Council provided interpreters and arranged for lawyers.

BIRTH OF THE SANCTUARY MOVEMENT

By then, Corbett realized the efforts of Fife and the Tucson Ecumenical Council were futile. Fife and his group were just buying time. In the end, refugees would inevitably be deported by the U.S. government back to Central America.

Fife and other members of his organization agreed to join Corbett to assist refugees in avoiding capture and deportation back to El Salvador. They brought undocumented refugees to Fife's church and introduced them to congregation members. Members in turn offered to provide them housing. Fife and some of his congregates met refugees who had crossed the Mexico-U.S. border illegally and drove them further into the U.S.

In early 1982, Fife's congregation voted to declare the South Side Presbyterian Church a sanctuary in the ancient tradition of the church. Fife's Church also decided to go public and ask churches across the country to make a similar statement. Four churches agreed — from Los Angeles, San Francisco, Washington, DC, and Long Island, New York.

On March 24, 1982, the Sanctuary Movement was born. Corbett and Fife held a press conference that day, at which time Fife declared his church a sanctuary. He released a letter sent the previous day to then Attorney-General William French stating that his church "will publicly violate the Immigration and Nationality Acts 274 (a)." This provision prohibits bringing into the U.S., transporting, concealing, harbouring or shielding any alien. The letter said the Church believed the U.S. government's policy and practice with regard to Central American refugees to be illegal and immoral.

At the press conference, Corbett said, "The human and legal rights of Salvadoran refugees captured in the U.S. are routinely violated in order to process them with maximum efficiency and minimum delay back to the murderous conditions they fled." The public declaration of sanctuary, he said, allows refugees and those wishing to help refugees know how and where to make connections.

Publicity about violations of international standards and domestic law could create public pressure to remove the violations. Corbett, Fife, and their colleagues could help only a few of the refugees in need of assistance. Publicity meant creating a mass sanctuary movement that would actually help refugees in need. If it became widely accepted that the U.S. was breaking its own laws and international standards, a change in government practice was more likely.

Above all, they believed the moral imperative of helping refugees justified public action and a call for participation by others. Openness about sanctuary proclaimed to the country the churches' heartfelt belief that they were doing the right thing. Secrecy would undercut the action's moral claim and mean silence about their own activities and about human rights violations. Morally, human rights violations had to be denounced in an effective way by publicizing the Sanctuary movement.

Another reason Sanctuary went public was the problem of coyotes — professional refugee smugglers. The 1980 abandonment of twenty-six Salvadorans, though dramatic, was not an isolated incident. A steady stream of stories tell how smugglers exploited and abused refugees. At best, coyotes charge refugees exorbitant sums of money for a few minutes' work. They steal from their clients, sexually assault the women, and abandon clients, leaving them to be picked up by police.

Refugees who cross the border with "professional help" become victims of others on the U.S. side. Notaries posing as lawyers take money for services never performed. Worthless documents claiming to give permission to refugees to stay are sold for large sums.

Thievery and sexual assault continue in the U.S. Refugees become easy targets for any criminal since they will not go to police for fear of being deported back to the country of persecution.

Refugee victims cannot ask the U.S. government to protect them because the government would deport the refugees back to their home countries. Although the Sanctuary movement could not stop those who preyed on refugees, at least it could reduce the temptation for refugees to fall into the clutches of bogus helpers.

THE MOVEMENT SPREADS

From the March, 1982 declaration, the Sanctuary movement spread quickly, climbing to a total of 222 declared sanctuaries by March, 1985. Members included 199 Christian sanctuaries, eight Jewish ones, ten universities, four city councils and one seminary. They were located in thirty-one states and the District of Columbia.

The Sanctuary movement is a grassroots initiative without a national organizational structure. Corbett and Fife are considered its founders, but have no power or responsibility to direct the movement.

Once started, the movement caught on particularly quickly in the Chicago area. In July 1982, Wellington Avenue United Church of Christ in Chicago declared itself a sanctuary and received a Salvadoran. In the Chicago area alone, 85 churches endorsed the action.

Corbett asked the Chicago Religious Task Force on Central America to co-ordinate the movement of refugees north from U.S.-Mexican border points. The Task Force agreed, and became the central clearing-house for information about the Sanctuary movement. In 1983, Sister Darlene Nicorgski joined the Task Force to co-ordinate the screening, orientation and transportation of refugees from Arizona and California to sanctuaries throughout the U.S.

THE MOVEMENT IS CHARGED

About 1,200 people registered to attend a movement-sponsored symposium in Tucson, Arizona in January, 1985. But two weeks prior to the symposium, the movement was in for a surprise. The authorities announced the indictments of sixteen people from the movement, including lay workers and leaders. Rev. John Fife, Jim Corbett, Philip Willis Conger and Sister Darlene Nicorgski were among those indicted. They were required to appear in court January 23, the day the symposium began. More than sixty aliens were arrested as unindicted co-conspirators.

Of the sixteen defendants, three pleaded guilty to reduced charges and were dropped from the case. Charges were dismissed against two more for health reasons. Eleven pleaded not guilty and had to be tried.

I attended the trial in Tucson, Arizona, on behalf of the International Commission of Jurists* and wrote a report on the trial based on my personal observations, transcripts, submissions and other reports.

By the time the trial had ended eleven accused faced thirty counts. The charges included bringing in illegal aliens; transporting illegal aliens; concealing, harbouring or shielding illegal aliens; encouraging or inducing or attempting to encourage the entry of illegal aliens; conspiracy; aiding and abetting; unlawful entry; and eluding examination or inspection.

PRELIMINARY MOTIONS — PROSECUTION

Donald M. Reno Jr. for the prosecution asked the court in a preliminary motion to disallow the Sanctuary movement from raising a number of defences. Judge Earl H. Carroll granted all of the motions.

Carroll excluded evidence of international law in the trial that might be used to show that the people being helped by the Sanctuary movement were legitimate refugees entitled to reside in the U.S. Although the foreigners helped by the Sanctuary movement might indeed be refugees, the judge said that did not validate their unlawful entry or entitle them to reside in the U.S. Carroll also ruled against the admissibility of evidence to demonstrate the danger civilians faced in any foreign country.

Further, Carroll excluded the defence that the Sanctuary movement's conduct was justified as a result of its members' religious beliefs. He said persons of religious conviction have the same obligation as all citizens to comply with the law.

Next, Carroll ruled that the motives and beliefs of the defendants did not constitute a legal defence to the charges in

---

* The I.C.J. is a non-governmental organization whose objective is promoting the rule of law and the legal protection of human rights. It headquarters are in Geneva, Switzerland. Its membership consists largely of lawyers, legal academics and judges.

the indictment. A refugee outside the U.S. is not entitled to enter and a refugee inside the U.S. is not entitled to remain except at the Attorney-General's discretion. Therefore, it did not matter whether the accused believed the foreigners they were helping were refugees.

Finally, Reno asked the judge to exclude the movement's defence of necessity. Carroll ruled no evidence would be received to prove the accused acted under duress or necessity for the surreptitious entry of a foreigner into the U.S.

The motions were requested, not just to prevent arguments from being raised, but to exclude evidence from being admitted in support of these defences. Reno's intent was to prevent the jury from hearing that the foreigners helped by the Sanctuary movement were real refugees, and that without the movement's help they would be sent back to persecution. As well, Reno did not want the jury to hear that the religious beliefs of Sanctuary movement members directed them to help refugees.

PRELIMINARY MOTIONS — DEFENCE

Whereas Carroll ruled in favour of every significant prosecution motion, each of the three significant defence motions failed.

First, the defence moved to dismiss the charges on the ground that the prosecution was an unconstitutional infringement on the right to freedom of religion because sanctuary work, saving lives, is religious work. Carroll found the enforcement of immigration laws does not constitute a violation of the defendants' right to freedom of religion.

The defence secondly argued charges ought to be dismissed because the infiltration of the Sanctuary movement by a government agent was outrageous government conduct, violating due process. Carroll ruled infiltration of churches by government informers is "not acceptable good conduct, but not outrageous," and not a violation of due process. Carroll called the government tactics unnecessary and suggested less intrusive means in future investigations, but he said the informers had a legal right to do what they were doing. He said the accused were not being investigated because of their religious interests.

Third, the defence asked for dismissal on the ground of selective prosecution: the state was prosecuting the Sanctuary movement but not ranchers who were inducing undocumented workers to enter the U.S., nor those assisting the family of El Salvador president Napoleon Duarte to enter the U.S. The selective prosecution motion, though a preliminary motion, was not introduced until after the trial had begun and not decided until the Sanctuary trial was over. Counsel for the defence asked either for dismissal of the charges or an evidentiary hearing to show selective prosecution had occurred. Carroll denied both requests. Between conviction and sentence, Carroll ruled no evidentiary hearing would take place and he dismissed the selective prosecution motion.

PROSECUTION OPENING STATEMENT
Opening statements began November 15, 1985. The prosecution divided the defendants into three tiers. The first tier, consisting of Reverend Fife, Jim Corbett, Philip Willis Conger and Sister Darlene Nicorgski, was dubbed the "chief executive officers" of the conspiracy — the generals of the underground railway. The second tier, consisting of Peggy Hutchison, Nena MacDonald and Wendy Le Win, was dubbed the "transporters and smugglers". The third tier, consisting of Father Tony Clark, Mary Espinoza, Father Quinones and Mrs. Socorro Aguilar, was dubbed the "Nogales Connection", in reference to the French Connection, a recent American movie about drug smuggling.

Reverend Fife was accused by the prosecution of allowing his church to be used as a place for harbouring illegals and as a meeting place for the conspirators to plan overt criminal acts. He was cited as the principal person at the top of the conspiracy.

The prosecution accused Philip Willis Conger of being the "nuts and bolts" organizer responsible for co-ordinating the conspiracy through the second tier, the transporters and smugglers, and the third tier, the Nogales Connection.

Darlene Nicorgski was described by the prosecution as a travel agent. Reno claimed Nicorgski organized transportation for the aliens to various destinations in the U.S. He said aliens were delivered to her apartment by second tier conspirators.

The prosecution claimed Mrs. Aguilar's house in Nogales, Mexico was a safe home, a drop house. Salvadorans and Guatemalans would stay there until the American defendants — the defendants other than Mrs. Socorro Aguilar and Father Quinones — made arrangements for their transportation and entry into the United States.

Aliens, Reno claimed, would go to the home of Father Quinones in Nogales, Mexico, who would tell them how to enter the U.S. illegally. On several occasions, he would provide fraudulent documents so they could enter the U.S. through a regular port of entry. He would take them to Mrs. Aguilar's home, where they would stay until they left for the U.S.

Reno charged Quinones would send the aliens through a fence hole on the Mexican-U.S. border and direct them to the Sacred Heart Church in Nogales, Arizona. Father Clark and Mary Espinoza would harbour the aliens at the Church until the Tucson defendants could co-ordinate the aliens' transportation to the South Side Presbyterian Church in Tucson. From Tucson the aliens were sent to various sanctuaries in the U.S. Transportation throughout the U.S. was arranged by Darlene Nicorgski.

DEFENCE OPENING STATEMENT

The defence opening statements were more in the nature of character references. Each defence lawyer provided a biographical sketch of his client, attempting to counter the prosecution's portrayal of the accused as a criminal conspiratorial gang. The defence described the accused as charitable, religious individuals with a deep-seated commitment to help others.

Le Win's lawyer said, "There is no crime, and there is no leadership here, no command structure; there is but one leader here — and that leader [God] is just beyond the reach of the immigration service." Conger's lawyer said, "They needed to respond to the need that was there." Aguilar's lawyer said, "No one in this case ever joined a criminal conspiracy... some of them had never met. They were brought together only when they were indicted." Fife's lawyer said, "What we have in this case, in a nutshell, is eleven people who have devoted their lives and activities to helping other people and, as a consequence, they have been indicted by the U.S. government." Espinoza's lawyer told the court that Ms. Espinoza treated refugees no differently from any of the other hungry and homeless people she helped.

The defence's attempt to portray the accused as charitable people motivated by religion was considered by the judge to be a violation of his previous preliminary motion ruling. He interrupted defence counsel several times during opening statements to remind them of his previous pronouncement.

The defence pointed out the inequity: while the prosecution was able to say the accused had bad motives, that they were a criminal conspiracy, the defence was not allowed to say the accused had good motives, that they were operating out of religious conviction.

Carroll rejected the defence concerns. "All I think is sought here is a continuing effort to have me mistry the case" (i.e., rule that there was a mistrial). A judge can declare a mistrial if the jury hears statements it should not hear. A judge can declare a mistrial on his own case. Carroll, who saw no imbalance in what each side could declare during opening statements, said, "the difference between what Mr. Reno said and what I heard from the other side is night and day."

THE PROSECUTION CASE

Criminal offences can be divided into two categories: *malum in se,* crimes that are bad in themselves, and *malum prohibitum,* crimes that are bad because they are prohibited. Crimes bad in themselves are articulations of community morality. Crimes bad only because they are prohibited have no moral commitment of the community behind them, and are just regulatory. In the absence of the laws, performing the acts prohibited by law would not be considered wrong.

A normal criminal trial involves one defendant and one alleged crime that is *malum in se.* The Sanctuary trial involved eleven defendants in a trial with seventy counts at the beginning, thirty at the end, one of which was a conspiracy charge alleging eighty-four overt acts. The crimes alleged were *malum prohibitum*. None of the defendants could be accused of doing anything evil. If the laws they were alleged to have violated had not existed, the defendants could not have been accused of immorality.

All of this contributed to the inanity of the trial and the prosecution. Months were spent attempting to establish whether Father Quinones had shown someone a hole in the fence, whether Reverend Fife had told an agent what highway to take to get from one place to another, and whether Wendy Le Win knew the legal status of someone she was driving.

It was not just that a volume of charges had been laid and the defendants were a crowd. The triviality of the alleged offences made the whole trial seem vacuous. Of course, the Sanctuary trial was really about murder and torture, about life and death, and about refuge for those fleeing persecution. To an observer unaware of the trial's context, the only danger of death would seem to be death from boredom.

The prosecution succeeded in its strategy of getting the jury to focus on the trivial and ignore the tragedy of the refugee plight. Virtually any evidence indicating the real issues at hand was excluded as inadmissible. The jury developed an artificial perspective in which it was not allowed to consider the context in which the charges against the accused had been brought.

Reverend Fife's lawyer called the prosecution's case a patchwork of incidents. No written agreement of a conspiracy existed among the defendants. The prosecution presented a pattern drawn from a jumble of discrete events.

THE DEFENCE CASE

On the other side, the defence claimed the defendants were acting as isolated individuals or groups of individuals trying to help refugees. The only common contact they had was Jesus Cruz, the State infiltrator.

No witnesses were called to testify by the defence, not even the accused. Instead, counsel relied exclusively on the testimony of prosecution witnesses. Counsel also parcelled out arguments about various legal components of the charge. The lawyer for Fife, for instance, talked about conspiracy, a charge faced by all the accused. He argued that there was no conspiracy but only a similarity of intent and a variety of disparate acts. Although the defendants visited and supported refugees, they did not recruit them to come to the U.S.

In addition to focussing on specific arguments, defence counsel developed common themes. Each repeatedly raised the question of reasonable doubt. Each attacked the credibility of Cruz and pointed to the good character and motives of their own clients.

A contrast was made between the evil of the prosecution and the good of the defence: the deception of Cruz and the defendants' willingness to help refugees. This contrast inevitably got defence counsel into trouble with the prosecution and the judge, since the prosecution had only to prove an intent to commit the acts, not evil motives.

Yet, since the prosecution presented the accused as evil, the defence inevitably tried to exonerate the accused and present them as good, caring human beings.

For instance, Reno introduced evidence that several defendants had told refugees to say they were Mexicans if caught by the INS in the U.S. In response, the defence argued that no attempts had been made to mislead the INS on the immigration status of foreigners. The accused had not counselled undocumented foreigners to say they were Americans or had status in the U.S. Foreigners wanted to avoid deportation back to El Salvador or Guatemala, where they would be killed or tortured, not to stay in the U.S. through deception.

The prosecution objected to this line of argument. The possibility of refugees being killed or tortured in Central America had already been ruled legally irrelevant by the judge. Referring to the dangers faced by refugees back home was viewed as an effort to win the jury's sympathy in spite of the law.

PARTIALITY OF JUDGE CARROLL

Adding to defence counsel problems was the partiality of Judge Carroll. He favoured the prosecution over the defence. Judgement must be suspended for impartiality to prevail. In a jury case, where the jury acquits or convicts, the judge's duty is to come to no conclusion at any time regarding the innocence or guilt of the accused.

In that sense Carroll was a partial judge. On a number of occasions he manifested a belief in the guilt of the accused. He implied that Sanctuary is "for the birds", said that Sanctuary has no defence, asserted that the defendants had openly admitted guilt on television, and claimed that "everybody says they did it and we are proud we did it." His certainty of the defendants' guilt may have had an effect on the jury and on the rulings Carroll himself had to make.

It seemed that although Carroll believed the defendants were guilty, he was determined to give them a fair trial. However, it is not enough for a judge to espouse a determination to conduct a fair trial. Once he expresses an opinion on guilt, the very fairness he seeks becomes impossible.

OUTCOME OF THE TRIAL

Eight of the defendants were convicted and three, Corbett, MacDonald and Espinoza, were acquitted. Convictions of aiding unlawful entry against Father Quinones and Father Clark resulted in sentences of six months each. All other convictions resulted in sentences of five years each. All sentences were suspended — those convicted did not actually have to go to jail. However, if any one them is convicted again for a similar offence during a five-year period, the court could sentence the person to jail for the original offence. Suspended sentences thus serve as a form of intimidation to prevent continued involvement in the Sanctuary movement. The defendants, nonetheless, said they would continue to take part in the movement.

The Sanctuary trial also intimidated those who were acquitted. Nena MacDonald, who was acquitted, spent more time in Tucson defending herself against the charges than she did helping the Sanctuary movement. The trial was so lengthy and demanding it was an ordeal in itself. For an extended period of time, the accused were neither church workers nor volunteers, but defendants.

After the conviction, the defendants were eventually allowed to present their defences in court, to the judge. The eight convicted defendants then explained in court, for the first time, INS refugee practices and the suffering of Central American refugees. The suspended sentences handed out by the judge can be explained by the fact that, at the level of sentencing, motive was relevant at last.

The eight Sanctuary movement workers and leaders appealed their convictions. On March 30, 1989, the U.S. Court of Appeals for the Ninth Circuit rejected the appeals of the convicted Sanctuary defendants.

Prosecution of the Sanctuary movement activists should never have been launched. American government practices, policies and laws amount to forced return of refugees to El Salvador and Guatemala.

The Sanctuary movement created a hole in the system by giving to refugees what the United States government was denying. Prosecuting Sanctuary movement leaders was an attempt to close the gap, make forcible return more certain, and shut off a safety valve.

The U.S. government has every right to be concerned with what it views as violations of its own laws. That concern, however, should have manifested itself by removing conditions that led to the Sanctuary movement's creation, by providing protection to refugees, not by indicting the Sanctuary movement.

Whether the prosecution should have been launched is an altogether independent issue from whether the trial was balanced or whether the conviction was rightly made. Even if the trial were fair, even if the accused were justly convicted, the U.S. government could not justify the prosecution simply on that basis.

On the contrary, the convictions make the prosecution more problematic. If the accused had been acquitted, the Sanctuary movement would not have been as harmfully affected. Even if the court was correct to look at the acts of the accused in isolation from the plight of refugees, the U.S. administration cannot similarly isolate itself. It is accountable for its failure to implement the Refugee Convention. Prosecution of the Sanctuary movement is part of the failure.

Chapter 13

A CANADIAN SANCTUARY MOVEMENT?

Will Canada develop a sanctuary movement of its own? If sanctuary does develop, what will its legal status be? Violation of the Immigration Act does not, in itself, make a sanctuary movement illegal. The Immigration Act must stand the test of the Canadian Charter of Rights and Freedoms before those giving sanctuary can be prosecuted.

Although Canada has a different legal structure from the U.S. for refugees, the outcome is the same. Under the Refugee Reform Act, the Canadian government can send refugees to what the government says is a safe third country, which may ultimately return refugees back to the country of persecution. Because of mistakes the system generates, even without a safe third country list, real refugees may be sent back from Canada directly to danger.

Two Salvadorans, Ricardo S. and S.M., an Iranian, Nasrin Peiroo, and an Ethiopian, Hussein Mohamoud, were given Minister's Permits by the Immigration Minister after a nation wide campaign on their behalf. They were all refugee claimants rejected in apparent error. Others have not been so lucky. Chhinder Pal Bhattia was forcibly returned to India. He has since disappeared. Abdi Aden was forcibly returned to Somalia. He was imprisoned on his arrival in Somalia. Hillary Adilei was forcibly returned to Nigeria. He has never been seen since.[1]

THE NEED FOR A CANADIAN SANCTUARY MOVEMENT

Refugee assistance agencies may be tempted to act in contravention of the Canadian legislated system, although not for the same reasons as in the United States. In the U.S., the system is so corrupted by foreign policy considerations, asylum applications by Guatemalans and Salvadorans are virtually hopeless. Refugees from these countries are tempted to enter illegally and remain illegally underground. Those who want to help refugees assist them in avoiding contact with INS officers.

That temptation does not exist in Canada, even under the new legislation, in part because Canada's foreign policy interests are not as extensive as those in the U.S. Under Canada's old system, the Minister of Immigration decided refugee claims. That created a potential for political interference, and in some cases the reality of interference. Since 1982, however, the independence of the Refugee Status Advisory Committee (RSAC) from government has worked against the politicization of the system. Furthermore, the new system, at least structurally, appears less political than the old. The Minister no longer has a power of decision, just a power of representation.

Nonetheless, Canadians may be tempted to break the law. Reverend Peter Flynn is rector of St. Matthews Anglican Church in Winnipeg and member of the St. Matthews-Maryland United-St. Paul's Catholic Refugee Committee. He stressed the importance of activist work. "Ordinary people engaged in activism believe intensely in compassion toward refugees," he said. "It's like a ministry that they are called to."

Where would their commitment lead them? Flynn, speaking before the system had got well underway, would not speculate on how far church members would go. "We don't know what we'd do until the Department does something, like deport a genuine refugee," he said. "And that's the greatest danger of all. Anything could happen."

A Vigil Network has been established which operates through a "telephone tree" set up in cities and towns across Canada. When the network is advised a refugee is in immediate danger, each local or regional vigil group is notified of the appropriate action, and the groups in turn inform their members. The Vigil Network plans non-violent action such as vigils, demonstrations, rallies, telephone calls and telegrams to the government.

PROBLEMS WITH SPONSORSHIP

Sponsorship is the first course of action for refugee activists. Many sponsored refugees are accepted each year. For 1989, the Canadian government estimates in its *Annual Report to Parliament on Future Immigration Levels,* 10,000 privately sponsored refugees and members of designated classes will come to Canada.

Sponsorship is a two-step procedure. The refugee claimant makes a refugee claim at a Canadian visa office outside of Canada, and outside of his country of nationality. The sponsor submits a sponsorship undertaking at a Canadian immigration office in Canada. The Canadian sponsor may be a group of five individuals or a corporation.

For refugee claimants neither step is automatic. The refugee claimant has to go through a refugee determination at the visa office abroad. The sponsors have to satisfy the Canadian immigration office that they have the financial and human resources and expertise necessary to fulfill an undertaking to sponsorship. Seventy national organizations have signed umbrella sponsorship agreements with the government. A local chapter of one of these organizations may sponsor a refugee without a separate assessment of its ability to sponsor.

However, sponsorship is not a recourse when the person is still in his home country. Gerry Weiner, Canadian Minister of

State for Immigration, asked the churches why, if they are so concerned about helping refugees, they do not help bring over refugees from refugee camps. They do. In fact, churches have been generous and well-organized supporters of refugees from abroad. But the existence of refugees abroad is no excuse for refusing people who turn up on our doorstep.

Canada does allow citizens in the political prisoners and oppressed persons class to seek protection from persecution at a Canadian visa office in their home country. Citizens of Chile, El Salvador, Guatemala and Poland are currently in this class. In 1988, Canada admitted 1,407 people for landed immigrant status under the category of political prisoners and oppressed persons.*

Citizens of countries other than these four do not have this option open to them, and must approach a Canadian visa office stationed outside of their country of nationality to seek protection from persecution. Simply in order to get access to the Canadian refugee claims system abroad, refugee claimants must be able to get out of their home countries and into a third country. If no third country will accept them, direct flight to Canada is the only alternative.

Sponsorship of refugees is also not a viable recourse where speed is crucial. Some people are in such danger they simply cannot wait out the lengthy sponsorship process. The problem of delays can be particularly acute where people are seeking protection from persecution while they are still waiting in their home countries, i.e., people in the political prisoners and oppressed persons class.

Beatriz Marroquin of Guatemala was abducted in mid-November 1985 by armed men believed to be members of the Guatemalan security forces. On release, she applied for entry to Canada. The visitor's visa requirement imposed on Guatemala prevented her from simply boarding a plane to come to Canada.

---

* In 1988, Canada admitted, in the oppressed persons and political prisoners class, 210 persons from Guatemala, 1,150 from El Salvador, seven from Chile, and forty from Poland.

Ms. Marroquin applied for a Canadian visa and because of her case's urgency, received it quickly. Canadian officials processed her request within days rather than the normal period of several months. However, even a few days' delay proved fatal. In early December, Ms. Marroquin was abducted again, tortured and killed. She was found dead forty kilometres from Guatemala City with evidence of torture on her body.

Amnesty International argued that Canada's visa requirement for Guatemalan refugees had allowed death squads enough time to find the woman. If she had been able to leave Guatemala immediately, she would not have been abducted a second time. Amnesty had no complaint with the officials who handled her visa request. They acted expeditiously. The visa requirement itself was the problem.

Death squads do not wait for delays in the Canadian processing system. People in imminent danger need to come to Canada immediately, even if it means circumventing the sponsorship and visa process.

Further, a refugee who applies for sponsorship may still need to enter Canada illegally. Overseas refugee determination is so faulty that it is more in the nature of a lottery than a fair determination. If sponsorship is rejected by a visa office abroad, those concerned with the fate of refugees are unlikely to acquiesce in a negative determination. They will be tempted to help the refugees in whatever way they can.

INCENTIVES FOR ILLEGAL ENTRY

Another appeal to illegality arises when the Canadian inland system generates mistakes. Because the system makes mistakes easily and has virtually no capacity to correct them, genuine refugee claimants will be rejected by the system. People concerned with refugees will attempt to help these claimants avoid forcible return to the country of danger.

For persons who illegally enter Canada, safe third country eligibility screening would not apply. A person who sneaks across the border, or lies to get entry as a visitor, may be prosecuted, but he could not be put into safe third country eligibility screening. The law creates an incentive for violation.

Once a safe third country list is drawn up, refugees who enter Canada illegally would be better protected under the legislation than those who did not. Canadians concerned with the fate of refugees will have to ask themselves whether they want to aid refugees to circumvent safe third country eligibility screening. Do they want to give assistance as in the U.S. and declare sanctuary? Do they want to violate both the new legislation and the old in order to protect refugees?

Winn Leslie is a leader in Winnipeg's St. Ignatius Catholic Church Refugee Committee and Co-ordinator of the Manitoba Coalition for a Just Refugee Policy. Leslie said point blank: "If it ever comes down to a genuine refugee being turned back at the border, and facing deportation back to the country of danger, we would be prepared to break the laws."

Father Bert Foliot, also of Winnipeg's St. Ignatius Church, echoed activists' concerns that sanctuary in Canada would not be easy. "It's not like in the United States where refugees could fade into the woodwork or be hired illegally for cash crops," he said. Refugees in Canada require a Social Insurance Number to work, and authorization to go to school or receive medical care.

Sanctuary in Canada could be used as a temporary measure, according to activists in the refugee assistance movement. Nancy Pocock, a leader in the Quaker Committee for Refugees and member of the Inter-Church Toronto Affairs Council, said a sanctuary movement in Canada could not provide a permanent hiding place. "A lot of people are thinking about a sanctuary movement here, but I don't know that it's realistic at this stage."

Refugees could not work and would have to stay inside day and night. "We would have nowhere to send refugees that we protected in hiding," Pocock said. "The U.S. would send refugees up here in the old days and we handled them. Now, no country is willing to accept them."

The notion that Canada protected refugees in the old days is a bit of an illusion. The 1978 legislated system was unfair. The Supreme Court of Canada forced an improvement by requiring oral hearings. Other defects in the system were masked by an ever-growing backlog. The delays generated by the backlog provided haven for real refugees and abusive refugee claimants alike. The erroneous rejection of real refugees was not as common, partly because the old system, on balance, offered more procedural protection, and partly because the old system operated so slowly fewer decisions were being generated, correct or incorrect.

For now, Pocock said, assistance workers ought to continue to fight the government to get a decent refugee policy. "We have a cruel, cruel government. Why couldn't the government have granted amnesty to the refugees backlogged in the old system? These people are more and more discouraged day by day. They have wives and children in El Salvador. At long last some of them [refugees in backlog] got work permits. So why can't they just get on with their lives? The government has shown no humanity to these people."

MISPLACED SANCTUARY—TURKISH REFUGEES

In the summer of 1987, thirty-seven Turks who had come to Canada to work claimed refugee status to prolong their stay. This was the only route open to them to become eligible for work permits. When the Turks were rejected as refugees and ordered deported, they sought and were granted refuge in a church basement. Quebec Minister of Immigration Louise Robic supported the Turkish refugees' claim. "These people have been here for more than two years, they have found work, and started to learn the language. Some have even had babies in Canada," she said.

In the end, some of the Turks were allowed to stay in Canada on humanitarian grounds, while others were deported back to Turkey and applied to re-enter Canada from there.

Should churches offer refuge to every refugee who has gone through the refugee determination process and is now waiting deportation? Should local churches open their basements to these people just as the Montreal East End church did for the Turks? My own answer is that churches should not open their doors to every rejected claimant. This would be illegal, unwise and unnecessary under the new legislation.

Refugee claimants can be divided into three groups: refugees who meet the Refugee Convention definition because they are people with a well-founded fear of persecution, refugees who have fled generalized violence but are not the targets of individualized persecution, and economic refugees who move in order to better their economic conditions.

At international law, countries have a clear duty to protect Convention refugees. If states fail to protect these refugees, churches cannot be faulted for offering that protection. International law condones and arguably even requires such action.

Countries also have an arguable duty of protection to refugees fleeing generalized violence. At customary international law, states arguably have a duty of temporary humanitarian refuge to non-Convention refugees fleeing general violence. For the state to deny protection to those people is an arguable violation of international law. International law arguably condones offers of protection to those people by churches.

However, economic migrants are not covered by any international duty of protection. A state has no obligation to protect these claimants. If churches try to offer economic migrants protection against state authorities, international law cannot help, since the churches' actions are illegal by any standard.

The Turks were economic migrants who claimed refugee status in a ploy to allow them to stay and work. They fled neither individualized persecution nor generalized violence. Churches' offers of protection to the Turks had no legal foundation.

CONSEQUENCES OF SANCTUARY[†]

While the Canadian legislation is not identical to U.S. law, a refugee who enters Canada without reporting to an immigration officer is committing an offence, and so is anyone who aids him.

Further, any Canadian assisting a refugee without proper documentation to come to Canada is committing an offence. Genuine refugees almost never have proper documentation:

[†] See Chapter 9 for further discussion on legal consequences of helping refugees.

- A refugee who obtains a visitor's visa to Canada by posing as a visitor is guilty of misrepresentation or fraud.

- A refugee from a country with a visitor's visa requirement who does not have a visitor's visa lacks the proper documents and is in violation of the law.

- A refugee from a country without a visitor's visa requirement still has problems because he is considered an immigrant. Immigrants from all countries require visas to come to Canada.

The Refugee Deterrents and Detention Act penalizes helping refugees without documents who arrive in Canada with five- to ten-year prison sentences and fines up to $500,000. The new legislation also prohibits assisting undocumented refugees to report to authorities, knowingly contravening or aiding any person to contravene the Immigration Act, and aiding or abetting a person not in possession of a valid visa, passport or travel document.

Winn Leslie, of Winnipeg's St. Ignatius Catholic Church Refugee Committee, is adamant activists will not back down in face of the new legislation. "C-84 provisions certainly strike fear in me, but won't stop us from protecting refugees," she said. In the past, her group regularly brought undocumented Central American refugees from Grand Forks, North Dakota to the Canadian border at Emerson, Manitoba. Once at the border they applied for refugee status.

Like refugee groups across the country, Leslie suspects her committee will be more cautious, but not let up. Her committee is now concerned with counselling refugees in the U.S. who may not have proper documents on how to make a claim in Canada.

AVAILABLE DEFENCES

How would a Canadian sanctuary movement fare in court? For one, the movement could challenge whether the provisions that generate the offences are constitutional. If provisions under the amended statutes contravene the Charter and international law, then those who comply with the legislation are in fact legally disobedient. Those who follow the requirements of the Charter and international law instead of the legislation are legally obedient.

For example, if the safe third country rule is brought into effect and found to violate the Charter by the courts, then the provision will be of no effect. Helping to violate that rule would not be illegal. A sanctuary movement could also challenge whether criminalizing aid to refugees is constitutional.

The government has a responsibility to comply with its international obligations set out in the Refugee Convention which it has signed. Canadian legislation must be interpreted, if at all possible, so as to be consistent with international law and Canada's international obligations. In keeping with the Refugee Convention, Canada should not prosecute those who protect refugees.

The Canadian Charter of Rights and Freedoms guarantees the right to life, liberty and security of the person and the right not to be deprived of these rights, except in accordance with the principles of fundamental justice. Whatever the scope of the phrase "fundamental justice", and there has been much debate about its meaning, one point is clear: deprivation of life, liberty or security of the person in violation of law is fundamentally unjust. An illegal detention is an unjust detention.

And that is the only point that needs to be made to demonstrate the fundamental injustice of prosecution of Sanctuary defendants, because such a prosecution would be a violation of international law.

Another possible defence has to do with a rule of state responsibility drafted by the UN International Law Commission. The rule says the conduct of an individual, not acting on behalf of the state,[2] shall not be considered as an act of the state. According to this rule, the actions of a private individual do not implicate Canada internationally or put Canada at fault.

However, a state breaches its international obligations if it takes a complacent attitude to the individual's wrongful action. A state is internationally responsible where it has not done everything in its power to prevent the act.

I suggest that it follows logically that just as a state must prevent its citizens from acting in conflict with one of the state's international obligations, so a state must not prevent its citizens from conforming with an international obligation of the state. A state is internationally responsible where it has hindered the rightful act of the private individual.

A Canadian sanctuary movement that is helping refugees is actually helping Canada adhere to its international obligations toward refugees. By prosecuting individuals who provide sanctuary, the Canadian government would be violating its international obligations.

Canadians who help a refugee coming directly from a country where his life or freedom would be threatened have an additional defence. The Refugee Convention includes a provision prohibiting penalties for illegal entry or presence of refugees. This provision protects not only refugees themselves, but also those who assist refugees.

For a Canadian sanctuary movement to be able to use this defence, the refugee must have presented himself without delay to immigration authorities[3]— not necessarily immediately, but within a period of time which is reasonable under the circumstances. A refugee can meet this requirement even if he is apprehended before he has had a chance to give himself up.[4]

THE DEFENCE OF NECESSITY

A sanctuary defendant in Canada could also use the defence of necessity, which is part of both international law and ordinary Canadian criminal law. In the war crimes trial of Friedrich Glick and five others before the U.S. Military Tribunal at Nuremberg, three of the defendants, Otto Steinbrinck, Odilo Burkart and Konrad Kaletsch, successfully invoked the defence of necessity under international law.[5] Although they were charged with being accessories to the use of slave labour, the use of prisoners of war in the manufacture of munitions, the tribunal acquitted them, holding that it was futile and dangerous to object to government orders. Any act appearing to obstruct or retard the war economy programmes of the Reich was considered sabotage and could result in severe penalties, sometimes death sentences.

Under domestic law, a defendant in a criminal case may be acquitted even if he committed the proscribed acts with sound state of mind, if he had a reasonable belief that his conduct was necessary to prevent some greater harm to himself or others. Members of a Canadian sanctuary movement might argue that they acted out of a reasonable belief that their actions directly prevented bodily harm to refugees.

The prosecution would no doubt point out a detailed administrative and legal process for reviewing a person's claim can result in claimants obtaining lawful refugee status. True, but refugees passing through listed intermediary countries would not be given protection by Canada. And the procedure itself is so faulty, it is impossible to have confidence in the results.

A judge does not have to decide in a sanctuary case whether the accused are exonerated by the necessity defence, only whether the jury could consider such a defence. In a number of U.S. protest cases where the judge left the necessity defence to the jury, the accused were acquitted. That happened in cases about accused protesting military aid to El Salvador,[6] deprivations of human rights in South Africa,[7] Navy participation in nuclear weapons proliferation,[8] and CIA recruitment at the University of Massachusetts.[9] The protests themselves involved some form of illegality, typically trespass.

Linking the allegedly illegal act and the harm to be prevented is a good deal more remote in protest cases than in refugee cases. Protest has only a speculative and uncertain connection with ending military aid to El Salvador, human rights deprivations in South Africa and so on. A sanctuary movement protects refugees more directly and effectively. It doesn't just protest the government's failure to protect refugees; it provides the very protection the government neglects to give. It does not simply influence, but acts directly to prevent harm.

FREEDOM OF RELIGION DEFENCE

Freedom of religion is an international standard and a domestic Canadian standard. It is guaranteed by the Universal Declaration of Human Rights,[10] the International Covenant on Civil and

227

Political Rights,[11] which Canada has signed and ratified, the U.N. Declaration on Religious Intolerance,[12] and the Helsinki Accord.[13] Freedom of religion is also guaranteed by the Canadian Constitution.

Freedom of religion is not just freedom of conscience or belief. It is also freedom to practice one's religion.[14] It encompasses more than prayer and piety. Religion is charity — helping people. To the clergy, every human being is made in the image of God. Promoting human rights is doing God's work.

Helping refugees is part of a sanctuary clergy's religious duties since the sanctuary concern for refugees is a human rights concern. Sanctuary is offered so that refugees can avoid being forcibly returned and subjected to human rights violations at home. The threat of prosecution only makes the religious work, the practice of the sanctuary clergy's religions, more difficult.

When sanctuary workers help persons fleeing religious persecution, they are working even more directly in line with their religious duties. Victims of religious persecution include the Bahai in Iran, or Ahmadis (a Muslim sect rejected by mainstream Muslims) in Pakistan.

Members of a sanctuary movement prosecuted for helping refugees cannot fully enjoy the freedom of religion supposedly guaranteed by international and Canadian law.

RIGHT TO PRIVATE DEFENCE

The Canadian Charter of Rights and Freedoms is subject to the rule of law. The rule of law is a standard or test by which laws themselves can be assessed. The rule of law means laws are not to be applied arbitrarily, but rather applied equally to all. When the rule of law is violated, fundamental justice is denied.

It is arbitrary when one law is applied and another is not, when the inculpatory provisions of a law are applied and the exculpatory provisions are not. For instance, the law of murder includes the right of self-defence. It would be arbitrary to apply the law of murder without regard to the right of self-defence. That would be a violation of the rule of the law, and a violation of fundamental justice. Yet prosecution of a sanctuary movement is like that.

In the criminal law, there is not only a right of self-defence, but also a right to defend others. If you defend somebody against a would-be murderer and in the process use force against the perpetrator, you can claim the right of private defence. You are justified in using reasonable force in defence of the victim because there is a general liberty to prevent an offence from occurring.[15]

That is really all a sanctuary movement does. Its members try to protect refugees from forcible return to the country of persecution. International law says the refugees are entitled to protection. Canadian immigration laws may say that rejected claimants must be returned and that it is an offence to prevent their return. But it is as arbitrary for a court to look at the immigration offence without regard to the international duty of protection as it is for a court to look at a murder charge without regard to the right of self-defence. If sanctuary defendants were to be prosecuted for an immigration offence without regard to the fact that they are attempting to bring Canada into compliance with its international obligations, the rule of law would be mocked and abandoned.

THE NUREMBERG DEFENCE

Even if Canadian law would lead to a conviction in a sanctuary trial, there is an additional international law perspective. Individuals are bound by international law. Defence counsel for Friedrick Glick and five others before the U.S. Military Tribunal at Nuremberg, in the trial previously mentioned, argued that the accused were not subject to international law because they held no public office. The Court rejected this defence of Glick and the others on the ground that "acts adjudged criminal when done by an officer of the government are criminal also when done by private individuals."[16]

International obligations binding upon individuals must be carried out, even if it means violating a state law or directive.[17] Anyone who knows of illegal activity and has an opportunity to do something about it is a potential criminal under international law unless the person takes affirmative action to prevent the commission of the crime.[18] Because individuals are responsible

The Nuremberg defence is a second order defence, and requires a prior finding of breach of international law. Disobeying state directives is justified if the state acts illegally. In a sanctuary case, the state activity would be illegal if it results in forcible return of refugees to intermediate countries, whether they would be protected there or not, or forcible return directly to the country of danger. This defence assumes that what the accused did was illegal according to Canadian law. The action becomes legal only under international law put against Canadian law.

Not every violation of domestic law in the name of international law justifies invoking the Nuremberg defence. If a person protesting against nuclear war violates local laws of trespass, the person cannot raise the Nuremberg principles in his defence. Abiding by trespass laws does not mean approval of the state's nuclear war strategy, even if we assume that strategy violates international law. There must be some nexus between the local law disobeyed and the local law violating international standards.

A sanctuary movement would not simply be violating an extraneous law in order to protest Canadian violation of international refugee law. A sanctuary movement would violate the very law that in turn violated international standards. So, for such a movement, the Nuremberg defence could be invoked.

PART FOUR

INTERNATIONAL RESPONSE TO REFUGEE PROTECTION

Chapter 14

EUROPE'S DENIAL OF PROTECTION TO REFUGEES

There are more refugees in the world today than the countries of refuge are prepared to accept. Yet governments are tied down by the Refugee Convention with a binding commitment that says they have to accept the refugees. Signatories to the Convention have found a way out of the dilemma by removing procedural protections such as appeal, access to counsel of choice, or even access to the system for refugees arriving in their territory. All countries with refugee determination systems are caught up in the game of competitive destruction of procedural safeguards.

If every country took its fair share of the refugee burden, then fair systems could prevail in all of them. Instead, as one country removes procedural protection and decreases its refugee intake, other countries are forced to take the overflow.

These countries, in turn, have pressure put on them to reduce protections in their system.

DESTRUCTION OF PROCEDURAL SAFEGUARDS

Each resettlement country has destroyed procedural protections in its system to produce the same result: a denial of protection to genuine refugees. An examination of seven Western European countries reveals a trend toward a world-wide "closing of the doors" to refugees. Not surprisingly, many countries employ the same tactics to eat away at procedural safeguards for refugees. Western European and North American countries share a zeal in chiselling away fairness in their refugee systems.

ITALY

Structural discrimination occurs when refugees from some countries are allowed access to the refugee system while others are not. Italy still takes advantage of an anachronistic option of the Refugee Convention allowing signatories to stipulate that only refugees from Europe can benefit from the Convention and Protocol,[1] even though European refugees are now only a small part of the world refugee outflow. On occasion Italy has admitted non-European refugees for resettlement, but these refugees have no general right to claim refugee status there. The Italian Constitution of 1947 grants aliens denied democratic liberties the right of asylum. However, no procedures are in place to implement this constitutional right. Non-European refugee claimants are referred to the UNHCR representative in Italy, and if the UNHCR representative recognizes them as refugees they are permitted to remain, pending resettlement in another country.

FRANCE

In France, decisions by the Office Francais de Protection des Refugies et Apatrides (OFPRA) may be made without oral hearings. OFPRA may reject a claimant after considering his application form, with or without an interview. OFPRA will always grant a claimant's request for an interview. However, by no means are all refugee claimants, even all refused claimants, interviewed.

If OFPRA does not notify a refugee claimant within four months of filing the claim, the silence is considered an implicit rejection of the claim. The claimant is entitled to appeal this implicit rejection within one-month of the four-month expiry period. A person who must appeal without notification of a decision is at an even greater disadvantage in arguing his appeal than a person who is given a decision but no reasons. A claimant may await the Office's decision, even if it takes more than four months, and then appeal.

At the appeal level, the Commission will question the foreigner, but does not provide interpreters. A foreigner who does not understand the proceedings is, in effect, denied an oral hearing. One observer was struck by the clear lack of under-standing on the part of some aliens as to what was being asked of them.

Discriminatory barriers in France include the failure of the OFPRA to present objections to the claimant and give him an opportunity to respond. As a result, there is a high reversal rate on appeal, and a high rate of revocation of the original decision once an appeal is launched. The Commission reversed twelve percent of OFPRA decisions on appeal in 1982. As well, OFPRA revoked its own decisions in thirteen percent of 1982 cases once an appeal was filed. A claimant finds out the objections to his claim and has a chance to respond only after it has been rejected. Many of the claimants' responses are obvi-ously satisfactory to authorities and cause them to reverse their decisions immediately.

Because of a lack of structured training programmes, OFPRA officers are uninformed on human rights developments abroad. OFPRA has no documentation centre of its own to compile data on refugee-producing countries.

Decision-makers are not independent of government moti-vations. The director of OFPRA is a career foreign service officer appointed by the Minister of Foreign Affairs. OFPRA officers serve under one-year contracts at the Director's discre-tion. OFPRA is considered independent from government, but is overseen by a council stacked with government representa-tives. Government officials admit that they occasionally ask

OFPRA to accept a claimant expeditiously or to delay processing a claim.

Changes in recognition rates have followed political shifts. Since President Francois Mitterand took power in 1981, OFPRA has granted refugee status to a substantially higher percentage of Haitian claimants, up to sixty percent in 1981, and increasing in 1982 to ninety percent.

SWEDEN

Sweden uses a manifestly unfounded claims system as a threshold requirement. The Aliens Police interview the claimant, and the Immigration Board usually talks only to interviewing policemen by phone. If they find the claim to be manifestly unfounded, the matter is closed and the claimant is expelled.

The 1983 report of the Swedish Committee on Immigration and Immigrant Policy recommended that the Immigration Board publish a code of regulations, including guidelines for deciding that a claim is manifestly unfounded. Outside of large cities, the interviewing officer is not a full-time specialist in refugee cases. Aliens Police officers have little knowledge of human rights conditions in origin countries.

Restricted access to counsel is a typical problem of refugee systems at the early, administrative stages of the proceedings. Once a refugee claimant gets to court or to quasi-judicial proceedings, access to counsel is usually not a problem. A claimant in Sweden is not entitled to counsel when his claim is being determined as manifestly unfounded. Only if he passes this initial hurdle, and his reasons for requesting status are not considered to be manifestly unfounded, would the refugee claimant be eligible for legal counsel.

The Swedish system suffers from fragmentation as well. Fragmentation of the determination system brings about a denial of an opportunity to respond. One official interviews, another decides. The claimant has an opportunity to respond to the interviewer, but not the deciding official.

If a claimant convinces the Swedish authorities his claim is not manifestly unfounded, then he is interviewed in detail by the Aliens Police. The Immigration Board decides the claim by taking into account a report of the interview, and other information such as human rights reports from the Swedish Ministry of Foreign Affairs, without giving the claimant an opportunity to comment.

Under the Swedish Aliens Act of 1980, a refugee claimant is denied the right to an oral hearing. An oral hearing may be granted on request, but requests are seldom successful. Appeals are administrative only. A claimant seeking an appeal has access to the Immigrations and Equality Division of the Ministry of Labour, not the court. At best, the claimant may be re-interviewed by the Aliens Police. A claimant at the border whose claim is determined to be manifestly unfounded, however, can be expelled even if he has submitted an appeal.

The Immigration and Equality Division has been criticized for not considering the facts of refugee claims cases. Different decisions have been made for identical situations. An executive committee, made up primarily of Members of Parliament appointed by government, heads the Immigration Board. The Board is partially autonomous from the Swedish government. It is not answerable to any ministry of the government, although it is answerable to its executive committee. As well, the Board's Director-General chairs the executive committee. While the Swedish government says the committee membership is politically balanced, the Board itself (other than the executive committee) consists of civil servants handling all immigration matters.

In Sweden, limited reasons are given for negative decisions. The applicant may be told that he does not fulfill the criteria for refugee status, but not be told which criteria. The government has developed biases based on a claimant's country of origin. For instance, a Turkish applicant has difficulty in being granted refugee status, while a Polish applicant has a good chance.

The Swedish government Committee on Immigration and Immigrant Policy recommended in 1983 that "doubtful cases be treated generously." It proposed guidelines for the Immigration Board, and recommended asylum applicants be given the benefit of the doubt. But no such guideline is on the Swedish books.

SWITZERLAND

Switzerland enforces a manifestly unfounded claims system similar to Sweden for port of entry or border claimants. The interviewing border guard discusses the merits of the claim with the Federal Police Office over the telephone. If the Federal Police Office, the immigration enforcement branch of government, considers the claim manifestly unfounded, the claimant will be refused entry to the country.

As well, inland claimants can be denied an oral hearing for manifestly unfounded claims. A claim is considered manifestly unfounded if the country of origin currently respects human rights, even though a particular individual may have a well-founded fear of persecution in a country generally deferential to human rights. Further, the person may have fled the country some time in the past, when it was guilty of human rights violations, although it now observes human rights. Compelling reasons may remain for refusing to return due to the previous persecution.

The UNHCR has recommended that a claim be considered manifestly unfounded only if it is clearly fraudulent or not related to refugee criteria. None of the systems examined throughout Western Europe has incorporated the UNHCR proposed safeguards in its laws.

Switzerland's Federal Police are faulted for handing down poorly reasoned opinions on claims. Refugee protection organizations have also criticized the government for giving preferential treatment to applicants from Eastern Europe. The government responded, not by recognizing more non-East European applicants, but rather by dropping dramatically the rate of recognition for East European applicants.

While the bona fide claims system is not fragmented as in so many other countries, the Swiss manifestly unfounded determination process is split between two decision-makers. For port of entry claims, the border guard interviews and the Federal Police Office decides, usually without even speaking to the claimant.

Normally, for inland manifestly unfounded claims, the cantonal authority interviews, and again the Federal Police decide. The Federal Police may question the claimant in person or by phone, but in most cases they decide without interviewing the claimant.

Interviewing officers in all but the major Swiss cities do not specialize in refugee cases. Officers have little knowledge of the political situation in countries of origin and no systematic access to country information.

In Switzerland, as in Sweden, access to counsel is denied at the border when the claim is being considered as manifestly unfounded or bona fide. Some Members of Parliament proposed in 1980 that claimants at the border be granted counsel. The proposal was defeated in Parliament.

The Swiss government allows claimants an administrative appeal to the Federal Department of Justice and Police, but no appeal to the courts.

UNITED KINGDOM

Access to counsel for refugee claimants in the United Kingdom is limited. Legal counsel may attend the initial refugee interview, but counsel is not allowed to participate. Counsel can request the interviewer to put specific questions to the claimant, but cannot ask questions of the claimant himself.

In refugee systems throughout Western Europe, the decision-making authority consults Departments of External Affairs reports about human rights violations in the claimant's country without giving the claimant a chance to comment on these reports and their accuracy.

The United Kingdom's determination process is split for all claims. An Immigration Officer interviews, the Home Office decides. The claimant has no opportunity to rectify an error of the deciding authority because the Immigration Office's interview report is not submitted to the claimant for correction. The deciding authority considers other information supplied by the U.K. Foreign Office without advising the claimant.

Countries with fragmented determination systems obviously do not have oral hearings. If a second level of determination is offered, an oral hearing might be guaranteed. However, usually that is not the case.

239

In the United Kingdom, a two-level appeal system is in place for claimants refused an extension of their temporary admission and claimants ordered deported. Claimants in these two categories can apply for asylum or a stay of the deportation order if they would have to be returned to a country of persecution where their life or freedom would be threatened according to Convention criteria. In these appeals, the immigration adjudicator and the Immigration Tribunal do not merely defer to governmental determination on refugee status. They make their own determinations.

However, claimants have no right to an oral hearing at either level of appeal. At the first level, an immigration adjudicator may determine the appeal without a hearing if he believes no issue of significance will arise, and that written statements in support of an appeal do not warrant a hearing.

At the second level, the Immigration Appeals Tribunal hears refugee appeals with leave of either the adjudicator or the Tribunal. In every case, the appellate authority must reject applications for leave without a hearing, unless special circumstances render a hearing desirable.

The English Court of Appeal ruled against a mandatory oral hearing on the application for leave. The Court rejected the contention that in every case where asylum is claimed, unless the claim is obviously unfounded or the applicant has had an oral hearing before the adjudicator, "special circumstances" exist justifying an oral hearing on the leave application. However, if leave is granted, normally an oral hearing is held.

Despite the need for claimants to be given the benefit of the doubt, and the UNHCR Executive Committee recommendation to this effect, this standard of fairness is commonly denied.

Until a December, 1987 decision of the House of Lords, the normal civil standard was used in the U.K.: the claimant had to establish on a balance of probabilities that his claim was well founded by proving it was more probable than not that he would be persecuted. As well, the burden of proof is on the claimant to show no country will accept him other than the one in which he fears persecution.

If the claimant wishes to provide details at his appeal for which he was not asked at his original interview, because he was not asked, the appellate authority will frequently suspect the additional information. Few appeals are successful.

United Kingdom appellate authorities have been criticized for failing to appreciate the difficulties claimants have in providing evidence. A person may have met the burden of proof, although gaps remain in the evidence.

Several commentators have admonished the balance of probabilities test as inappropriate for asylum-seekers. They petitioned that it be replaced with the House of Lords test applied for fugitive offenders. The House of Lords has said that a court should not ignore the possibility of danger merely because the odds of it happening are fractionally less than even. For example, if there is a thirty percent rather than a fifty-one percent chance of danger, the danger must still be taken into account. The test, instead, should be whether a "reasonable chance" or "a serious possibility" exists that the person might be punished. The lesser degree of likelihood is appropriate because of the gravity of consequences of error. An error may result in death.

This principle was initially applied to fugitives who might be punished in their country of origin for reasons of race, religion, nationality or political opinion. In December, 1987, the House of Lords accepted the analogy between refugee claimants and fugitive offenders. It held that for refugee claimants, too, this lesser degree of likelihood is appropriate.

Lack of independence in determining refugee claims is a universal problem. In the United Kingdom, officers in the Immigration and Nationality Department of the Home Office carry out the interview and make the decision. The Department has overall responsibility for immigration enforcement.

Like many other countries, the British local officer who interviews is not a refugee specialist. He is typically a junior officer without any training in refugee law or human rights violations abroad. Interpreters are often not used. Questions relevant to assess immigrants are covered thoroughly, but inquiries pertinent to refugee status are given cursory treatment. The deciding officer has no formal training for his job.

Despite the seriousness of the refugee decision, many countries such as the U.K. deny port of entry claimants the right to appeal. According to the Immigration Act, a person is not entitled to appeal a refusal of leave to enter so long as he is in the U.K., unless given prior entry clearance. Yet an appeal abroad is of little use to the claimant.

In September, 1987, Sivakumaran and five others from Sri Lanka applied for refugee status on arrival in the United Kingdom. All were refused and returned to Sri Lanka in February, 1988. Lawyers for five of the six filed appeals after removal.

Amnesty International reported that two of the six were arrested and tortured following their return. A third was detained for three months and ill-treated. Another was rounded up and held for ten hours.

An adjudicator allowed the appeals in March, 1989 and ordered the five be returned to the U.K. "with minimum delay." In April, 1989, the Immigration Appeals Tribunal upheld this ruling. In May, 1989, the High Court of the U.K. gave the U.K. authorities leave to have judicial review of this decision and suspended return of the five Sri Lankans until the review process was completed. As of writing, over a year after their removal, the five remain in Sri Lanka.

Those who entered illegally cannot appeal denials of refugee status. An illegal immigrant can be removed from the U.K. with a direction for removal. A deportation order is not necessary. The claimant may appeal the decision that he is illegal, but only after he has left the country. In this appeal, he cannot raise the issue of refugee status.

Finally, a claimant convicted of an offence punishable with imprisonment and recommended for deportation by the sentencing court cannot appeal a negative refugee determination. He has the right to appeal his conviction and sentence within the criminal courts system, but not the right to raise his refugee claim. He has a right to appeal a direction for removal to a particular destination, but he can argue only for removal to another country, not for the right to stay. If no other country will take him, he has no argument at all.

In the U.K., overstaying is an offence punishable with imprisonment. So, if a claimant overstays, he could lose his right to appeal his refugee claim. The British courts have said, in the case of a port of entry refusal, that judicial review by the courts is available because the right of appeal to the immigration adjudicator and immigration tribunal is useless.

Presumably, the courts would also consider appropriate a judicial review of refused claims made by illegal entrants or by entrants recommended for deportation by a criminal court judge in sentencing. But judicial review requires leave of the court, and is rarely granted to a refugee claimant.It is unlikely such a leave would be given. The Court of Appeal has said :

> "The courts are not concerned with the political systems which operate in other countries. The court has no knowledge of those matters over and above that which is common knowledge; and that may be wrong. It would be undesirable for this court or any other court to express views about regimes which exist outside the United Kingdom."

Another difficulty refugee claimants face is the Home Office's refusal to gives reasons for a rejected claim. An unfavourable decision says the applicant has failed to show he qualified for asylum. If the applicant has a right of appeal, and does appeal, the Home Office will deliver a scantily detailed explanatory statement.

FEDERAL REPUBLIC OF GERMANY

Like its neighbouring countries, the Federal Republic of Germany uses the concept of manifestly unfounded claims. If the Federal Agency rejects a refugee claim as manifestly unfounded at the first level of determination, the claimant is served with a deportation order at the same time as the decision on his claim comes down. The claimant may appeal the deportation order to an Administrative Court judge in a summary proceeding, but a further appeal is not permitted.

A claimant rejected by the Federal Agency for reasons other than a manifestly unfounded claim is told he must leave. He is issued a deportation order only in the event of non-compliance. The claimant may apply for a full review by a panel of Administrative Court judges. If unsuccessful, he may go on to the Administrative Court of Appeal with leave.

The Federal Republic of Germany also has a fragmented system. Before the present law came into effect in 1982, thousands of claims were denied without an interview by the Federal Agency, based on a claimant's statement to local authorities. The 1982 law provides that one Federal Agency officer interviews at the first level of determination, another decides. The deciding authority also considers information not communicated to the claimant, including Foreign Ministry reports.

Refugee claimants in Germany do not have the right to oral hearings. When the claim is not considered to be manifestly unfounded, and a full review is granted, the Administrative Court may request that the claimant appear before the Court for questioning. The claimant is not entitled, as of right, to appear before the court. As a result, an increasing number of determinations are based solely on a written report.

In virtually every country, the immigration department, or the external affairs department, or both, are involved in the refugee determination process. West Germany is no exception. The Minister of the Interior appoints the director of the Federal Agency that decides refugee claims. Agency interviewers and decision-makers may be appointed for one-year terms. Opponents of this system have claimed that if the one-year appointees do not follow government policy, they can be removed. Civil servants hoping to advance their careers may have difficulty ignoring the Minister's political stand.

Refugee interviewers in West Germany also mix refugee work with other work. Most West German Federal Agency refugee claimant interviewers have no special qualifications. They are given training sessions after they have begun work.

When procedures are faulty, a scope for bias exists. Unfair procedures lead to unfair results. Critics have charged that West Germany selectively applies restrictions in favour of Eastern European applicants and against applicants from countries such as Turkey and Pakistan. An upsurge in xenophobia — fear of foreigners — has affected non-European seekers of political asylum.

In 1980 the recognition rate for asylum applicants in West Germany from Eastern Europe was 51.8 percent. For applicants from Asia it was 21.8 percent. Two years later, 40.8 percent of Eastern European asylum applicants were accepted, and 3.8 percent of Asian refugee claimants.

BELGIUM

Access to counsel is denied, once again, this time in Belgium. Prior to July, 1987, claimants were denied access to counsel at the initial interview that determined the application's admissibility. Admissibility was recognized, depending, *inter alia*, on whether the claimant had made his claim promptly on arrival in Belgium. The Aliens Office interview did, on occasion, inquire into the claim's nature, though it had nothing to do with admissibility determination. Results of this inquiry were available to the refugee decision-maker, who was the United Nations High Commission for Refugees representative in Belgium.

Under the new system the border police make a summary determination of claims. The claimant generally has no access to a lawyer or to any other type of advocate to help present his case, and is not entitled to an interpreter.

Until July, 1987, the UNHCR representative decided refugee claims in Belgium. Critics claimed the representative's independence was compromised because the UNHCR depends heavily on government financial support and co-operation. The member governments of the UNHCR are often governments of countries from which claimants are fleeing.

Belgium denies appeals to refugee claimants. Until July, 1987, Belgium said that because the refugee decision was made by an international official, the UNHCR representative, it was outside the jurisdiction of Belgian courts. The UNHCR official could have re-opened a case and sought the advice of UNHCR headquarters.

In July, 1987, the system changed, but the lack of appeal remained. Under the prior system, refugee claimants enjoyed universal access. Any claimant at the Belgian border could enter and make a claim. Under the new system, a person can be turned away at the border for a number of different reasons, including a manifestly unfounded claim or a judgement that the entry of a refugee is a threat to public order.

From this decision, no appeal to the courts is allowed. The claimant can only apply for administrative review from the Council of State, but cannot remain in Belgium pending this review. A claimant can stay only if he can persuade a local judge that his life or liberty will be in danger back home. Appeal from the local judge's decision is not possible.

Occasionally, no reasons are given for rejecting a claim. More often, only scanty reasons are given. In Belgium prior to July, 1987, the UNHCR representative gave no reasons for a negative decision. Nor did the claimant or his lawyer have complete access to the file on which the decision was based. The new law does not provide for informing a claimant, rejected by a border guard after summary proceedings, of the basis for the decision denying entry.

While proper procedures can prevent the exercise of bias, Belgium's unfair procedures foster discrimination. In Belgium, under the old system, government authorities were reported to have reached a tacit understanding with the UNHCR that Zairois were not to be recognized as refugees. For political and economic reasons, Belgium does not want to incur the anger of the present regime governing Zaire, a former Belgian colony. There remain substantial economic ties between Belgium and Zaire. The countries are on friendly terms politically. UNHCR representatives in Belgium presumed that Zairois were not bona fide refugees.

Under the new system now in place, no agreement with the UNHCR is necessary. Since border police can summarily exclude claimants from entry without an effective appeal, the government is free to implement this Zairois policy on its own.

Convention signatories must institute fair determination systems if they are to uphold their professed commitment to human rights. Denial of fairness is denial of a human right. The legal requirements of fairness or natural justice or fundamental justice are often found in the constitutionally entrenched statements of human rights in the countries examined. Imposition of unfair standards in refugee systems must be halted if refugees are to be protected. Otherwise, genuine refugees will be refused asylum, and returned to their home countries of persecution.

Chapter 15

CANADA AND THE UNITED NATIONS HIGH COMMISSION FOR REFUGEES

The government of Canada has the distinction of being a leader among resettlement countries. In the past Canada set an example of protection. Now Canada is setting a negative example. The Refugee Deterrents and Detention Act contains generalized detention provisions, offences for helping refugees come to Canada, and widened powers of search and seizure. Combined with the Refugee Reform Act's denial of appeal to correct errors of fact and commitment to return refugee claimants by group to countries of first asylum, Canada is set apart from other resettlement countries. While one country or another has accepted some of these Draconian measures, only Canada has adopted the full set. Canada stands alone among all countries with established refugee determination systems in denying the possibility of appeal on the merits to correct erroneous refusals of refugee status.

UNITED NATIONS HIGH COMMISSION FOR REFUGEES

The international community established the United Nations High Commission for Refugees on January 1, 1951 for a period of three years to aid refugees and displaced persons in Europe who had fled their home countries during and after the Second World War. Since then, the mandate of the UNHCR has been extended to cover refugees around the world. Its mandate has been renewed every five years, and it now cares for twelve million refugees. It is financed mainly by governments. Part of its administrative expenses are borne by the regular budget of the United Nations.

The head of the UNHCR is a High Commissioner, an international civil servant. The High Commissioner is elected by the UN General Assembly on the nomination of the UN Secretary General. Since January 1, 1986 Jean Pierre Hocke has served as High Commissioner.

The UNHCR has two main functions: protecting refugees and finding durable solutions for them. Durable solutions can take one of three forms: voluntary repatriation to the country fled, local integration in the country of first asylum, or resettlement in a third country other than the country fled and the country of first asylum. Until a durable solution is found, the UNHCR provides both emergency aid and long-term assistance to refugees. Emergency relief includes water, food, shelter, and medical aid. Longer-term assistance includes education and the introduction of income generating activities.

The Executive Committee of the UNHCR — an advisory body of forty-three states — gives guidance to the High Commissioner. The Executive Committee also approves the assistance programmes of the UNHCR and sets financial targets for their implementation.

Canada, a member of the Executive Committee, has used its membership on the Committee to weaken refugee protection standards, authorize its own actions, and encourage other states to follow its example.

Unlike state members of the United Nations Commission for Human Rights, state members of the High Commission for

Refugees are not elected for a fixed term. Thus, there is no mechanism for reviewing the membership of an individual country which may have an abysmal record with respect to refugees. Canada has sat on the UNHCR Executive Committee since its inception in 1959, even though Canada did not ratify the Refugee Convention until 1969.

The UNHCR committee system leaves itself open to abuse. Turkey and Iran, which are both Executive Committee members, themselves create refugee outflows by violating human rights. Their presence on the Committee must be questioned.

But among resettlement states Canada has been a lead abuser. In recent years at the United Nations, Canada has favoured weakened international refugee protection standards at the same time as it has introduced its own immigration legislation, the Refugee Reform Act and the Refugee Deterrents and Detention Act.

THE CCR CHALLENGE

I attended the 39th Executive Committee of the UNHCR meeting in Geneva, Switzerland in October, 1988 as a Canadian Council for Refugees (CCR) delegate. Non-governmental organizations can observe Executive Committee proceedings and submit statements. Canada's harsh new legislation and other initiatives prompted the Canadian Council for Refugees to question Canada's membership on the Executive Committee.

The United Nations system is universal and should remain so. Human rights violators and states generating mass exoduses are properly part of the system. However, the Executive Committee of the UNHCR is not universal. It does not include all U.N. member states. Membership should be linked to a state's behaviour.

The CCR condemned the Canadian legislation for denying an appeal on fact, allowing access to courts of law by leave rather than by right, and providing for forced return of refugee claimants by group to third countries. These provisions violate both the Refugee Convention and past Executive Committee conclusions.

The CCR pointed to an Executive Committee conclusion of 1979 that asylum should not be refused solely on the ground it could be sought from another state.[1] Also, according to the Refugee Convention, expulsion or return is individual in nature and cannot be denied because the person comes from a particular country or belongs to a particular group. Denial of protection based on group membership violates the Convention.

In 1977, the Executive Committee concluded that if an applicant for refugee status is not recognized by the government to which he applies, the applicant should be given a reasonable time to appeal.[2] The Committee concluded in 1983 that even unsuccessful claimants of manifestly unfounded or abusive applications should be eligible for a review of a negative decision before they are rejected.[3]

In addition, CCR noted, the Refugee Convention states a refugee should have access to courts of law of all contracting states.[4]

THE "IRREGULAR MOVEMENTS" INITIATIVE

The CCR rebuked Canada's "irregular movement" initiative, presented to the Executive Committee at its 1984 and subsequent meetings. The initiative was an attempt to involve the UNHCR in forcible return of refugees who had moved in a fashion Canada considered irregular. For Canada, a movement of a refugee from one country to another was "irregular" if the refugee travelled to a country without prior permission of that country. The refugee would be forcibly returned to the country of provisional asylum he had left.

This concept, known domestically as the "safe third country" rule, became the basis of a Canadian drive almost immediately after the government changed from Liberal to Conservative in the 1984 federal election. Denying access to refugees was not part of the Conservative platform in 1984, but it was a bureaucratic initiative to which the Tories were ideologically receptive.

The bureaucrats themselves were not acting out of a conservative ideology, but out of an agenda of control: they wanted Canada to choose refugees rather than have refugees choose Canada. Access of refugee claimants to Canada was to be cut off so that bureaucrats could select, based largely on the immigration criterion of the likelihood of successful establishment, which refugees could come to Canada from refugee camps abroad.

No one single official can be blamed for the Department of Immigration's bureaucratic agenda. The philosophy behind Bills C-55 and C-84 was widely shared among department officials. But Raphael Girard was head of refugee policy for the Immigration Department, and later head of the departmental task force responsible for drafting Bills C-55 and C-84. Girard, who spoke on behalf of Canada to the High Commission's Executive Committee in 1984, revealed immigration officials' classic concern that refugees are really immigrants. He stated, "It could not be said merely that the movements of asylum-seekers were being enmeshed in migratory flows; in fact, some refugee movements were themselves migratory flows."[5]

Girard introduced the term "irregular" to describe international movements of refugees. "Irregular arrivals, even in small numbers, undermine the host country's support for the refugees," he said. Girard called on the High Commission to study the matter, hinting at his desired solution — in his words, "return to the country of first asylum."

Canadian behaviour at the UN on refugees has been worse even than of the typical human rights violator. Typically, abusers respond to accusations of human rights violations by claiming they are not happening, that they are beyond their control, or that other countries are doing the same thing or worse. It is unusual for a human rights violator to come to the United Nations to say, "We are violating human rights. We are right to be doing it, and the standards should be changed to condone what we do."

Yet Canada is seeking approval at the UN for weakening its protection to refugees. Canada's "irregular movement" or "safe third country" initiative at the Executive Committee was an attempt to have the UN system endorse the return of refugees and asylum-seekers to countries of first asylum.

As a result of Canada's initiative in 1984 and other interventions, the High Commission appointed consultant Gilbert Jaeger from Belgium to study "irregular" movements. The August, 1985 Jaeger report⁶ recommended a number of initiatives. As an immediate response, Jaeger urged protection and assistance to refugees. Secondly, he recommended a vigorous aid and development policy aimed at urban refugee populations in countries of departure of irregular movements. Finally, as a long-term solution, Jaeger advocated tackling the root causes of the refugee problem to avert new flows of refugees.

Jaeger did not recommend simply returning refugees and asylum-seekers who have moved irregularly back to the country of first asylum. Nonetheless, Canada chose to pursue the safe third country initiative. In 1985, in an unusual move, Canadian delegates presented the Subcommittee on Protection of the Executive Committee with a draft resolution.* Canada asked the Executive Committee to recommend that refugees and asylum-seekers who move irregularly to any other country may be returned to their country of first asylum.† Only one proviso was added, that those returned had to receive protection against forced return to the country of danger fled.

Thanks to input from the Office of the High Commission, two other provisos were added to Canada's resolution. Firstly, for a person to be returned to the country of first asylum he must be able to remain there. Secondly, for a person to be returned he must be treated in accordance with recognized minimum standards until a durable solution is found.

Canada found these provisos were more lenient than it wanted, but they were acceptable. Canada began lobbying Executive Committee member states to favour the conclusion.

The Canadian Council for Refugees in 1988 urged Executive Committee participants to reject any resolution on irregular movements comparable to Canada's 1985 draft conclusion on irregular movements. Canada's draft referred to the use of

---

* It is unusual for country delegations to present resolutions. Normally, resolutions are presented by the Secretariat of the UNHCR, and drafted as a consensus from discussions held by country delegations.

† A country of first asylum is a country of provisional asylum where temporary protection is given to refugees. It is usually a neighbouring country or country of proximate refuge to the country a refugee fled.

fraudulent documentation as unjustified or unacceptable, not recognizing that circumstances may compel fraud where physical safety or freedom is endangered.

Firstly, the CCR objected to the use of the terms "irregular", "unjustified", and "unacceptable", which may imply condemnation of improper behaviour. Refugees and asylum-seekers are not in fact behaving improperly by seeking refuge without correct documentation. The Executive Committee has a duty to assist in protection of refugees and asylum-seekers, not to denounce those without proper papers.

The draft conclusions focussed on "irregular" movements of refugees who have already found protection in one country and then move to another. The CCR noted that there are often good reasons for this movement, including unjustified detention and other deterrents, and the absence of educational and employment opportunities and durable long-term solutions. "Irregular" movement sometimes occurs because family reunification is denied in the country of first asylum, or there is lack of due process in handling of refugee claims. Standards of fairness are violated, and incorrect decisions result. As well, movement can be caused by overly narrow, politicized, or inconsistent application of the refugee definition.

Governments that impose deterrents, deny due process, and politicize the Refugee Convention behave in an irregular, unjustified, unacceptable manner. Concern should be focussed on government's behaviour, not the reaction of refugees and asylum-seekers.

Canada's draft conclusions further stated refugees may be returned to countries in which they have already found protection. The CCR responded that if refugees and asylum-seekers are fleeing a "protection" country because of an intolerable situation, they may end up with no place to go except the country they originally fled. Thus, forcible return to a "protection" country may amount to disguised refoulement through an intermediary.

Involving the UNHCR in forced return to the first asylum country, as recommended in the draft resolution, is particularly reprehensible, according to the CCR. The UNHCR's purpose is to protect refugees, not to become part of the process of forced return.

Irregular movements would be more appropriately termed "instigated movements" because governments are often responsible for subjecting refugees and asylum-seekers to intolerable conditions leading to movement. The CCR called on the Executive Committee to deal with instigated movement, not by blaming the victims, but by concentrating on root causes. The movement of refugees can be stopped by ending deterrence measures, giving asylum-seekers a fair refugee determination process, and applying the refugee decision in a depoliticized way.

No consensus was reached on the Canadian government resolution and provisos at the 1988 Executive Committee meeting. The matter was put over for another year. However, it is not at all clear that this Canadian initiative can be blocked indefinitely. According to informal reports, opposition to the Canadian proposal in 1988 came at the last minute from only one country. While there was no consensus of the Executive Committee, the overwhelming sentiment was in favour of the Canadian initiative. Unless the Canadian bureaucratic agenda changes, Canada will continue to press this matter at the Executive Committee.

OTHER INITIATIVES

Canada's irregular movement initiative at the Executive Committee was not the only attempt to weaken international standards for refugee protection. Canada also took initiatives on detention.

In 1986, the High Commission brought the issue of detention before the Subcommittee on Protection of the Executive Committee. The High Commission was concerned about the increasingly frequent use of detention and unduly protracted internment to deter further refugee arrivals. However, some of the countries abusing refugee detention sit on the Executive Committee, including Canada, which was moving toward mass, indefinite detention as set out in its new law. Once the issue of detention was raised, Executive Committee members, including Canada, grabbed at the chance to justify the incarceration of refugees.[7]

The High Commissioner was embarrassed, and in his 1988 note on protection[8] attempted to qualify and restrict conclusions reached by the Executive Committee two years earlier. Normally, the Committee and the Commissioner agree how to carry out the Commission's mandate to protect refugees. In the case of detention provisions, however, the High Commissioner attempted to set his statements apart from the Executive Committee, and soften the Committee's far-reaching, reactionary recommendations.

The original discussion paper of the High Commission stated that restriction of freedom of movement of asylum-seekers may be justified to verify identity. A fair reading of that statement is that it may be sufficient to require the person to stay in the region of the country where the claim is made until his identity is confirmed, rather than imposing detention as recommended by Executive Committee members.

In his 1988 note, the High Commissioner wrote that asylum-seekers who arrive without documentation because they were unable to obtain any in their country of origin should not be detained solely for that reason. The High Commissioner argued that the Executive Committee conclusion recognized what he was advocating.

However, the Executive Committee conclusion recognizes no such thing. It says that those with no documents, fraudulent documents or those who have destroyed documents may be detained, whether there was an intention to mislead the authorities or not, simply in order to verify identity.

This distinction is important because it is the foundation for the new Canadian law of detention. Canadian law provides for systematic detention, not just restriction of movement, of undocumented asylum-seekers until their identity is verified. Whether asylum-seekers or refugees intended to mislead authorities is irrelevant. Through the Executive Committee, Canada received international sanction to justify its policy despite efforts by the High Commission to the contrary.

ICAO INITIATIVES

Finally Canada, attempted to disintegrate standards of refugee protection at an International Civil Aviation Organization (ICAO) session held September 7 to 23, 1988 in Montreal. Canada proposed two amendments[9] to the standards annexed to the Convention on International Civil Aviation, which was first signed in Chicago in 1944. Unlike the Refugee Convention, the Chicago Convention has virtually universal membership. Only a handful of countries have not signed.

Canada proposed that states which are party to the Chicago Convention should accept any person returned to the departure state from his destination point because he was found to be inadmissible. According to Canada's proposal, the person could be returned if he was allowed even temporary entry there, or if he had been in direct transit in this state for more than seventy-two hours.

Canada wanted to make its policy of forced return to a safe third country workable. Although a safe third country list was not drawn up when the new legislation took effect, it can be imposed at any time. Denying claimants access to Canada is academic as long as claimants who arrive are stuck here. If no country will take them back, then the new legislation requires the refugee claimants be put into Canada's refugee determination system.

Under the Canadian ICAO resolution, it would not matter whether the asylum-seeker would be prosecuted, mistreated, denied access to the refugee determination system or even entitled to remain in the first asylum country.

When the UNHCR heard of the Canadian resolution and others like it being introduced by several resettlement countries in Montreal, an official of the High Commission attended, something that does not normally happen for ICAO meetings, and objected.

Some states, in turn, objected to the High Commission's atypical presence at the meeting. Canada's resolution passed with some slight changes in wording. But thanks to the UNHCR, a note was appended to the resolution stating that nothing in the standard proposed by Canada is to be construed so as to allow return of an asylum-seeker to a country where his life or freedom would be threatened on account of his race, religion, nationality, membership in a particular social group, or political opinion.

The standard still requires first asylum countries to accept return of rejected asylum-seekers who have travelled to resettlement countries like Canada without permission.

Canada's second initiative at ICAO concerned fines for airlines that bring refugees to an asylum country. Prior to ICAO's 1988 meeting, the relevant Chicago Convention provision said, "Airlines shall not be fined in the event that any control documents in the possession of a passenger are found by a contracting state to be inadequate or if, for another reason, the passenger is found to be inadmissible by the state."[10]

Even though Canada was a signatory of the Chicago Convention of the time, it legislated airline fines in 1978. But the Refugee Deterrents and Detention Act makes matters worse. The new legislation increases fines regardless of whether the offence was committed knowingly. It also gives the government power to require airlines to hold passports and hand them over directly to immigration officials, and to require airlines to provide evidence to establish the concerned person's identity.

At the ICAO meeting in Montreal, Canada proposed that the Chicago Convention be amended to allow fines where the person concerned does not have proper documents and evidence suggests the carrier was negligent in ensuring passengers comply with the receiving state's documentary requirements.

UNHCR officer Erica Feller has written[11] that carrier sanctions inhibit entry and access to asylum procedures for persons who would otherwise seek asylum. Carrier sanctions cut across basic principles of refugee protection, and reinforce a state's ability to reject asylum-seekers at the border. They may lead to refoulement of genuine refugees.

Despite objections, Canada's second resolution also passed. Again, when a conflict arose between international standards protecting refugees and state behaviour threatening protection, the international standards gave way. And again Canada led the assault on the standard of refugee protection.

Chapter 16

NGOS AND THE UNHCR

The non-governmental community in Canada has as its unifying voice the Canadian Council for Refugees. As an umbrella organization representing eighty refugee assistance organizations and agencies across the country, the CCR is an instrument for effecting change. It has been involved in advocacy work to ensure the protection of refugees in Canada by proposing changes to strengthen protection, and opposing changes that could weaken protection. During debate over the recent legislative changes in Canada, the CCR argued for alterations in the Bills reflective of the non-governmental organizations' concerns. In the past, the Canadian Council for Refugees has also taken action at international fora. It submitted statements to the Executive Committee of the United Nations High Commission for Refugees meeting in October, 1988 condemning Canada's new legislation and questioning its membership on the Committee. (See Chapter 15.)

CHANGES AT THE UNHCR

Protection for refugees has been weakened internationally, not only by diminished standards, but also by the breakdown of protection through administrative changes at the UNHCR. Not just in Canada, but everywhere — not just governmentally, but intergovernmentally — we are witnessing a deterioration of protection for refugees. When the individual nations of the world lose their will to protect refugees, not surprisingly, the United Nations intergovernmental system falters as well.

The UNHCR was created to protect refugees, yet it cannot campaign against its own member governments without losing the financial and political support necessary for its survival. The UNHCR's annual budget for 1989 is U.S. $428.7 million. The Office of the High Commissioner has 100 offices and 2,000 staff members in over ninety countries.

UNHCR Commissioner Jean Pierre Hocke of Switzerland has been accused of weakening the High Commission's protection function. However, problems surfaced even under his predecessor, Poul Hartling of Denmark.

In the late 1970s and early '80s, Guatemalan and Salvadoran refugees were forcibly relocated from refugee camps inside the Mexican border. Mexican authorities arrested refugees refusing to relocate, burned their crops, and cut off food and medical supplies. Mexican authorities denied access to service organizations, the UNHCR, the press, and international human rights organizations.*

During this life-threatening period for Central American refugees in Mexico, the UNHCR was not as much help as it could have been. True, the UNHCR was limited in its ability to intervene because Mexico is not a signatory to the Refugee Convention. Yet, the High Commission refused even to criticize the forced relocation of refugees. On the contrary, UNHCR described the relocation as regular and orderly.

---

* See Chapter 11 for greater detail on the Mexican forced relocation of Central Americans.

Americas Watch, an NGO, called on the UNHCR to fulfill its mandate to protect the rights of Central American refugees in Mexico, stating that UNHCR had not always met its responsibilities in dealing with these refugees.[1]

Until 1984 the High Commission protested frequently and vigorously to Mexico about the deportation of refugees to Guatemala. In turn, the Mexican Government protested to the UN High Commissioner for Refugees, Poul Hartling, regarding the local representative's role. The local representative in Mexico was recalled, and replaced in early 1984 with a new representative who refrained from public criticism and confrontation with the government of Mexico on refugee issues.

THE HOCKE ADMINISTRATION

Before Hocke became High Commissioner and reorganized, two hierarchies existed at the UNHCR — one for protection, and the other for assistance. Each regional bureau had an officer with authority over assistance, and an officer with authority over protection.

Beneath the regional bureaus are a number of desks, responsible for geographical sub-groupings of the region. Beneath the desks in the hierarchy are the individual offices of the UNHCR in the field. The individual offices are the local representatives responsible for overseeing the local refugee situation and implementation of local programmes.

With the advent of the Hocke administration in January, 1986, matters took a dramatic turn for the worse at the UNHCR. Hocke has a Red Cross background and, although the Red Cross is involved in some refugee protection work, Hocke's experience at the Red Cross was in assistance — the provision of food, clothing, shelter and medical aid. His expertise and commitment in assistance brought him to the UNHCR.

Introducing his own thinking on how the High Commission should be organized, Hocke began his term by undercutting its protection function. Protection was shifted to one side. The position of regional protection officer ceased to exist. A new bureau of refugee law and doctrine assumed protection functions. However this bureau is only advisory to the various subregional desks and is not part of the chain of authority as was the previous protection officer. Now, the subregional desks make the final decisions on protection matters.

With Hocke's shift, protection officers at UNHCR headquarters in Geneva have had difficulty ensuring protection principles are applied by their own people. Not every desk officer is a lawyer and able to function as a protection officer. On occasion they do not understand protection principles or are not interested in applying them.

Even within UNHCR ranks there is a resistance to protection. Headquarters protection officers are considered obstructionist and doctrinaire. Officers involved in assistance work closely with governments, and they are reluctant to confront these same governments by insisting on protection.

Hocke has an organizational justification for his changes. A unified chain of authority allows for a more direct link between headquarters and the field. Nonetheless, Hocke's reorganization downgraded protection in the UNHCR.

THE 1988 NGO CONSULTATION

At a consultation with UNHCR before the 1988 Executive Committee meeting, the International Council of Voluntary Agencies (ICVA), a non-governmental agency, said that responsibility for protection had been diffused. Field officers did not feel they had the backing needed when pushing protection. Staff morale had been weakened.

Other NGOs at this annual consultation complained the UNHCR was not speaking up about blatant violations of protection. Pat Taran of World Church Service said he wanted the High Commissioner to speak about interdiction[†] and refoulement of Haitians from North America. The United States was preventing Haitians from landing by boat.

Frank Kiehne of World Alliance of Young Men's Christian Associations reiterated the NGOs' need for a public UNHCR statement to rally around when quiet diplomacy is not enough.

[†] Interdiction is the turning back of boats (of refugees) from landing.

Quiet diplomacy, making polite suggestions behind closed doors to authorities of the states violating protection to cease their violation, can on occasion be effective. If effective, it is because a sanction can be imposed should the suggestion not be accepted. The international community cannot impose its will on sovereign states. The sanction it can impose is public criticism and condemnation — what the former director of the UN Human Rights Division, John Humphrey, called "the mobilization of shame."

If a government is never publicly criticized, then quiet diplomacy has little hope of being effective. Like silence, quiet diplomacy alone is surrender. The NGOs can criticize publicly whether or not the UNHCR speaks out. But the very silence of the UNHCR becomes a defence that violating states can raise to exonerate themselves. They have claimed that when the UNHCR says nothing publicly, the state's behaviour is acceptable.

Refugees International's S.C. Lowman said the UNHCR had not been complaining publicly about Thai push-offs — pushing boats of Vietnamese refugees away from Thai coasts instead of allowing them to land. The NGOs had no answer when the Thai government pointed out the UNHCR has not objected.

NGOs are accused of political partiality and are essentially handicapped when the UNHCR is silent, Mrs. H. Taviani of France Terre d'Asile said. The UNHCR is known to be the political expert, and so must take positions more frequently.

Public statements by the UNHCR criticizing governments are a legitimate part of a protection strategy, UNHCR spokesman Dennis McNamara responded, but there is a high price attached to such statements. McNamara said public criticism alienates governments, and makes co-operation more difficult in areas such as channelling assistance.

UNHCR TIMIDITY AND FALSEHOODS

In the world of diplomacy, the value of public statements will always be debated. Non-governmental organizations judged that the UNHCR has been far too timid in its response to obvious contraventions of the Refugee Convention, including denial of protection and the refoulement of refugees to countries of danger.

In any case, the UNHCR clearly should not make false public statements, for example, that refugees face no danger in a country when they do. Yet, the UNHCR has been criticized for saying the Tamils' situation in Sri Lanka was becoming safe when it was not.[2] Tamil refugees were encouraged to return to situations of persecution. In a letter to European governments and UNHCR national offices in April, 1988, the High Commission maintained Sri Lanka's security situation was stabilizing so that Tamil asylum-seekers might be forcibly returned to Sri Lanka's Mannar and Colombo areas. Tamil refugee organizations were surprised by this assessment and discouraged by its implication. European refugee organizations were concerned the UNHCR might be imprudent to suggest forced return of Tamil refugees could take place when conditions were so uncertain.

In early 1988 Jean Pierre Hocke ordered 130,000 copies of the UNHCR monthly magazine *Refugees* to be burned because the magazine contained a fourteen page article critical of West Germany for its declining commitment to refugee asylum.[3] Since West Germany contributes ten percent of UNHCR funds, it appeared that Hocke ordered destruction to appease a major donor.

Joel McClellan of Friends World Committee for Consultation expressed regret, pointing out that UNHCR's *Refugees* had been prepared, on occasion, to step on government toes. It was considered relatively independent, and provided some critical perspective.

Many observers have questioned *Refugees'* courage and commitment since the critical issue was banned. The magazine has become anodyne, laundered — a propaganda magazine for governments. The change in the magazine signals UNHCR's step back from its protection role: the High Commission is not prepared to confront governments when they are not protecting refugees.

OTHER INTERGOVERNMENTAL ORGANIZATIONS

The UNHCR is only one of a number of international governmental groups dealing with refugees. The Council of Europe, consisting of all twenty-one Western European states, has established an *ad hoc* committee of experts on legal aspects of territorial asylum, refugees and stateless persons called CAHAR, for short, after its French acronym. CAHAR is now considering a draft agreement that would provide guidelines of circumstances in which countries can deny protection to asylum-seekers.

As well, the European Economic Community, most notably through the Trevi Group, works jointly on refugee initiatives. The Trevi Group is composed of officials in ministries of justice and the interior of member states who deal with asylum policy. Currently, the Group is preparing a list of nationalities which will require visas to enter countries of the European Community, and a list of countries considered safe for purposes of expulsion.

Within the European Community, the Schengen Group, consisting of France, West Germany and Benelux, discusses harmonization of asylum policy. International immigration barriers within the European Economic Community are to be removed in Europe by 1992. The Schengen Group wants to have a common policy in place by then.

The UNHCR and European governments meet in consultations structured around an annual series of confidential meetings. Working groups have been established and policy meetings at the ministerial level have occurred.

Although Canada and the United States are not technically part of the European deliberating bodies, they participate in many European meetings and are key players. Government refugee policy is being developed in a trans-Atlantic manner.

Due to the UNHCR's move away from protection, it is imperative the international NGO community work collectively to be effective in strengthening protection for refugees.

NORTH-NORTH DIALOGUE

Partly in response to intergovernmental activities, NGOs in Europe and North America developed the North-North dialogue. Members are the European Consultation on Refugees and Exiles (ECRE), the Canadian Council for Refugees, and the Committee for United States Action on Asylum Concern (CUSAAC). All three groups are umbrella organizations for NGOs concerned with refugees.

Since 1987, North-North has been meeting regularly, alternating between Europe and North America. Canada has hosted two North-North meetings. The United States hosted its first dialogue in June, 1989 in Washington, D.C.

North-North is at a very early formative stage. It is still exchanging information, and has yet to take stands on substantive issues. With no staff, headquarters or officials, North-North operates as a collective, not unlike its component organizations, ECRE, CCR and CUSAAC. The component organizations will have to assume leadership responsibilities if North-North is to accomplish anything in a co-ordinated fashion.

THE NGO AGENDA

All NGOs agree on certain rudimentary policies. They reject out of hand government attempts to blame refugees for moving from intermediate countries to resettlement countries. They acknowledge that maltreatment of refugees in first asylum or intermediate countries instigates outflows of refugees.

Maltreatment of refugees in intermediate countries is not just a refugee flow problem, but a human rights concern as well. Denial of human rights suggests both a solution and strategy. Future North-North meetings should take an initiative on the following issues: maltreatment of claimants in intermediate countries, de facto refugees, protection procedures and detention.

Integrating Human Rights Issues

Firstly, to combat maltreatment of refugees in first asylum countries, the NGO community should approach not only international refugee institutions, but also international human rights organizations. Integrating refugee treatment to human rights principles is more effective than isolating each issue.

De Facto Refugees

Secondly, NGOs should raise the issue of de facto refugees — refugees who are recognized in fact, but not in law. De facto refugees are offered protection even if they do not meet the refugee definition.

Canada has given protection to a number of different groups of people without formally calling them refugees. From time to time Canada has established temporary humanitarian programmes and offered protection to people within the self-exiled class, the Indochinese designated class, and the political prisoners and oppressed persons class. But these people do not have to meet the refugee definition, do not receive refugee status, and do not receive the benefits accorded to refugees. They are the Canadian version of *de facto* refugees.

The *de facto* refugee notion has not been fully developed in Canada. By and large, persons who are refugees are recognized as such. For some European countries the distinction between *de facto* and *de jure* refugees is rigorously made and maintained. Canada under the old law had a thirty percent acceptance rate for refugees. Europe has had the same rate, but it has broken it down to ten percent *de jure* (legal) refugees, recognized as such, and twenty percent *de facto* refugees.

The *de facto* category exists because of an overly restrictive application of the refugee definition that ends up excluding people who are refugees, such as potential victims of generalized violence. Even governments who exclude these people, because of a failure to meet a requirement they impose that refugees must be potential victims of individualized persecution, see the inequity. Rather than send these potential victims of generalized violence back home, a clear cruelty, governments offer them protection as *de facto* refugees, but little else.

De facto refugees are treated differently, and often far worse, than *de jure* refugees. In some countries, *de facto* refugees face a system of deterrence, in which governments attempt to discourage them from making or pursuing claims.

Deterrence schemes cause *de facto* refugees to flee from one country to another. Governments complain regularly about irregular movements, which frequently result from deterrence schemes inflicted on *de facto* refugees.

The NGO community should be pushing for assimilation of the categories of *de facto* and *de jure* refugees into one category. The Netherlands courts have already held the distinction between *de facto* and *de jure* refugees cannot be maintained.[4] NGOs cannot sit idly by while real refugees are given second class treatment.

Protection Procedures

Thirdly, the non-governmental community should take an initiative on protection procedures. The UNHCR Executive Committee has stated some conclusions on procedures, and the High Commission has also set out guidelines for procedural protection. But neither document supplies sufficient detail to cover all potential due process problems.

The Canadian NGO community has been greatly exposed to procedural issues, partly because of Canada's old, complicated system, and partly because of the extensive debate surrounding the new legislation. Canada's community can draw on its experience to offer leadership internationally.

For example, one acute procedural problem that has been faced in Canada is the need for an independent decision-maker. None of the Executive Committee conclusions or UNHCR guidelines deals with the fact that refugee decisions in many countries are made by people involved in external affairs or immigration.

North-North should propose a set of procedural safeguards to make refugee determination procedures fair. NGOs affiliated with North-North should then attempt to achieve international endorsement of these procedural safeguards. Irregular movements of refugees, a concern of governments, would be greatly reduced if every country established a fair refugee determination system.

Detention

Lastly, non-governmental organizations should take an initiative on detention. Even with Canada's new legislation, detention is not as systematic as in other countries. Wholesale detention elsewhere has been used a deterrence measure, leading to refugee movements to Canada.

Despite recommendations by the High Commission, the Executive Committee passed in 1986 a wide-ranging, hostile conclusion on detention.[5] Detention is authorized far beyond what is necessary to protect the public or ensure compliance with the legal procedures of the country of asylum. The Executive Committee's conclusion needs to be qualified or elaborated to avoid condoning detention simply for the purpose of deterrence.

NGO RESOURCES

NGOs are at a tremendous disadvantage in dealing with governments because they consist mainly of volunteers. They are typically financially threadbare, and use any available funds for the pressing needs of refugees. Governments, on the other hand, seem to consist of endless streams of people with bottomless resources.

It is difficult enough to muster effective representation even nationally. NGOs resources are stretched to the limit in attempts to have an effect at international fora, which are convened regularly around the world.

The CCR has been around since 1977, earlier as the Standing Conference of Canadian Organizations Concerned with Refugees. Some Canadian activists take it for granted. However, United States NGOs did not set up a comparable umbrella organization until 1988, the Committee for U.S. Action on Asylum Concerns. Previously, the American NGO community marched in disorder, one component often unaware of what another was doing. The North-North dialogue had no American component that could take a full and proper part in its discussions.

Canadian NGOs were united in their opposition to the government's new immigration bills. The Canadian Council for Refugees helped to create a more effective and united front of opposition, and to develop a shared awareness of the true impact of the new legislation.

The CCR needs to assume a still greater leadership role on the international scene. Only in 1988 did the Council set up, for the first time, a small secretariat in Montreal. Policies on fundamental issues such as *de facto* refugees and worldwide refugee protection procedures must be developed. The complex problems refugees encounter in a world bent on denying protection to refugees make it mandatory the CCR develops communication links with other NGOs, as those committed to refugee protection grapple with the ramifications of new laws and governmental initiatives.

The battle over refugee protection is being fought around the globe. If each NGO restricts the battle to its own country, it is sure to lose. Each NGO must widen its horizons and add to its allies if it hopes ever to carry the day.

PART FIVE

CONCEPTS AND PRINCIPLES FOR REFUGEE PROTECTION

Chapter 17

HUMAN RIGHTS AND MASS EXODUSES

n May, 1988, tens of thousands of Somali refugees began pouring into neighbouring Ethiopia. The influx of Somali refugees peaked in June, when 4,000 persons were arriving daily. By mid-October, approximately 389,000 Somalis had found refuge in refugee camps in Hararghe, a remote rural area in Eastern Ethiopia.

The mass exodus of Somalia's Issak clan followed what eyewitnesses described as large-scale suffering of entire civilian populations as the result of combat between the rebels and government troops.

At the end of the 1970s and early 1980s, the Vietnamese boat people crisis occurred. It was a dramatic mass exodus caused by rampant human rights violations. To this day, millions of these boat people remain in first asylum countries waiting to have their refugee status determined or to be resettled in another country.

Meanwhile, hundreds of thousands of refugees have fled Guatemala, El Salvador and other Central American countries as a result of civil and political upheaval. They flee widespread deprivation of human rights, including the denial of political freedoms, torture, death squad killings, and disappearances. In Mexico alone, some 45,000 Guatemalans, 120,000 Salvadorans and 11,000 people of various Central and South American origins have sought protection.

During the late 1970s and 1980s, mass exodus due to human rights violations has become an all-too-familiar and alarming scenario: Haitians fled Jean-Paul Duvalier's regime of terror; Tamil refugees exited Sri Lanka *en masse* due to wholesale infractions of their rights; and the suffering faced by the Sahrawi in the Maghreb resulted in a mass exodus.

Sometimes, human rights violations are ended and refugees are repatriated. For instance, after the Macias Regime in Equatorial Guinea ended in 1979, a majority of 150,000 Guinean refugees returned home. When India and Pakistan ended hostilities and Bangladesh was proclaimed a new state, millions of refugees were repatriated. When white minority rule in Rhodesia ended, many refugees returned to the newly-renamed nation of Zimbabwe. Since the withdrawal from Afghanistan in early 1989 of Soviet troops, some 3.0 million Afghan refugees from Pakistan and another 2.35 million from Iran await repatriation.

The plight of refugees is inextricably linked with human rights violations. Indeed, the plight of refugees and human rights violations are not two problems, but different facets of the same problem. Human rights violations are a root cause of mass exoduses. The difficulties refugees face once they have fled the source of danger are also often human rights violations. Focussing on mass exoduses provides a strategy for elevating human rights standards and establishing human rights mechanisms. Focussing on human rights standards provides a strategy for improving the plight of refugees.

DIFFERING TRENDS — HUMAN RIGHTS AND REFUGEE RIGHTS

Regrettably, we cannot count on universal respect for human rights in the immediate future, nor can violations be expected to

cease where they occur. Meanwhile, the human rights of refugees are also being violated in countries of proximate refuge.
Refugees frequently endure treatment in countries of proximate
refuge little better than the conditions they fled.

While governments world-wide are strengthening and
proliferating human rights standards, refugee standards are
languishing, even disintegrating. International compliance with
human rights conventions is far from ideal, but at least the trend
is in the right direction. Refugee standards are getting worse
rather than better.

There is an important indirect effect on the work of NGOs.
Even when they are not effectively implemented, human rights
standards serve a purpose. NGOs can call governments to
account for failing to apply in practice what they say in theory.
Domestic courts, applying constitutionally entrenched bills of
rights, can draw on international standards to create domestic
remedies. But when international standards themselves lapse,
as they are lapsing for refugees, the work of NGOs becomes
more difficult.

Politics is the cause for differing trends in human rights and
refugee rights. Countries find it politically useful to attack each
other's human rights records measured against universally-
accepted standards. United Nations votes in favour of improved
human rights standards are easy to win. States can demonstrate
they are concerned with the principles of human rights, even if
they may fail to apply these principles in practice.

For example, Syria acceded to the International Covenant
on Civil and Political Rights in 1969. This Covenant provides
every human being with the right to life and freedom from
torture, cruel, inhumane or degrading treatment or punishment,
and arbitrary arrest or detention. Yet Syria under President
Haafez al-Assad's dictatorship since 1970 has consistently
violated its citizens' human rights. Amnesty International has
issued a sequence of reports detailing various abuses in Syria
such as abduction or disappearance of alleged political opponents of the Assad regime, widespread use of torture to extract
"confessions" during interrogation and prolonged solitary
confinement of untried political detainees, lack of basic legal

safeguards and secret trials for political prisoners by special security courts, and the use of the death penalty for both political and criminal offences.

REFUGEE RIGHTS

Only the First World (the West) and the Third World are involved in the refugee problem internationally. The Soviet Bloc has been absent. Historically, this happened because the Refugee Convention was developed after the Second World War to protect citizens of occupied Eastern Europe fleeing persecution by the Soviets, and the Soviet bloc wanted no part in the system. Today, the bulk of refugee outflow comes from the Third World, not Eastern Europe. Nevertheless, the Soviet Bloc — except for Hungary, which signed the Convention only in 1989 — remains an outsider.

Relationships between Third and First World countries are often tense because of arguments over the division of responsibilities. Third World countries are countries of proximate refuge or first asylum for the majority of today's refugees. Countries of resettlement in the First World argue that Third World countries could offer greater protection to those fleeing neighbouring countries. Proximate refuge countries in the Third World counter that First World countries could be doing more to resettle.

The Refugee Convention clearly states that signatories have an international obligation not to return a refugee to a country where his life or freedom would be threatened because of his race, religion, nationality, membership in a particular social group, or political opinion. However, the United Nations Refugee Convention makes only general statements about sharing the burden of helping refugees who are outside the boundaries of a signatory state in a country of proximate refuge. States are left to arrange among themselves how the burden is to be shared.

The refugee debate is distorted by the nexus between proximate refuge and resettlement and financing. First and Third World countries do not face each other as equals. Even though the West is not doing what it can to settle and protect refugees — in fact, it is doing less each year — the West also spends large portions of foreign aid money supporting proximate refuge states. Countries of proximate refuge are client states that receive international aid money, while countries of resettlement are donor states providing foreign aid. For some Third World countries, refugee aid is a significant part of their economies. As a result, the West, by and large, gets agreement on the lessened protection it wants to give.

First asylum countries are chiefly concerned with the amount of aid given by resettlement countries, not with the principles of protection. If resettlement states want to weaken the principle of protection, proximate refuge states will not object.

First asylum countries also depend on the goodwill of resettlement states to accept influxes of refugees. If they aggressively confront countries of resettlement, these countries might refuse to accept large numbers of refugees.

Forcibly returning refugees and asylum-seekers from resettlement states to first asylum countries is a form of weakened protection benefitting only resettlement states. Sometimes, refugees and asylum-seekers leave the first asylum country of their own accord due to disincentive and deterrence measures, or an unfair refugee determination procedure, or an arbitrary application of the refugee definition. Forcibly returning refugees to the country of first asylum weakens protection by necessitating a choice between staying in intolerable conditions in the refuge country or returning to the country of danger.

Nonetheless, first asylum states will approve of such weakened protection because they find nothing improper with their own imposed disincentive and deterrence measures.

HUMAN RIGHTS

The UNHCR has been disinclined to get involved in condemning human rights violations, even when they are the root causes of mass exodus. Commission staff fear talk of human rights violations would lead to a confrontation with governments, politicize the UNHCR, and make assisting and protecting refugees more difficult.

Nonetheless, the international community is clearly involved in mass exoduses. The community provides refuge in neighbouring countries, resettlement, and aid. Thus, a state cannot claim that its human rights violations are just an internal matter, and point to the UN Charter principles articulating non-interference in domestic matters.[1] International human rights institutions, whose involvement might otherwise be rejected, have pursued human rights remedies to a limited degree in countries generating mass exoduses.

The international community recognized the connection between human rights violations and mass exoduses when the Vietnamese boat people tragedy occurred. While there is reluctance to interfere in the internal affairs of an abusive regime, almost no matter how flagrant human rights abuses may be, mass exodus is everyone's business.

Canada responded to the Vietnamese boat people crisis in two ways. Firstly, Canada opened its door to refugees — in 1979 and 1980 some 60,000 boat people were admitted. Of those, about 40,000 refugees were sponsored by private organizations or groups of five or more individuals. Secondly, Canada took a number of initiatives through the United Nations system to do away with human rights violations that result in mass exoduses.

CANADIAN UN INITIATIVES

At the United Nations in 1980 Canada focussed on removing the root causes of mass exodus as a strategy to improve conditions in countries systemically denying human rights. Ideally, the goal is removal of human rights violations around the world.

Canada proposed two human rights resolutions to the 1980 United Nations General Assembly. As part of the Canadian delegation, I was involved in drafting, negotiating and lobbying for the resolutions. One, dealing exclusively with mass and flagrant violations of human rights, failed. This resolution, known as the "good offices" resolution, proposed the Secretary General of the UN offer assistance to the governments of countries suffering mass and flagrant human rights violations, with a view toward full restoration of human rights. The proposition did not require establishing a new institution, position, or bureaucracy. It merely restated the duties of the Secretary-General.

The Secretary-General said it was already his responsibility to exercise his good offices in human rights matters and he would continue to assist in any way possible. Previously, when the Secretary-General had been requested in specific situations by UN bodies dealing with human rights to contact directly violating governments, he had sent designated representatives to these countries.

The Canadian proposition did not call on the Secretary-General to condemn or publicize human rights deprivations, or to send fact-finding missions, only to assist if the concerned government consented. The Secretary-General was not required to make contact, only to consider it. The Canadian resolution noted that mass and flagrant violations of human rights are not simply internal affairs, but legitimate matters of international concern.

When Canada introduced the good offices resolution in the Third Committee of the General Assembly in December, 1980, India proposed an amendment that assistance be given to the government "at its request" rather than "with its consent". This amendment, which passed by a narrow margin, destroyed the purpose of the resolution since it denied the Secretary-General the right to take the initiative, rather than merely respond to a request from a human rights violator. On an Irish proposal, supported by Canada, Canada's resolution was withdrawn and ceased to be considered.

Why did Canada's original resolution, which seemed so beneficial and harmless, fail? Opponents of the resolution argued that, in the absence of a mass exodus, direct contact by the Secretary-General on human rights interfered in the concerned government's internal affairs, thus exceeding what was permitted by the Charter of the United Nations.

Canada's resolution failed, as well, because of the generally weak human rights records of most countries. If the Secretary-General were authorized to make direct contacts in cases of human rights violations, this power could be frequently used against a large number of countries. If the good offices resolution had passed, supporters would likely be at the receiving end of pressure by the Secretary-General to change their practices.

CANADA'S SECOND RESOLUTION

A second Canadian resolution was successful. This resolution asked the UN Human Rights Commission to recommend action on human rights violations linked to mass exoduses. The resolution proposed the UN make direct contact with concerned governments only in situations where mass exoduses occur, as a step to restore full human rights, bring an end to mass exoduses, and allow those who left to return home.

Canada's resolution on mass exoduses passed the Third Committee of the UN General Assembly December 3, 1980, without opposition or formal amendments.

Countries generating mass exoduses are few in number, thereby curbing the fears of member states that a vote in favour of Canada's mass exoduses proposition would in the long run be used against these supporting states.

The successful UN resolution said, in part, that the General Assembly requests a special representative be responsible for an early warning system, to gather information about human rights violations that would lead to mass exoduses. Any human rights violations would be brought to the attention of those involved with root causes to try to prevent a mass movement. The special representative would also be responsible for seeing that the operation was kept under review by the relevant bodies.[2]

THE SPECIAL RAPPORTEUR

At the next meeting of the Commission of Human Rights, in 1981, Canada proposed, again successfully, a resolution that the Commission appoint a special rapporteur, or independent expert, to study the question of human rights and mass exoduses.[3] Canada secured the appointment of former UN Commissioner for Refugees Sadruddin Aga Khan as Special Rapporteur.

Aga Khan submitted his report in February, 1982 to the Commission on Human Rights in Geneva. It remains to this day a useful and positive contribution. The report examined carefully each article of the Universal Declaration of Human Rights and the effect of article violations on the movement of people. Additional push and pull factors that lead to mass exoduses, besides human rights violations, were also discussed.

The report stated:

> The phenomenon of mass exodus would practically disappear if states respected — or, in the case of economic rights, had the means to respect — the rights elaborated in the Universal Declaration. In the world of the eighties, the Universal Declaration of Human Rights holds out promises which are utopian. The Declaration and its relevant articles are an ideal backdrop, a shimmering mirage which we strive to attain... Exodus could be prevented or circumscribed only if conditions were to be drastically different at the point of departure... Such conditions are not about to be established. We live in an imperfect world.[4]

The report has been criticized for discussing human rights violations in abstract terms, thus omitting country-specific findings of human rights abuses. "Reading the report, one almost loses the sense that human decisions contribute to the persecution, suffering or privation that drives people out," one commentator said.[5]

In fact, the report originally contained descriptions of twenty-seven mass exoduses from 1972 to 1982, but these were excised following objections from those who felt the report was either too generous or too harsh.

The section removed was composed of three annexes. Annex I contained a selection of twenty-two mass exoduses between 1972 to 1982, such as Equatorial Guinea in Africa, and El Salvador in Central America. Annex II detailed four case studies — Afghanistan, Ethiopia, Indo-China and Mexico — chosen because of their magnitude, importance and geographical spread. Mexico was included because of the phenomenon of migrant labour to the U.S. Annex III was a global overview of the diversity and scale of mass exodus, continent by continent.

Removal of these annexes from the final report reflects a common United Nations problem: the reluctance to name names. Aga Khan's report noted that refugee-producing countries and refugee-receiving countries are rarely on talking terms when a mass movement is underway. Relief develops in a vacuum, without any relation to the root causes and solutions. Relief agencies refrain from going into the background of mass movements on the ground that they cannot concern themselves with political matters.

If the report seems pessimistic, it nonetheless contained a number of positive proposals. It called for the appointment of a special UN representative for humanitarian questions. The special representative would be responsible for an early warning system — to gather impartial information from proven sources about human rights violations that could lead to mass exoduses, and to bring human rights violations to the attention of those in the UN who deal with causes, such as the Secretary-General, in order to encourage preventive action before the start of a mass refugee exodus.

Aga Khan's report reinforced the belief that human rights violations rarely provoke action until refugees are on the move. A special representative for humanitarian questions could help to remedy that lapse by encouraging concern before the outflow occurs.

Secretary-General Javier Perez de Cuellar announced in March, 1987 that an early warning unit would become part of this office. The unit is not restricted to refugees, or even human rights. Its mandate covers political and security matters as well. James O.C. Jonah currently holds the position of Assistant Secretary-General for Research and Collection of Information. Whatever the weaknesses and failings of the early warning unit, its very existence improves the chance of halting a mass exodus generated by human rights violations.

Canada can justifiably take pride in the creation and operation of the early warning institution. But it is not enough that Canada was instrumental in giving the Secretary-General the power to intervene in situations where governments are generating mass exoduses. Canada must see that the authority is used.

It is ironic that very states attempting to link mass exodus and human rights violations are denying protection to refugees and urging a weakening of international standards for protection. Canada has shown leadership in its resolutions to have the United Nations attempt to stop human rights violations. Why then has Canada taken such giant strides to weaken refugee protection? The connection between human rights protection and refugee protection is evident: refugee outflows are created by human rights violations; they are the product of the violations Canada wants stopped. How Canada can be simultaneously a champion of human rights protection, a destroyer of refugee protection at home, and an advocate of weakened international refugee standards of protection abroad?

Chapter 18

RESETTLEMENT OR ASYLUM? — THE SAFE THIRD COUNTRY CONCEPT

The world community has moved beyond the notion of voluntary protection of refugees. It accepts in principle the legal obligation to protect refugees. However, the obligation is not a positive one, to allow refugees to enter and seek asylum, but only a negative one, not to return refugees forcibly to the country of danger fled once they have already entered.

A near world-wide consensus has been reached on the need for protection. But there is not a consensus about who should protect whom. Neighbouring countries cannot provide asylum to every refugee. Signatories to the Refugee Convention have an obligation to share the burden of the refugee problem. But international law does not set out how much of the burden each country is to assume.

Refugees arriving in a country spontaneously are the point of conflict: a refugee moves without permission from a neighbouring country of temporary asylum to a third country in which he wishes to resettle. The resettlement country cannot send the refugee back to his home country that he fled because that would violate the Refugee Convention. In theory, the resettlement country could send the refugee back to the country of temporary asylum. Superficially, such action would not violate the Refugee Convention.

By and large, resettlement countries reject the whole concept of spontaneous arrivals. When they share the refugee burden, they want to choose their refugees from among the refugees in temporary asylum abroad. They do not want refugees to choose how the refugee burden is spread by moving to resettlement countries without permission.

This issue was really at the heart of Bill C-55, with its safe third country concept. Refugees who arrive in Canada from listed countries can be returned to these temporary asylum countries without access to the Canadian refugee determination system. The listed countries have been called safe third countries — third countries because they are countries other than Canada and the home country fled.

So far no country has been put on the list. However, the debate about the safe third country continues. Bureaucrats, who lobbied for the concept in the legislation and won, are now lobbying for the power in the legislation to be used.

This chapter discusses that debate from two perspectives. It looks at the safe third country concept as it has been articulated in Bill C-55, and at the issue of principle.

Should Canada be a country of first asylum for refugees who choose to come here? Or should we be a country of secondary resettlement only for those refugees the government of Canada chooses to admit? While the government claims Bill C-55's mandate is to control abuse, its silent if not hidden agenda is to deny protection to real refugees, who the government says could be protected elsewhere. Essentially, Canada is attempting to select refugees rather than permit refugees to select Canada.

The government argued that the Immigration Act never intended for refugees to come to Canada to claim refugee status, and that Bill C-55 merely reinforces this intention. However, the Immigration Act of 1978 clearly allowed for refugee claims from within Canada, or else the issue of how to deal with these claims now would not have arisen. Under the guise of amending an existing law, the government stripped the law of its original purpose and intent, which was to provide protection to refugees. It replaced this objective with a new objective of closing Canadian doors to refugees who may be protected elsewhere.

SELECTION FROM ABROAD — THE GOVERNMENT CASE

Refugees are selected from abroad in two different ways: by private sponsorship and government sponsorship. The government will admit as many privately sponsored refugees each year as Canadian private groups wish to sponsor. There is an annual global and geographic quota for government-sponsored refugees. For 1989, the global total allocated among regions of the world is 13,000: 3,000 for South East Asia, 3,400 for Eastern Europe, 3,400 for Latin America, 1,000 for Africa, 1,800 for Middle East and West Asia, 100 other, and 300 in reserve.

The breakdown is even more specific than that. Within the regional quotas, different visa offices are given their own quotas to fill. A visa office meets its quota of government-sponsored refugees by looking at two factors: whether the person meets the refugee definition, and whether the person is likely to successfully establish himself in Canada.

Government officials say Canada should not be a country of first asylum because it is not geographically proximate to any refugee source. For instance, Sri Lankan refugees ought to seek first asylum in India, not Canada. Neighbouring countries are often culturally similar, making it easier for refugees to adapt, government officials say. Ideally, a refugee problem is solved by ending the situation which created the refugee outflow and repatriating the refugees; and repatriation is more effectively carried out from a geographically proximate country than from a geographically remote country such as Canada.

If the Canadian government selects a refugee abroad, the person will enter Canada as a permanent resident or as a desirable candidate for permanent residency. He is free to work or go to school and has access to the services and benefits available to Canadians. However, if a person comes here on his own as a refugee claimant, he will be here for months — or even years — while his claim is being processed. During that time he is in a state of limbo. He is considered a temporary resident until his status is determined, and he is severely restricted in his access to work, school, medicare, and all government services and benefits. The government argues that a person is better off coming here for resettlement rather than for first asylum.

Government officials say they admit refugees to meet a refugee need, not to cater to refugees' preferences. By selecting refugees abroad, the government says it can make a determination based on priority needs. If the government allowed refugees the choice of coming to Canada as a country of first asylum, then officials say Canada's refugee resources would be used up on those who chose Canada, rather than resettling Canada's fair share of the world's refugees.

REFUGEE NEEDS AND CANADIAN NEEDS

This government reasoning is faulty. The government does not select refugees from abroad merely based on refugee needs. It also considers Canada's needs.

The government admits refugees for resettlement from the refugee pool abroad based on their likelihood of successful establishment in Canada.[1] Canada notoriously chooses the skilled, young, educated and healthy refugees from camps. The unskilled, old and ill refugees left behind are often ignored by other resettlement countries as well. These refugees are left as a burden to the country of provisional asylum, making first asylum more onerous for those who provide it. A group of refugees arriving in Canada on its own is likely to include a more representative sample from camps than the cream of the crop group hand-picked by government. The Canadian obligation of sharing the world's burden of refugees would be better met by accepting refugees who come here than by accepting only those Canada chooses.

287

The government often accuses refugee claimants of only pretending to be real refugees when they are actually seeking economic betterment. Yet, ironically, Canada chooses refugees who will cost least and contribute most to the economy. (Even by this criterion, self-selected refugees should be admitted. Self-selected refugees tend to have initiative and enterprise. They are capable of doing things for themselves and taking care of themselves. These people are more likely to be economically successful in Canada than people who cannot organize themselves to get here on their own.)

In principle, there are some good reasons for giving preference to refugees abroad over refugees in Canada. The refugee abroad may have stayed longer in a camp or suffered more severe persecution than refugees who came to Canada. Refugees abroad may be physically weaker than refugees who came. Canada could give preference to the weaker refugees in camps over the more hardy refugees who make it to Canada on their own initiative. Canada could give preference to those in the camps with family ties here over refugees who come on their own who have no relatives here.

Self-selection results in age and sex discrimination. Those who come on their own are overwhelmingly adult males, while women and children disproportionately stay behind. Canada could counter this imbalance by selecting among those who stay in refugee camps over those who come on their own.

All these reasons for giving preference to refugees abroad are acceptable. However, none of them is now relevant given current Canadian immigration policy. Canada does not give preference to refugees abroad who have waited longer in camps or suffered more acute persecution. It does not give preference to those who are less able to resist camp hardships, those who have family ties in Canada, or women and children. Canada does have a selection preference system for refugees in camps, but these humanitarian considerations simply do not enter into the selection process.

Refugees who have suffered severe persecution or prolonged stays in refugee camps are more likely to be ill than refugees who have endured minor persecution or shorter stays.

Canada is less likely to admit these people because their ill health makes them more likely to place demands on Canadian health services.[2]

Further, women and children, who are less able to support themselves than adult males, are less frequently selected by the government to enter Canada. Women and children can accompany a refugee admitted from a camp as his dependants, but relatively few single mothers with children are admitted by the government from refugee camps. In 1987, out of 19,000 refugees accepted by Canada, only 2,660, or fourteen percent, were female heads of families. A mere ten were single mothers whose lives were in danger.

As well as demonstrating a likelihood of successful establishment and good health, refugees in camps must also jump other hurdles that refugees here do not have to face. A refugee in a camp must convince Canadian authorities he will not engage in crime upon his arrival in Canada.[3] A refugee in Canada can be expelled only if he has committed a major crime, not simply because authorities believe he will commit a crime.[4]

The Canadian refugee selection system abroad is geared to what is good for Canada, rather than what is good for refugees. While an immigration policy cannot be faulted on that ground, a refugee policy can. Refugee policy should be humanitarian, with its purpose to help refugees, not to help Canada.

DIRECT ADMISSIONS SYSTEM

The oppressed persons and political prisoners class, designated in 1982, allows the Canadian government to extract people from a situation of immediate peril before they have actually fled the country. However, Canada's direct admissions system for those in danger in home countries suffers from all the defects of Canadian procedures in third countries, including the criterion for successful establishment. In addition, the claimant must face the hazards of remaining within the reach of authorities in his home country. A claimant may be denied access by the local military to the Canadian embassy. Even if he is allowed access, the Canadian embassy may be under local military surveillance and a person may jeopardize his safety simply by approaching a Canadian embassy to make a claim. Or he may fear there is surveillance even when none exists, and be too frightened to approach the embassy.[5]

Once a claim is made at a Canadian post abroad, processing can take six months or more. During that time the claimant remains in his home country, although he is in danger and needs immediate refuge. Canadian posts abroad employ some domestic staff who are nationals of the host country, causing a refugee claimant to fear the confidentiality of his claim may be jeopardized. He will be reluctant to put forward all the details of his claim in such a context.

When a person in danger makes a claim in his own country, others may not be willing to assist him in putting forward his claim for fear of jeopardizing themselves. For instance, while doctors in Canada are quite willing to examine refugee claimants and provide medical reports of the sequelae of torture, doctors in the country of torture may be reluctant to provide such reports.

The oppressed persons and political prisoners designated class is not useless. Indeed, it is a welcome addition to the Canadian panoply of protection for persons in danger and should be maintained. However, permitting oppressed persons and political prisoners claims to be made in one of the listed countries is not an adequate substitute for processing claims within Canada for those refugees who manage to arrive here.

REFUGEE DETERMINATION IN THE RESETTLEMENT PROCESS

Opponents of refugee self-selection, such as Progressive Conservative Senator Richard Doyle, asked during discussions of Bill C-55 why a person who has money to buy an airline ticket to Canada to make a refugee claim should have a better chance of being accepted than a person who applies from a refugee camp abroad. Why, Doyle asked, should we have a system of self-selection for refugees who are financially able to come to Canada rather than a system of government selection?

In reality, Doyle's question is really an argument. The argument is that refugees should not be given an artificial preference by Canada just because they manage to arrive here on their own. Doyle argues that people who arrive without permission should not benefit, and those who stay in refugee camps until they are processed should not suffer.

But Doyle's contention is erroneous because of the differing legal regimes for refugees in Canada and abroad, the unfair refugee determination component of the resettlement process abroad, poor conditions in camps, deterrence schemes, and procedural unfairness.

A refugee lawfully in Canada has a right to remain and will be given permission to stay if no other country has already given him protection. A refugee outside of Canada, on the other hand, has no right to enter even if he has no protection from any other country.

The refugee determination component of the resettlement process in Canadian visa offices abroad is unfair. The decision-maker is not independent from Immigration and External Affairs. Refugee status is determined by the local officer in charge of the visa office, who is normally not an expert in refugee law and human rights conditions in persecuting countries. A refugee applying for admission to Canada from abroad has no right to appeal, no access to Canadian courts, no right to counsel. Counsel are routinely denied the opportunity to participate in the refugee interview abroad.

A refugee has no right to an oral hearing before the person deciding. Nor has he any right to an interpreter. One person, an immigration officer, interviews. Another person, the officer in charge, decides. A person doesn't even have the right to make a refugee claim abroad. The visa officer can simply refuse to consider the claim. Where a refusal is given, a refugee has no right to reasons for the refusal.

Because a refugee in Canada is more likely to be recognized as such by Canada than a refugee abroad, refugees have good reason to come to Canada. By coming to Canada on their own, refugees have a far greater chance of being recognized. Once in Canada, a person has a legal right to remain until his refugee claim is determined.

CONDITIONS IN THE COUNTRY OF ASYLUM

It is false to assume a refugee in a camp is protected, and that we should not worry about sending him back, as proposed under Canada's safe third country concept. Practically speaking, a country neighbouring the persecuting country may not be an appropriate refuge.

Refugee camps bordering the country fled are often viewed as guerilla camps and are subject to bombing or cross-border military attacks by the persecuting country's armed forces. Often, neighbouring countries are ideologically similar to the country of persecution. On occasion, they persecute refugees within their borders.

As well, refugee camps often lack hygiene, adequate shelter, and proper food. Refugees are given no work, no schooling. They are restricted to the camps, and may end up staying there for long periods of time. They are forced to endure a life of unmitigated misery, squalid poverty, hunger, disease and enforced inactivity in the camps.

If the international refugee burden-sharing system worked effectively and moved refugees out of the camps quickly, the camps might be a viable first step. However, in light of the prolonged delays and conditions it is cruel to insist that all refugee claimants be returned to these camps.

Much the same argument holds true for refugees coming from other Western resettlement countries where they have been deterred from seeking protection. Western countries have set up harsh deterrence schemes to discourage would-be refugees. Refugees may be detained and then subject to harsher treatment than common criminals. In Western countries as in the Third world, work, education and mobility are denied. Refugees are forced to lead lives of idleness, wasting their formative and productive years.

Furthermore, refugees in the West are denied protection procedurally. Unfairness in refugee determination is a disguised form of expulsion. Due process safeguards are denied refugee claimants, leading to inaccurate results and forced return to the country of danger fled.

THIRD WORLD "SCREENING" —
THE COLLAPSE OF FIRST ASYLUM

Third World countries of proximate refuge that do not want to provide protection to refugees have imitated First World countries' deterrence schemes, detentions, and rejection of refugees. Instead of just rejecting the refugees as a group, stopping them at sea, pushing their boats off, closing the borders, or sending them back, Third World countries have started to introduce the unfair and distorted selection systems characteristic of the Western world.

Since July, 1985, the Thai government has been screening new arrivals from Laos. Since June, 1988, the Hong Kong government has been screening Vietnamese boat people and detaining them under horrible conditions. These screening systems have all the due process failings of the Western screening systems.

The Association of South East Asian Nations (Asean) — Brunei, Indonesia, Malaysia, the Philippines, Singapore and Thailand — announced in March, 1989 that Vietnamese seeking asylum will no longer be automatically regarded as refugees eligible for resettlement to a Western country. The refugees will have to go through procedures similar to those now in place in Hong Kong. The six countries and Hong Kong have borne the burden of providing temporary refuge to Vietnamese refugees who were awaiting resettlement in the West.

Asean countries want those who fail screening put in holding camps. Asean officials say that the holding camps should be sufficiently uncomfortable to persuade the Vietnamese to return home.

If the South East Asian first asylum countries were simply to send refugees back without screening, the West would object and pressure for change as it has in the past. When countries like Thailand and Hong Kong reject refugees by mimicking the procedures the West has used, the West is in no position to complain. Indeed, Gordon Fairweather, the head of the Canadian Immigration and Refugee Board, has gone out of his way to praise the Hong Kong system.

The West's obsession with stopping spontaneous movement of refugees from countries of first asylum is generating the collapse of first asylum. We are seeing not so much a crude and indiscriminate rejection of all refugees, but rather a sophisticated simulation in first asylum countries of the techniques developed in Western resettlement countries.

The collapse of first country asylum will occur ever more swiftly, ever more surely, once safe third country policies are put in place. When Canada accepts a refugee from a third country, intermediate protection by that third country for other refugees becomes more likely. When Canada rejects a refugee that has come to Canada from a third country and sends him back, protection for other refugees by that third country becomes less likely.

When Canada rejects refugees on the basis that they might have been protected elsewhere, Canada is denying burden-sharing in a tangible and glaring way. Canada has protested other countries' denial of protection. Those protests will have little credibility if Canada returns refugees from those countries.

For instance, Canada has protested the denial of protection by Thailand of refugees from Vietnam and Kampuchea. How can those protests remain credible if Canada sends Vietnamese refugees who have come to Canada from Thailand back to Thailand? Canada's rejection of Vietnamese refugees makes the Thai acceptance of them less likely.

THE SAFE THIRD COUNTRY CONCEPT

Originally, Bill C-55 denied access to anyone who came from a government-deemed "safe third country." As amended, the Act denies access to a refugee from "a country that complies with Article 33 of the [Refugee] Convention."[6] Article 33 commits signatory states not to return refugees to countries where their lives or freedoms would be threatened. Though the terminology has changed, the concept remains the same.

However, the safe third country concept is dubious. Just because a country is generally safe does not mean it is safe for all persons. A glaring example is the United States, which has mistreated Salvadoran and Guatemalan refugees. Indeed, in the case of *Orantes Hernandez v. Meese,*[7] a United States District

Court decided April 1988, that the U.S. is unsafe for Salvadoran refugees. If the United States is on the safe third country list, a Salvadoran who has spent time there before applying for refugee status in Canada would automatically be sent back to the U.S. Even though Salvadoran refugees are systematically denied protection there, nobody in Canada could question whether the Salvadoran was safe or unsafe in the U.S. before sending him there.

To take another example, because of the United Kingdom's restrictive application of the refugee definition, Sri Lankans are generally not considered refugees. If Sri Lankans were sent back to the U.K. from Canada, they would be removed from England.

If the safe third country system is implemented, the Canadian Cabinet will devise the list of safe third countries. There is no room for argument if the Cabinet determination is considered wrong. A country that may initially be safe may subsequently be unsafe. In the past, the government of Canada has taken at times six months to react to changes in country conditions as they affect temporary humanitarian programmes. The government is slow to change and, when a situation deteriorates, tends to believe that the refugee concerns are fabricated, or that a refugee faces no real danger on return.

A breakdown in law and order in a remote corner of the world is not immediately apparent worldwide. A refugee claimant in Canada can give evidence of the disorder during a hearing, if he gets a chance. If the country he fled is on the safe third country list, the claimant never gets an opportunity to detail the dangers of the third country. He will automatically be declared ineligible to have access to the Canadian refugee determination process and will be returned to the so-called safe third country.

Bill C-55 provides that when determining whether a country is a safe third country, the Cabinet must have regard to the record of the country in terms of its policies and practices with respect to Convention refugee claims.[8] But what does that mean? If that provision is applied to encompass refugee determination systems, then even many Western democratic countries would not meet the safe third country standards. Indeed, Canada itself would not meet this standard under the new legislation. On the other hand, if Canada were regarded as a country that is safe, even under Bill C-55, hardly a refugee determination system in the world could fail to make the list.

Presumably, the new legislation is concerned only with a country's record with respect to expulsion of refugees without consideration. As long as the claim is considered, no matter how unfairly, then the country must be regarded as safe. If that is the law's true meaning, then return to so-called safe third countries would mean inexorable disaster for those returned.

Under the law, a person recognized, and who claims refugee status in Canada, as a refugee in a provisional asylum country, can put in evidence of a well-founded fear of persecution in the provisional asylum country.[9] If the Canadian system acknowledges a credible-basis for that fear, the claimant in Canada passes eligibility screening and goes to a credible-basis hearing on the claim that he has a well-founded fear of persecution in his home country.

However, and this is quite bizarre, a person who has never been recognized as a refugee in the intermediate country has no similar opportunity to describe his fear of persecution in that country. Cabinet decides whether the intermediate country generally respects human rights, without consideration of any particular claimant. As long as the claimant is a member of a class that has a right of entry to the intermediate country or a right to have the merits of a refugee claim determined in that intermediate country, back he goes, no matter how serious the impending persecution.

ADVISORY COMMITTEE — PREJUDGED CONSTITUTIONALITY

Canada's new legislation provides for an advisory committee to advise the government on countries to be placed on the safe third country list.[10] Gordon Fairweather, chairman of the Immigration and Refugee Board, is also a member of the advisory committee. This is totally inappropriate. Fairweather should resign. In advance of any argument or testimony, it appears he has made a *de facto* decision on the constitutionality of the safe third country concept even though Fairweather may one day be called to make that decision from the bench in his role as chairman of the IRB.

Consider what would happen if the advisory committee recommended that a country be designated as safe, and the government accepted and legislated the designation by Order in Council. A refugee from that country would then be denied access to Canada's refugee determination system by a Refugee Board member and an adjudicator. But the refugee might challenge the constitutionality of that designation when appearing before the Refugee Board member and adjudicator, arguing that the situation is not safe for him regardless of the general situation in that third country.

What could the Refugee Board member say when the Chairman of the Board has already said the country is safe? The Board member deciding may be Fairweather himself. What could Fairweather say to the refugee when he has already decided the country is safe? How could the refugee have a fair determination of that point in those circumstances?

Indeed, Fairweather's behaviour in relation to the whole legislation has been questionable: he has touted, promoted, endorsed, and advertised the law. "'Immigrants have nothing to fear from the law," he said. "I do not think the new system has anything to do with any increase in smuggling human flesh."

The Immigration and Refugee Board put out a pamphlet in 1989 titled *Refugee Determination: What it Is and How it Works.* Gordon Fairweather says in the pamphlet's introduction, "Fairness, compassion and openness are at the heart of the new refugee determination system..."

How will Fairweather deal with a constitutional challenge saying the system is not fair? In advance of hearing any arguments, he has made up his mind the system is fair.

His behaviour is unheard of for someone in a quasi-judicial capacity. Canadians would be astonished if the head of the Tax Court went around the country presenting virtues of Canada's Income Tax Act, or if the chairman of the Court Martials Appeal Tribunal extolled the Defence Act.

Fairweather's actions compromise not only him, but the whole Immigration and Refugee Board. The Board has the power and duty to deal with the constitutionality of all aspects of the law, in addition to the safe third country concept. The Board cannot assume its own legislation is valid until the Federal Court rules to the contrary. According to the Canadian Charter of Rights and Freedoms, remedies for Charter violations can be given in a court of competent jurisdiction.[11] The Board is a court of competent jurisdiction for refugee Charter challenges.[12]

In exercising its Charter jurisdiction, the Board has to follow the same legal principles as it would in exercising other components of its jurisdiction. The Board must hear both sides and decide on material before it, not in advance of the hearing. All of these principles are violated when the Chairman promotes the law openly. In attempting to enhance the law's credibility, Fairweather has undercut the Refugee Board's credibility.

AN EMPTY LIST

The new legislation sanctions designating third countries as safe. But this power need not ever be used. For instance, the government has never used the Immigration Act power to require licensing of paid non-legal counsel before they can represent persons at immigration inquiries and at the Immigration and Refugee Board.[13] If the government can refrain from invoking the power to license counsel, it can also refrain from using the power to designate safe third countries.

Canada's Immigration and Refugee Board Documentation Centre circulated a background paper by Guy Goodwin Gill setting out criteria and guidelines for choosing safe third countries. The paper said "threats incidental to daily life would not normally be included as a criterion for deciding a country was unsafe."

The paper also suggested recognition rates of refugee claimants from that country be analysed. The implication was that a country with a high recognition rate of refugee claimants as refugees, according to the Immigration and Refugee Board, would be considered safe.

However, a discussion of criteria for designating safe third countries, just as for assessing persecution, is meaningful only if circumstances of individual cases are considered. But when individual circumstances are irrelevant, a safe third country criteria discussion lacks a context.

The safe third country concept is not only unfair to individuals, but also unworkable by government if it were implemented in a comprehensive manner. There are 160 countries in the world to designate as safe or unsafe. But the system is more complex than this. It also allows separate ratings for different classes of people who might be sent back to each country. For example, the United States could be unsafe for Salvadorans and Guatemalans, but safe for all others. If we start looking at categories of nationals for every country and determining if they are safe or unsafe in every other country, the number of categories to be considered is 160 multiplied by 160, or over 25,000. To keep current information on 25,000 plus categories is an impossible task for government. It is far simpler to examine each claimant individually to determine whether or not he would be safe or unsafe in the third country.

Canada should keep the safe third country list empty. This would please the refugee support community. It would also make eminent sense from the government's perspective. The safe third country concept was the most controversial and criticized provision of the law. While several components aroused concern and dissatisfaction, eliminating individual consideration from the refugee determination process was at the top of virtually everyone's list of concerns.

A decision not to establish a safe third country list would do more to mend relations between the government and the refugee concern community than any other possible single step the government could take. It would indicate a willingness on the part of government to pay attention to the non-governmental community's concerns. Although it would not mean that NGOs approve of the legislation, at least the fervour and depth of criticism would be diminished.

It would also avoid offending countries which did not appear on the list. For example, the U.S. government would no doubt take umbrage if Canada made a decision to leave the U.S. off the list for Guatemalan and Salvadoran refugees. Canada would be caught in a dilemma: leave the United States off the list, in whole or in part, and risk offending the U.S., or put the U.S. on the list and risk refugees' lives.

At one point, an Immigration Department official said the government was considering putting on the safe third country list only Western European and North American countries. Third World countries were not being considered. If it did that, Canada would offend developing countries by suggesting only the West is safe. Again, the best way to avoid this implied criticism is to have no list.

An empty list would be viable. More people would enter Canada's refugee determination process, but not a flood. An expeditious, efficient system could handle the load while discouraging spurious claims, which have been a problem in the past. Additional people in the system could be easily managed.

Any safe third country designation is bound to be challenged in the courts, creating legal costs for the government. An empty list is more difficult to challenge.

In December, 1988, Immigration Minister Barbara McDougall said she was "prepared to proceed with no country on the safe third country list... We think the new system will be able to function well without it." McDougall's statement is not the final word. When and if a backlog develops in the new system, Departmental pressure will increase to implement the list.

THE NGO RESPONSE TO THE SAFE THIRD COUNTRY RULE

What countries should be on the safe third country list? What criteria should be used for deciding when a country should be on the list, and when it should be taken off the list? The United Nations High Commission for Refugees refused to answer these questions when the government of Canada asked. The High Commission focuses on individuals and will determine an individual's safety in a country, but it will not judge whether a country as a whole is safe or unsafe. The refugee definition is, after all, an individualized definition based on individual circumstances. For the UNHCR to assist in creating Canada's safe third country list would, I believe, mean abandoning its mandate.

Major NGO players have recently formulated a number of different proposals dealing with the controversial safe third country concept. The European Consultation on Refugees in Exile (ECRE), a non-governmental organization, sets out five conditions which must be met before an asylum-seeker can be returned to an intermediate country:

1. The asylum-seeker must be assured protection and assistance if returned.

2. The asylum-seeker must have effective access to local refugee determination procedures of the first asylum country.

3. The asylum-seeker must have in the first asylum country effective access to opportunities for resettlement elsewhere.

4. There must be facilities for temporary local settlement of asylum-seekers.

5. Asylum-seekers must be able to return voluntarily to their home country once returned to the first asylum country.

Amnesty International has produced a similar proposal, which sets out four conditions to be met before a refugee or asylum-seeker can be forcibly returned to an intermediate country:

1. A person must be allowed to enter and have access to a fair refugee determination system. AI goes beyond ECRE in stipulating that local procedures must be fair.

2. AI proposes the intermediate country be a signatory to the Refugee Convention. ECRE proposes only that, whenever possible, countries should be party to the Convention.

3. Amnesty International proposes, as a parallel to ECRE's requirement of protection, that the intermediate country respect the spirit *de facto* of the Refugee Convention. AI is concerned that an overly narrow, legalistic approach to the

Convention may mean that the purpose of protection is frustrated.

4. AI submits that the safe third country determination should be done on an individual basis. ECRE's proposal is quiet on this point, although it is unlikely ECRE anticipated a safe third country rule like Canada's that would make determinations of safe countries *en bloc* without a thought to individual circumstances.

Amnesty International's recommendations have nothing to match ECRE's conditions of assistance, resettlement, temporary settlement and voluntary return. AI's mandate prevents proposals on such matters.

The Canadian Council for Refugees differs from AI and ECRE in that it is totally opposed to the safe third country concept, under any conditions. Regardless of what intermediate country refugees pass through, the CCR says they should be allowed access to Canada's refugee determination system. Refugees should not be forcibly returned to an intermediate country.

The differences among non-governmental organizations may be more theoretical than real. Both AI and ECRE believe their conditions are unrealistic. If accepted, no one would ever be returned to an intermediate country.

DENMARK'S THIRD COUNTRY RULE

Denmark has in place a safe third country rule that has proved disastrous. An October, 1986 amendment to the Danish Aliens Act said refugee claimants without visas would be denied entry.[14] According to a proviso, the foreigner could not be expelled to a country in which he risked persecution as set out in the Refugee Convention, or to a country in which the foreigner would not be protected against further expulsion to a country of persecution.

An alien is stopped by Danish police at the port of entry. Police submit the person's case to the Directorate for Aliens, by telephone or fax. Access to the Danish Refugee Council and to all other counselling is denied. The asylum-seeker can appeal a denial of entry to the Minister of Justice, but is removed pending appeal.

The Danish Refugee Council (DRC) conducted a study of the safe third country system after its first year in operation.[15] The Council followed twenty-six asylum-seekers who had come to Denmark without proper documentation. Four were allowed to stay, and twenty-two were expelled. Of the twenty-two, only six were admitted immediately to Denmark's "safe third countries."

Of sixteen remaining, three were sent back to the country of persecution, two asylum-seekers disappeared, presumed forcibly returned to the country of persecution, five were eventually admitted to Denmark after an attempted expulsion failed, and three became refugees in orbit, travelling back and forth after being expelled.

In one respect, Denmark's system is stricter than the Canadian system. The Danish safe third country structure covers asylum-seekers who were in transit in third countries, whereas Canada's system excludes claimants merely in transit from being forcibly returned to those countries.

In another respect, the Danish system is better than Canada's in that safe third country determination is individualized, and not done by groups. Nevertheless, the law turned out to be essentially unworkable. Because the Canadian system prevents individualized determination, the Canadian experience would presumably be even more catastrophic.

During the first year of Denmark's safe third country system, 791 persons were expelled. If, as DRC believed, the twenty-two expulsions studied were a representative sample, they show the Danish system functioned as intended only one third of the time.

The Danish Refugee Council concluded: "It seems reasonably established through the experience of the Danish Refugee Council concerning expulsion of asylum-seekers that expulsions, in the way they are carried out, involved grave risks for the asylum-seekers and, in many cases, are carried out to 'non-safe' destinations."

Since Denmark's safe third country rule was implemented, the principle of refugee protection and non-refoulement have been violated. Do we want Canada to have a similar record of forcibly returning refugees to countries of persecution?

Self-selection should be allowed alongside Canadian selection abroad. A refugee is someone out of his country by reason of a well-founded fear of persecution. In other words he has left out of fear. He has chosen to leave. He has not left because an asylum country has invited him or chosen him.

The Refugee Convention obliges signatories to give protection to those who have selected themselves to escape dangers in their home countries. Rejecting self-selection repudiates the Refugee Convention's obligations. Signatories are not free to choose whether or not to protect refugees. They are obliged to do so.

Chapter 19

WHY PROTECT REFUGEES?

The starting point for refugee protection is the need to help those in danger. The Jerusalem Talmud says, "Whoever preserves one life, it is as if he has saved a complete world." The Old Testament and the New Testament both say, "Love your neighbour as yourself." Denying protection to refugees is a rejection of a moral imperative incumbent upon us all. We have a duty to help other people in distress, to do unto others as we would have them do unto us. In any humanitarian system, people must support the less fortunate and those who need assistance in times of crisis.

A LEGAL DUTY

Protection of refugees constitutes more than just a moral duty. It is also a legal duty. It is a legal duty to save another's life, and it is an offence for a person or a government to stop someone from saving a life.

The Quebec Charter of Rights and Freedoms provides:

> Every human being whose life is in peril has a right to assistance. Every person must come to the aid of anyone whose life is in peril either personally or by calling for aid, by giving him the necessary and immediate physical assistance, unless it involves danger to himself or a third person, or he has other valid reasons.

In Belgium, France, Germany, Greece, Italy and Poland, it is an offence under the penal codes to fail to render reasonable aid in case of danger. In the United States, the State of Vermont penal code makes it an offence to refuse aid to those exposed to grave physical harm.[1]

Many states require assistance to people in peril in the open seas. United States Navy Captain Alexander Balian was court-martialed for failing to rescue a group of eighty Vietnamese boat people in the South China Sea in June, 1988. Captain Balian ordered his men not to throw life belts to refugees who abandoned the boat and swam to his ship, and one refugee who climbed a line hanging from the ship was shaken off by the crew. The Vietnamese were later rescued by Filipino fishermen after thirty-seven days at sea in a broken-down drifting boat. They had resorted to murder and cannibalism of three of their group in order to stay alive.

Canada's Criminal Code makes it an offence to prevent or impede, without reasonable cause, any person who is attempting to save another's life. That Code provision alone means the government of Canada will break the law if it impedes protection to refugees.[2,3]

The Law Reform Commission of Canada recommended that failure to rescue be inserted as a crime in the Criminal Code. It would read: "Everyone commits a crime who, perceiving another person is in immediate danger of death or serious harm, does not take reasonable steps to assist him." An exception is proposed where the person cannot take reasonable steps to assist without risk of death or serious harm or where he has some other valid reason for doing so.[4]

ASYLUM AND ROOT CAUSES

Historically, one of the arguments raised against refugee protection is that the refugee burden is the responsibility of the true culprits, the human rights violators themselves. Violators should cease their violations and the refugee outflow will stop. Innocent countries like Canada have done nothing to generate the refugee outflow and should therefore not be expected to cope with the burden.

We have learned from history how shallow and pointless such an argument is. Refusing to grant asylum to refugees does nothing to end human rights violations. On the contrary, refugees are simply returned to countries of danger, and the persecutor is fortified in his belief that the world community cares little about his infractions, or even supports them. The oppressor is awarded a *carte blanche*: he can persecute with impunity.

If the ultimate goal is to end human rights violations, providing protection to refugees is necessary. Without refuge, it is a mere sham to express any concern for human rights violations.

Before and during the Nazi murder of six million Jews in Europe and the attempt to exterminate the whole Jewish people, a Jewish refugee population in the hundreds of thousands attempted to flee the Holocaust. These Jewish refugees were turned away everywhere and had nowhere to go. They were sent away from Canada and other countries around the world to extermination in Europe's death camps.

Canada's record of admissions during this sordid period was arguably the worst. Canada failed to provide refuge to Jewish refugees because of anti-Semitism and the government's denial of the concept of protection. Hume Wrong, the Deputy Under-Secretary of State for External Affairs said, on December 17, 1942, that the Allies knew definitely two million Jews had already been massacred by the Nazis. When asked whether the government intended to admit Jewish refugees to rescue them from the Holocaust, he replied the solution was not to admit them to Canada "but to defeat Germany."[5]

The Allies defeated Germany in May, 1945, two and one-half years later. By then the death toll had risen from 2 million to six million. Canada's refusal to admit Jewish refugees showed that whatever motive Canada had for fighting Nazi Germany, saving lives of helpless victims of the Nazi killing machine was not one of them.

The tragedy of the Holocaust illustrates that an emphasis on root causes alone cannot avert disaster. Wrong cited the hideous violence of Nazism as a reason for defeating Germany, but Canada refused to do what it could to curb the effects of that violence.

RACISM

A certain percentage of Canadians hold racist sentiments. B'nai Brith Canada's League for Human Rights asks two indicator questions about Jews, Italians, Poles and Blacks to determine attitudes: "Do you think [Jews, etc.] have too much power?" and "Would you vote for a person of [Jewish, etc.] descent, if nominated by the party you normally vote for in your riding?" A summary of the League's survey results from 1983 to 1986 shows 15.1 percent of Canadians think Jews have too much power, and 9.6 percent would not vote for a Jewish candidate nominated for their party. Even for Poles, who were subject to the least discrimination in the survey, the corresponding results are 3.8 percent and 8.1 percent respectively.[6]

Discrimination based on race is reflected in attitudes to immigration and refugees. Some racists advocate that entry to Canada be restricted to immigrants from Europe, the United Kingdom, and Scandinavia. Peter Hope, a Confederation of Regions Party (COR) candidate against Joe Clark in Yellowhead in the 1988 federal election, supported a "white only" immigration and refugee policy. Hope said the Canadian immigration mix should return to more traditional patterns, which he referred to as basically Caucasian.

Douglas Collins, a Vancouver area candidate for the Reform Party in the 1988 federal election, wanted a return to immigration policies of the 1950s and 1960s, when quotas were imposed on non-whites. He said Canada should have fewer

Third World immigrants. "For years now you [Parliament] have been keeping white folk out and letting every other SOB in. We're entitled to our own cultural traditions," Collins wrote.

The party leaders of Hope and Collins distanced themselves from their candidates' position, but only half-heartedly. COR leader Elmer Knutson said Hope should choose his words more carefully in the future, but he did not expel or discipline him. Reform Party leader Preston Manning refused to sign nomination papers for Collins unless the candidate abjured racism. Collins refused and sat out the election. But Manning also said the Reform Party hoped to exploit the issue of immigration in the election. He referred to the theory that the Trudeau government opened up non-white immigration deliberately to break up English-speaking Canada's homogeneity. Manning neither agreed nor disagreed with the theory.[7]

Hope and Collins' arguments are evidently steeped in racism. When someone talks of returning to traditional patterns of immigration, it is worth pointing out Canada's culturally "homogeneous" immigration policy was a result of the government's traditional exclusion of people according to race.

The notion that Canadian culture is threatened by providing protection to Third World refugees is misplaced. Despite the significant numbers of immigrants and refugees from abroad each year, the totals represent about one-half of one percent of Canada's population. To suggest a relatively small, dispersed and disparate group threatens Canadian culture is far-fetched. In fact, the greater threat is to immigrants and refugees, who are inevitably pressured to conform to the majority culture. Immigrants and refugees risk losing their own cultural heritage.

The impression of a homogeneous Canadian culture threatened now by immigrants and refugees is false. Canada is a multicultural nation, and has long been so. Canadian immigration and cultural patterns, originally French, then British, have evolved over time. Eastern European immigration before the First World War was as dramatic a shift in Canadian immigration patterns as the increase in Third World immigration recently. Canada was originally native, not British and French. It is historically selective to suggest that European immigration is traditional. It insults our original peoples and ignores the traditions they contribute to Canada.

Third World immigrants and refugees do not threaten Canada. They benefit Canada economically and culturally, contributing richness and variety. Canada would be culturally stunted if all immigrants were drawn from European cultures.

Racists often say they are concerned about the unfairness against whites, but Canada does not discriminate against whites in favour of non-white immigrants. Race is no longer a criterion for immigrants and refugees. If anything, in the operation of the law, as Chapter 1 demonstrates, the problem is the reverse — Third World immigrants and refugees suffer from systemic discrimination.

Many racists fail to distinguish between immigrants and refugees. Immigrants come here willingly for family or economic reasons with an intention to stay. Refugees come to Canada not by choice, but because they are forced to flee. If the danger disappears, they may want to return to their country of origin. True, refugees come disproportionately from Third World countries. But Canada does not favour Third World refugees over First or Second World (Eastern European) refugees. It just happens that the Third World now produces a far larger refugee outflow than the First World or Second World.

To restrict entry by refugees from the Third World in favour of entrants from Western Europe denies protection to refugees. During the Second World War, Jews fleeing the Nazi threat constituted a real and significant refugee outflow from Western Europe. Racists then did not talk of the need for immigrants from Europe, because that did not serve their racist purpose.

Racism is unjustifiable as a basis for immigration policy. It is particularly heinous as a basis for refugee policy. Immigrants refused entry on the ground of race lose the opportunity for economic betterment. Refugees denied protection because of their race may lose their lives. Refusing protection to refugees on the basis of race is a form of racist violence.

Some people espouse racist immigration and refugee policies, yet reject the racist vocabulary. In September, 1987, a group that calls itself the Immigration Association of Canada ran an advertisement in Canadian newspapers which said that the present rate of immigration from Third World countries threatens to make English- and French-speaking Canadians "minorities in their own land" by early in the next century. "The story of mankind is filled with the scattered remnants of once great powers that forgot to stand guard," the advertisement said.

One of the people responsible for the ad was Kim Abbott, a former director of the Canadian Immigration Service, the predecessor of the present Immigration Department. To criticize the ad as racist was "name-calling," and "emotional labelling," Abbott said. "This is an emotional area and it is legitimate to have differing points of view," he said.[8]

But criticizing the Immigration Association of Canada's policy is not name-calling. It is an attempt to point out that their policies are implicitly if not explicitly racist. English and French are not in danger of becoming a minority in Canada. Yet, the immigration and refugee policies of those who advocate restricting entry to preserve Canada's traditional way of life would be racist in their effect.

Abbott also said the new refugee legislation was exactly what Canada needed, but that it should have been excluded from the Charter of Rights and Freedoms provisions. Abbott and his association, virtually alone in the non-governmental sector in its support for the new laws, apparently believes the legislation violates the fundamental rights and freedoms of Canadians. Abbott would keep out Third World refugees rather than abide by the Charter's guarantees of equality.

REFUGEES AS QUEUE-JUMPERS[9]

Refugees are sometimes called queue-jumpers. Everyone else waits their turn to be processed abroad, proponents of this argument say, while refugees come here without waiting, jumping ahead of all those who try to comply with Canadian immigration requirements.

However, refugees are processed separately. They do not affect the numbers of economic immigrants or family class immigrants who come to Canada. If refugee numbers are greater than expected, there is no corresponding cutback in non-refugee immigration.

The metaphor of queues or lines waiting to be dealt with by immigration authorities is totally misconceived. When a queue is jumped, those at the back of the line end up waiting longer because someone has jumped ahead. However, those non-refugee immigrants who apply from abroad are processed at the same pace, and receive visas at the same time, regardless of whether refugees apply from abroad or in Canada.

When refugees apply in Canada they are not jumping ahead of economic and family immigrants in an immigration queue. When refugees are abroad, they are not waiting or lined up in the same queue as economic and family class immigrants.

Economic immigrants who come to Canada to claim refugee status are in fact queue-jumping. But they are not refugees. They are abusing the system. Abuse of the refugee system is no reason to close down the system, but a reason to weed out abuse.

REFUGEES AS TERRORISTS

Another argument is that Canada has become a safe haven for foreign terrorists. Critics say that terrorists can come to Canada, claim refugee status, and remain in Canada, though they fail to meet Canadian security requirements.

But if we look at one particular case of a convicted terrorist who came to Canada and claimed refugee status, Mahmoud Mohammad, we see that the real problem is not the refugee system. It is government incompetence. Mohammad originally came here as a landed immigrant. He was able to enter and stay, not because he was a refugee, but because the government bungled.

Mohammad and Maher Suleiman attacked and destroyed an El Al jetliner in Athens in 1968, killing an Israeli man. They identified themselves as members of the Popular Front for the Liberation of Palestine. Mohammad was sentenced by a Greek court in 1970 to seventeen years in jail, Suleiman to fourteen years and three months. Four months later, Palestinian terrorists hijacked an Olympic Airways plane and threatened to blow it up with fifty-five people on board unless Greek authorities freed seven prisoners, including Mohammad and Suleiman. The Greek government gave in, and Mohammad was released.

In 1986, Mohammad applied to come to Canada as a landed immigrant from Spain. A security check by the Canadian Security and Intelligence Service (CSIS) in Spain turned up no record of his past terrorist activity or criminal conviction. He was granted landed status. CSIS in Ottawa knew about Mohammad, but the CSIS agent in Spain saw no need to check with headquarters.

At the last minute before Mohammad was to come to Canada, CSIS issued an alert to the Toronto airport warning Mohammad was on his way. If he had been stopped at the airport, he would have been denied landing. However, the shift changed, and the new shift was not told of the alert. Mohammad was landed, on February 25, 1987.

The immigration inquiry should have been launched immediately, but it was not scheduled until February 15, 1988, fully a year after his arrival in Canada. It probably would not even have been scheduled then if Mohammad's presence in Canada had not been made public by the media. The Mohammad case has documented obvious failings in Canada's immigration security system.

However, this case does not suggest that we should deny all refugee claimants access to Canada for fear some may be terrorists. Although Mohammad has claimed refugee status, neither Canadian law nor the Refugee Convention requires Canada to give protection to security risks or people who have committed serious criminal offences.

The best way of preventing a repetition of this incident is to prosecute terrorists in Canada. Hijacking is an offence under Canada's Criminal Code. A person can be charged with the offence no matter where the crime was committed, provided the person is found in Canada.*

---

* Because Mohammad did not serve his sentence he could not argue "double jeopardy" if prosecuted in Canada for the hijacking. The Canadian Charter of Rights and Freedoms prohibits prosecution for the same offence a second time only where the person has served his sentence, if found guilty the first time.

If terrorists, hijackers and war criminals know they can be prosecuted in Canada for international criminal law offences they have committed, they will be reluctant to come here.

REFUGEES AS AN ECONOMIC BURDEN

Some people maintain refugees are taking jobs from Canadians or adding to welfare costs. Charity, it is said, begins at home. We should use our scarce resources to help disadvantaged Canadians rather than refugees from abroad.

This economic argument against refugees is misplaced. We do not protect refugees to make money or to help the Canadian economy. We protect refugees because they need protection. How can a nation justify carrying out any humanitarian programme if it must be judged by its economic benefit? The point is to help people.

In any event, refugees do not hurt the economy. Don DeVoretz of Simon Fraser University concludes newcomers have been economically successful in Canada regardless of the particular immigration policy in place at the time. Immigrants and refugees do not take jobs away from native-born Canadians or take more from the public purse than they contribute, according to DeVoretz's studies.[10]

A study by the Committee for Economic Development of Australia found immigrants and refugees have had a positive effect in the Australian economy. They "have higher labour force participation rates and are prepared to work long hours in order to establish themselves in their new country."[11]

Rather than being economically undesirable, refugees are often economically highly desirable. The persecuted in many countries are educated, professional, trained and articulate. They are less likely than the unskilled and the illiterate to be submissive to tyrants or to accept the propaganda of tyrants as truth.

Even where persecution is not directed specifically against the educated, the educated may be the first to flee. They see the pattern of what is developing more quickly, are in closer contact with the hierarchy imposing the persecution, and are the first to suffer. As a refugee poster reminds us, Albert Einstein was a refugee.

Refugees create jobs for Canadians by adding to the demand for goods and services. Refugees arrive with few possessions, and tend to spend a disproportionate amount of their income on Canadian goods once they start work.

Immigrants and refugees also help to stimulate the international trade between Canada and their countries of origin. They tend to import goods from their home countries and send Canadian goods back home.

Canada needs immigrants and refugees. Because of the low birth rate of native-born Canadians, combined with emigration, we need newcomers to sustain our population and economy. *The Annual Report to Parliament on Immigration Levels* for 1987 notes the annual rate of population growth in Canada has declined from about three percent in the 1950s to 0.9 percent in 1985. The fertility rate has remained low, at 1.65. The *Levels Report* predicts the Canadian population growth rate after the turn of the century could become negative. A sufficient immigration and refugee inflow would block this anticipated decline. But the current levels are insufficient: even to maintain a zero growth population would require large increases in the influx of immigrants and refugees.

No charitable organization calls for Canada to cease protecting refugees. They are prepared to assist refugees as well as Canadians. Charity may begin at home, but it doesn't end there.

Refugees face danger and privation greater than even the most disadvantaged Canadians. Canadians do not go to sleep every night wondering whether death squads, torture units, or "salvaging" operations by the military or guerillas will attack their homes.[†] Young Canadian boys are not arrested simply for belonging to the wrong ethnic group or living in the wrong ethnic area. Canadian mothers do not have to watch their children being shot or maimed. The Canadian government does not rule by force. Canadians do not have to worry if a sister or brother will be jailed or tortured for participating in a peaceful demonstration against the government. Opponents of the Cana-

---

[†]Salvaging is a term used in the Philippines to refer to the killing of everyone in a village and salvaging of the supplies.

dian government are not made to disappear because they disapprove of government actions.

Protecting refugees means helping people who need help and putting a generous face on Canada to the world. Denying protection to refugees means refusing to help the helpless and painting Canada as a cruel and mean-spirited nation. In the end, the judgement Canadians make about refugees is a judgement we make about ourselves. If Canadians would rather have it said of us that we cared, we tried, and we did what we could to save those in danger, then we owe it to ourselves to make every effort to protect refugees.

Introduction

1. Nichols, *Religion, Refugees and the U.S. Government During World War II*, paper presented to the Oxford Symposium on Refugees (August, 1985), Oxford paper.

2. ABELLA AND TROPER, NONE IS TOO MANY (1982).

3. WYMAN, THE ABANDONMENT OF THE JEWS (1984).

4. Melander, *The Concept of the Term Refugee,* paper presented to the Oxford Symposium on Refugees (August, 1985).

5. Boshyk, *Between East and West*, paper presented to the Oxford Symposium on Refugees (August, 1985).

6. Loescher and Scanlan, *The Politics of Escape,* paper presented to the Oxford Symposium on Refugees (August, 1985).

7. Saloman, *Refugees in the World War,* paper presented to the Oxford Symposium on Refugees (August, 1985).

8. Section XVI.

Chapter 1

1. 9-10 Edward VII S.C. Chapter 27, section 28(c).

2. 9-10 George V Chapter 25 Section 13.

3. P.C. 1203 (June 9, 1919).

4. P.C. 1204 (June 9, 1919).

5. P.C. 2115 (September 16, 1930).

6. CANADA GAZETTE PART II, 548, Regulation 21 (1956).

7. P.C. 1954-1351, Regulation 20.

8. P.C. 1956-785.

9. P.C. 1962-36.

10. 6 Edw VII Chapter 19 Section 20.

11. CANADA GAZETTE, Volume XLI, 3276.

12. Section 37.

13. 6 W.W.R. 1347 (1914).

14. 48-49 Victoria, S.C. Chapter 71, Section 4.

15. 63-64 Victoria S.C. Chapter 32, Section 6.

16. 3 Edward VII S.C. Chapter 8, Section 6.

17. 13-14 George V S.C. Chapter 38.

18. 9-10 Edward VII S.C. Chapter 27, Section 38(a).

19. P.C. 735 65 (1945).

20. 1946 S.C.R. 248; 1947 A.C. 87.

21. ABELLA AND TROPER, NONE IS TOO MANY (1982).

22. CANADIAN JEWISH CONGRESS, RACE RELATIONS AND THE LAW, 93 (1988).

23. Section 9(1).

24. Section 87.

25. Singh v. M.E.I. (1985) 1 S.C.R. 177.

26. Recommendation 28.

27. Immigration manual IS 2 Annex I, Appendix A.

28. Immigration manual IS 28.

29. Recommendation 30.

30 Regulation 14(2).

Chapter 2

1. 15 Columbia Human Rights Law Review 39 (1983).

2. GRAHL-MADSEN, THE STATUS OF REFUGEES IN INTERNATIONAL LAW, Volume 1, 192 (1966).

3. Article B(1).

4. Article A(2).

5. Immigration Manual I.L. 7.

6. I.L. 7.

7. Coles, *Approaching the Refugee Problem Today* (unpublished paper).

8. S.C. Chapter 35 section 48.07(1) (b) (1988).

9. Conclusion III (3).

10. Article I (1).

11. Takkenberg, *Country Report for the Netherlands*, to meeting of European Consultation on Refugee and Exiles, Geneva (October 1 and 2, 1988).

12. Article 3.

13. Article 1.

14. Article 4.

15. Article 45.

16. Immigration Case No. A26 949 415.

17. Article 147.

18. A.I. U.S.A. LEGAL SUPPORT NETWORK NEWSLETTER, 54 to 56 (fall/winter, 1988).

19. Article 6.

Chapter 3

1. Article 33.

2. Conclusion 30 (XxXIV) paragraph (a).

3. Paragraph 199.

4. Singh v. M.E.I. (1985) 58 N.R 1, 64.

5. Conclusion 30 (XXXIV) paragraph (e) (i).

6. Paragraph 196.

7. Conclusion 8 (XXXVIII) paragraphs (e) (vi) and (vii).

8. Conclusion 30 (XXXIV) paragraph (e) (iii).

Chapter 4

1. Regulation 19(4) (k) (ii).

2. Regulation 20(2) (c).

3. CANADA GAZETTE Part II, 1058 (January 31, 1985).

4. CANADA GAZETTE, Part II, 2828 (June 26, 1986).

5. T-2041-88.

6. I.E. 8.19(2) (d).

7. Annual Report, Employment and Immigration Canada (1987-88).

8. Regulation 14.1.

9. Chapter I.E. 8.22.

10 Re Pirbhai 49 B.C.L.R. 275 (1983).

11. Revised Statutes of Canada, Chapter F-1 Section 3(1) (1985).

12. Regulation 3(a).

13. I.E. 8.17(2).

14. PLAUT, REFUGEE DETERMINATION IN CANADA: PROPOSALS FOR A NEW SYSTEM, 153 (1985).

15. Matas, *The Plight of Refugee Claimants*, REFUGE, Volume 4, Number 4, 22 to 24 (May, 1985).

16. Section 87(1).

17. Matas, *The Plight of Refugee Claimants*, REFUGE, Volume 4, Number 2, 22 to 24 (December 1984).

Chapter 5

1. Sevhetoglu, Canadian Law Information Concil 4.14 (1979).

2. Haidekker, 11 Immigration Appeal Cases 442 (1977).

3. Kovar 8 I.A.C. 226 (March/April, 1975).

4. Andrew, *Role of a Canadian Diplomat Abroad*, INERNATIONAL PERSPEC- TIVES, 56 (1974).

5. GRAHL-MADSEN, THE STATUS OF REFUGEES, Volume 1, 191 (1966).

6. April, *Examining the Right of Asylum*, INTERNATIONAL PERSPECTIVES, 46 (May/June, 1974).

7. Mingot (1975) 8 I.A.C. 351 at 356.

8. GRAHL-MADSEN, THE STATUS OF REFUGEES, Volume 1, 201, 208, 215 (1966).

9. *Question of Diplomatic Asylum*, REPORT OF THE SECRETARY GENERAL, U.N.G.A., A/10139, Part I, 17.

10. CASTEL, INTERNATIONAL LAW, 519 (3rd edition, 1976).

11. Andrew, op.cit.

12. CANADIAN YEARBOOK OF INTERNATIONAL LAW, 335 (1976).

13. Question of Diplomatic Asylum, op.cit., Part I, 11.

14. Question of Diplomatic Asylum, op.cit, Part II, 121.

15. Montevideo Treaties of 1933 and 1939; The Havana Convention of 1928 and the Caracas Convention of 1954.

16. GRIEG, INTERNATIONAL LAW, 448 (2nd edition, 1976); April, op.cit.

17. Convention on the Prevention and Punishment of Crimes Against Inter- nationally Protected Persons (1973).

Chapter 6

1. Matas, *The Refugee Claims Procedure: An Overview*, REFUGEE, Vol 3 No. 4, 3 (1984).

2. See Chapter Seven.

3. 99 D.L.R. (3d) 525 at 528 footnote 3 (1980).

4. Re Boun-Leua and M.E.I. (1981) 113 D.L.R. (3d) 414.

Chapter 7

1. T-3857-78, (Unreported).
2. 104 D.L.R. (3d) 664 (1980).
3. 104 D.L.R. (3d) 236 (1980).
4. 36 N.R. 332 (1981).
5. 36 N.R. 305 (1981).
6. 38 N.R. 170 (1981).
7. T-2835-84 (Unreported).
8. 17 D.L.R. (4th) 422 (1985).

Chapter 8

1. Chapter 1 S 6.
2. 89-T-601.
3. S.C. Chapter 35 Section 48.01(7) (1988).
4, Section 45(2).
5. Section 30(2); Regulations.
6. Section 51(l) (b).
7. Section 4 8 (3).
8. Section 4 8 (2).
9. Re Salvatierra and M.E.I. (1980) 99 D.L.R. (3d) 525 at 528 footnote 3.
10. Section 48.01(6)(b).
11. Section 83.1 (1), 83.3 (1).
12. Article 16.
13. Sections 83.2(2); 85.1.
14. Re Singh and M.E.I. (1985) 17 D.L.R. (4th) 422.
15. Section 71.1(12).
16. Sections 83.3 (1.1) ; 83.1 (1) ; 51 (1) (b).
17. T-2040-88.
18. 56 D.L.R. (4th) 82 (1989).

Chapter 9

1. 35-36-37 Eliz. II S.C. Chapter 36 Section 12(1) Adding Section 104.1. Future references are to sections as amended.
2. Article 31(1).
3. Article 3 1 (2).

4. Article 9.

5. Section 98.1.

6. Section 115 (p.1).

7. Section 91.1.

8. Section 48.1.

9. Section 41.

10. Section 95.1.

11. Section 95.2.

12. Section 9 5 (1) (a).

13. Section 95(l)(b).

14. Section 9 5 (1) (i).

15. Section 9 5 (1) (j).

16. Section 103.02(5).

17. Section 103.03.

18. (1984) 11 D.L.R. (4th) 641.

19. Section 103.02(1).

Chapter 10

1. Senate Debates (May 11, 1988).

2. S.C. Chapter 35 Section 30(2) (1988).

3. Section 83.1(1.1).

4. A.C. 176 (1934).

5. 50 D.L.R. (4th) 669 (1988).

6. 52 D.L.R. (4th) 681 (1989).

Chapter 11

1. Sources for this chapter can be found in MATAS, THE SANCTUARY TRIAL (1989).

Chapter 12

1. Sources for this chapter can be found in MATAS, THE SANCTUARY TRIAL (1989).

Chapter 13

1. TORONTO STAR (May 11, 1989).

2. *Article II, Draft Articles on State Responsibility*, YEARBOOK OF THE INTERNATIONAL LAW COMMISSION, VOLUME II, 60.

3. GRAHL-MADSEN, THE STATUS OF REFUGEES IN INTERNATIONAL LAW, VOLUME II, 217 (1966).

4. UN Doc. E./AC.32/SR40, 8–9, quoted in Grahl-Madsen, *loc cit.*

5. 9 L.R.T.W.C. 1 at 18.

6. State of Vermont v. Jeanne Keeler, 26 Santa Clara Law Review 320.

7. Chicago v. Allen Streeter, 26 Santa Clara Law Review 325.

8. People v. Ann Jarker, 26 Santa Clara Law Review 324.

9. Amy Carter Trial, GLOBE AND MAIL (April 15, 16, 1987). WINNIPEG FREE PRESS (April 14, 1987). NEW YORK TIMES (April 7, 1987).

10. Article 18.

11. Article 18.

12. U.N.G.A. Resolution 36/55 (Nov 25, 1981).

13. Article VII.

14. See Article III, American Declaration of the Rights and Duties of Man.

15. Smith and Hogan, CRIMINAL LAW, 326–327 (5th Ed.).

16. 9 L.R.T.W.C. 1 at 18.

17. U.S. v. Von Lees 11 T.W.C. 462 (American Military Tribunal) (1950).

18. Campbell, *Non-Traditional Nuremberg Defense*, 16 CALIF. W.I.L.J. 93 at 95.

19. BEDAU, CIVIL DISOBEDIENCE, 173 (1969).

Chapter 14

1. Sources for this chapter can be found in Matas, *Fairness in Refugee Determination*, MANITOBA LAW JOURNAL (1988).

Chapter 15

1. 15 (XXX).

2. 8 (XXVII).

3. 30 (XXXIV).

4. Article 16(1).

5. A/AC. 96/SR 373.

6. Jaeger, *Study of Irregular Movements of Asylum Seekers and Refugees,* WG/M/2 (August, 1985).

7. 44 (XXXVII).

8. A/AC.96/713.

9. FAL/10-WP/230.

10. Standard 3.36, Annex 9.

11. DANISH REFUGEE COUNCIL , THE ROLE OF AIRLINE COMPANIES IN THE ASYLUM PROCEDURE, 6 (July, 1988).

Chapter 16

1. AMERICA'S WATCH COMMITTEE, GUATEMALAN REFUGEES IN MEXICO 1980–84, 3 (September, 1984).

2. DANISH REFUGEE COUNCIL, REPORT ON A FACT FINDING MISSION TO SRI LANKA, (1988).

3. WASHINGTON POST (September 13, 1988).

4. See Chapter 2.

5. See Chapter 15.

Chapter 17

1. UN Charter Article 2, paragraph 7.

2. Resolution 35 (196).

3. Resolution 29 (XXXVII).

4. E/CN.4/1503.

5. Martin, A.J.I.L. 598 (1982).

Chapter 18

1. Regulation 7 (1).

2. Act 19 (1) (a).

3. Act 19 (1) (d).

4. Act 55 (1) (6).

5. Matas, *Canada as a Country of First Asylum*, REFUGE, Volume 4 Number 2 (1984).

6. Act 48.01 (1) (b).

7. See Chapter 11.

8. Act 115 (1) (R).

9. Act 48 01 (2).

10. Act 115 (5).

11. Article 24.

12. Law v. Solicitor General of Canada 144 D.L.R. (3d) 549 (1983).

13. Act 115 (1) (v).

14. The Aliens Act, Section 48(2).

15. Danish Refugee Council, Current Asylum Policy and Humanitarian Principles (1984).

Chapter 19

1. Law Reform Commission of Canada, Working Paper 46, *Omission, Negligence and Endangering* (1985).

2 Globe and Mail (December 12, 1988).

3. Criminal Code, section 262.

4. Law Reform Commission of Canada, Report 31, Recodifying the Criminal Law, *Failure to Rescue* (1987).

5. Abella and Troper, None is Too Many, 100 (1982).

6. League for Human Rights of B'nai Brith Canada, Annual Review of Anti-Semitism (1987).

7. Globe and Mail (October 31, 1988).

8. Globe and Mail (September 19, 1987).

9. Article 11(h).

10. Globe and Mail (January 15, 1988).

11. Winnipeg Free Press (July 4, 1987).

ADJUDICATOR. An immigration judge appointed by the Public Service Commission of Canada who presides at immigration inquiries.

ALIEN. An American legal term for a foreigner in the U.S.

ASYLUM-SEEKER. A person who seeks protection as a refugee.

BILL C-84, THE REFUGEE DETERRENTS AND DETENTION BILL. Introduced in the House of Commons August 11, 1987 and given Royal Assent July 21, 1988. It came into effect in its entirety January 1, 1989. It legislates a number of provisions to deter refugees from coming to Canada and to detain them once they arc here.

CREDIBLE-BASIS HEARING. The initial hearing under the present Canadian refugee determination system. The refugee has to pass a credible-basis test in order to go on to a full hearing. A claim without credible-basis is manifestly unfounded.

DE FACTO REFUGEES. Refugees in fact, if not in law. They may not meet the Convention refugee definition, but are nonetheless fleeing man-made dangers and need protection.

DE JURE REFUGEES. Refugees in law who meet the Convention refugee definition.

DEPARTMENT OF IMMIGRATION. A government of Canada department responsible for the administration of the Immigration Act.

DEPARTURE NOTICE. A notice that states the person must leave Canada by a certain day. If a person does leave by that day he can return at any time provided he meets normal Canadian immigration criteria. An adjudicator gives a departure notice to a person inland who wishes to remain in Canada but is prohibited from remaining by the Immigration Act.

DEPORTATION ORDER. A bar to entry for life except with the consent of the Minister of Immigration. An adjudicator gives a deportation order to a person in Canada who is prohibited from remaining by the Immigration Act.

EXCLUSION ORDER. A bar to entry to Canada for one year, except with the consent of the Immigration Minister. An adjudicator issues an exclusion order to a person at a port of entry who wishes to enter Canada, but is prohibited from entry by the Immigration Act.

EXTENDED VOLUNTARY DEPARTURE. A term used in the United States to refer to temporary humanitarian refuge. Extended voluntary departure is typically granted by group to citizens of countries where there is a breakdown of law and order. With permission, any refugee may depart the U.S. voluntarily. The period of time before which he must depart is extended for these groups.

HUMANITARIAN LANDING. Permission to stay in Canada as a permanent resident for humanitarian reasons without the prior grant of a landed immigrant visa abroad.

THE IMMIGRATION AND REFUGEE BOARD. A board which began operation January 1, 1989. The Board has two divisions: a Convention Refugee Division and an Immigration Appeal Division. The Convention Refugee Division decides refugee cases at full hearings. It provides one panel member at credible-basis hearings.

IMMIGRATION APPEAL BOARD. In operation until December 31, 1988. It used to hear redeterminations of refugee claims where the Immigration Minister had decided the person was not a refugee. The Board continues for one year until

December 31, 1989 to complete only those cases that began before December 31, 1988.

LANDED IMMIGRANT VISA. Permission given by the government of Canada to a person to enter Canada as a permanent resident.

LEAVE TO APPEAL. Discretionary permission to appeal given by the court which hears the appeal.

MANDATE REFUGEE. A refugee who falls within the mandate given to the United Nations High Commission for Refugees to protect or aid refugees.

POLITICAL PRISONERS AND OPPRESSED PERSONS CLASS. Consists of citizens of Poland, Guatemala, Chile and El Salvador who are inside their country of citizenship and are political prisoners or persons with a well-founded fear of persecution.

PORT OF ENTRY. Not necessarily a port and not always at the Canadian border. Any Canadian immigration office which deals with new arrivals is a port of entry. Ports of entry are located at airports, seaports, and land border points.

POST-INQUIRY PRE-REMOVAL REVIEW. A review before removal that unsuccessful refugee claimants in Canada go through to determine whether they should be granted humanitarian landing.

PRE-INQUIRY REVIEW. A review that refugee claimants in Canada go through before inquiry to determine whether they should be granted humanitarian landing.

REDETERMINATION. A second look, after an initial refusal, at the question of whether or not the claimant is a refugee.

REFOULEMENT. Forcible return of a refugee to the country of danger he fled by the authorities of the state from which he seeks protection.

REFUGEE CLAIMANT. A person who claims refugee status by invoking the legal procedures available.

REFUGEE DETERMINATION. A decision by the competent authority whether or not the claimant is a refugee.

THE REFUGEE STATUS ADVISORY COMMITTEE. In place under the Immigration Act from April 10, 1978 to December 31, 1988. The Committee advised the Immigration Minister whether inland or port of entry refugee claimants were refugees.

RESETTLEMENT COUNTRY. A country that resettles refugees for the duration of time they require protection, a country of secondary asylum. Resettlement is a form of durable solution to refugees' problems.

SAFE THIRD COUNTRY. A country listed under Bill C-55 designated by the government of Canada as safe.

SCREENING PANEL. The panel that decides whether a refugee claimant passes the credible-basis test. It consists of an adjudicator and Refugee Board member.

THE SECURITY INTELLIGENCE AND REVIEW COMMITTEE. Committee appointed by the Cabinet which, until December 31, 1988, heard appeals from governmental decisions that a person had to leave Canada as a security risk.

SELF-EXILED CLASS. Consists of citizens of Eastern Europe who are outside of Eastern Europe, outside of Canada, and unwilling or unable to return to Eastern Europe.

SOURCE COUNTRY. The home country of the refugee or the country the refugee fled.

TRANSIT VISA. A type of visitor's visa which gives permission to enter Canada solely for the purpose of passing through on the way to another country.

THE UNITED NATIONS HIGH COMMISSION FOR REFUGEES. A United Nations bureaucracy established in 1951 with the mandate of protecting and assisting refugees.

VISITOR'S VISA. Permission given by the government of Canada abroad to a person to visit Canada.